DEDICATION

To His majesty, our Lord Jesus Christ,
who is the very substance we are made of and without
whose love and sacrifice our second birth would be
impossible; and,

to my daughter Keilah Maia, and to every born again
superman of God.

The Marvel Of The New Creation Superman
the Unordinary Jaggernaut That is the Christian

Joseph Kyalo

PUBLISHED by PARABLES
Earthly Stories with a Heavenly Meaning

The Marvel Of The New Creation Superman
The Unordinary Jaggernaut That is the Christian

Copyright ©Joseph Kyalo
December, 2017

Published By Parables
December, 2017

All Rights Reserved. No part of this book may be reproduced or utilized in any form or by any means, electronic or mechanical, including photocopying, recording, or by any information storage and retrieval system, without permission in writing from the author.

Unless otherwise specified Scripture quotations are taken from the authorized version of the King James Bible.

    ISBN978-1-945698-37-8
    Printed in the United States of America

Readers should be aware that Internet Web sites offered as citations and/or sources for further information may have been changed or disappeared between the time this was written.

"There is nowhere in this book I dignify satan by affording him any special treatment; even the least one of beginning his name in capitals. I disregard him to the extent where I have purposed to flout canons of grammar to deny him any glory."

The Marvel Of The New Creation Superman
the Unordinary Jaggernaut That is the Christian

Joseph Kyalo

PUBLISHED by PARABLES
Earthly Stories with a Heavenly Meaning

CONTENTS

Acknowledgments	2
Introduction	3
CHAPTER ONE: THE NEW CREATION: FAR FROM AN ORDINARY HUMAN BEING	6
A. Righteousness defined	18
B. God shared his glory!	28
C. Righteousness by faith only	50
D. The new creation: a brand new species of being	52
CHAPTER TWO: MAN: GOD'S STRATEGIC CREATION	64
A. The make-up of man	79
B. The soul explained	84
(i) The thinker (intellect, imagination and memory)	84
(ii) The conscience	88
(iii) Emotions	92
(iv) The will (chooser)	109

CHAPTER THREE: ATTRIBUTES OF THE NEW CREATION — 115
1. The New Creation: A Brand New and Perfect Spirit — 115
  (i) The new creation is not a "sinner saved by grace" — 118
  (ii) The new creation has no past — 128
  (iii) What about spiritual growth? — 138
2. The New Creation are Vital Sons of God — 143
3. The New Creation are One Entity With God — 149
4. The New Creation are a Species of gods — 163
5. The New Creation is God's Ultimate Delight — 177
6. The New Creation is Not Limited To Life in the Three Dimensional Natural World — 180
7. The New Creation are Citizens of Heaven, not Earth — 185
Your new spirit trains, develops, teaches and renews your soul, not vice versa — 191
8. The New Creation has all Past, Present and Future Sins Forgiven — 199
9. The New Creation Owns all Things — 209
10. The New Creation is Invincible — 214
11. The New Creation has Access to all Authority on Earth — 219
  (i) God is sovereign but not in control in the earth; — 225
  (ii) Men allow bad things in the earth, not God — 230
  (iii) Neither God nor satan is to blame for troubles on earth, men are — 240
  (iv) What is authority? — 247
  (v) God has the power, we have the authority — 250
12. The New Creation is a Champion for Ever — 261
13. The New Creation can Defy Aging — 267
14. The New Creation is in Eternity Already — 271
15. The New Creation is Unlimited: Knows no Impossibilities — 274

CHAPTER FOUR: AN EARNEST INVITATION TO JOIN THE GOD CLASS — 279

ACKNOWLEDGMENTS

No man or woman of God is self-made. Not even Paul who authored more than half of the New Testament was a man of his own invention. Everything he taught and wrote down for generations after him came from Jesus. Likewise, none of us can claim to know anything independent of the Holy Spirit who teaches us all things and reminds us all the things Jesus said. Every serious and mature believer is a product of the work of many men and women of God, and the overarching tutelage of the Holy Spirit who is in every one of us who believes.

He is the primary source of our revelation and inspiration. He is the first one I profusely thank for the massive treasure chest of revelation I have come to accumulate over the years I have been studying God's word. Not only so, He has brought into my life several of His men in whom He has also invested heavily the revelation of the gospel of grace. I would like to acknowledge the foremost two of the ministers who have by far impacted my life the greatest: Andrew Wommack and Joseph Prince. I was born again and stuck in a depressing and powerless Christian religion for two decades until these two generals came into my life and quashed all those toxic rules and traditions of men that had insulated the power of God from working in my life. Both run enormous ministries of God's unconditional love, grace, faith and hope in the US and Singapore respectively. Andrew is the founder and president of Andrew Wommack Ministries (AWMI) and Charis Bible College in Woodland Park, Colorado. Joseph is the President of Joseph Prince Ministries and senior pastor of the New Creation Church in the tiny but powerful city state of Singapore. Notably also, other ministers who have greatly impacted my life include Pastor Chris Oyakhilome, Creflo Dollar, brother Curry Blake and my own pastor, Judah Kalinga. The Lord has used many more men to speak into my life and to mold me and for that, I am absolutely grateful.

INTRODUCTION

New creation is the term the Bible gives to anybody who has believed in Jesus Christ as personal savior and Lord. The new creation person is far from an ordinary human being. Although he is in the world and dwells in a seemingly ordinary body similar to that of a natural man, he is a brand new and perfect spirit. His new spirit is a direct offshoot of God; with the nature, character, image and capability of God.

One of the most sensitive and powerful pieces of information the devil has tried to hide from the body of Christ throughout the millennia is about their real identity in Christ. If he can successfully keep it from their reach as he has done to a large extent; then, he can comfortably keep them from being manifested as sons of God. That is the thing he fears most. You see, manifested sons of God put that old crook where he belongs. They never give him rest or any fighting chance. They run him throughout the world and destroy his dirty works. They prevent his wicked dominion from being established in their spheres of influence. They snatch as many people as possible from his strangle-hold. However, wherever he encounters ignorant Christians, he ensures they don't reign on the earth to make the will of God happen here as it does in heaven in order to liberate creation from his tyranny. The whole aim of satan is to steal, kill and destroy and one of the strategies he employs to arrive at those goals is by impeding people from: knowing their true identity in Christ; knowing what is theirs in Christ; and, knowing their capabilities in Christ. Once that happens, he has just succeeded in incapacitating them from doing what they are capable of doing, and that is carrying out their purpose on earth and exploiting their full potential. There is no question the devil's number one tool is ignorance. With this one, the Bible says he destroys God's people. Having been spoilt and stripped of all authority by Jesus, all he has are tricks and wiles that he employs to craftily steal the inheritance of God's children.

THE MARVEL OF THE NEW CREATION SUPERMAN

I have identified one of the greatest tragedies in Christianity as the ignorance Christians have of their true identity and of the treasures available to them in Christ. There is so much unawareness in the body of Christ around the issue of who Christians really are, what they are capable of doing and what they have in Christ that the devil has a field day exploiting it in order to hamper the advancement of God's kingdom on earth and at the same time further his evil cause. Until Christians have an accurate grasp of who they are and what they have and can do in Christ, they will continue to malfunction and be ineffective in life; and, the kingdom of God will continue to be somewhat disadvantaged. If all the Christians had a proper understanding of the full glory of this reality called "to be in Christ" or the new creation, the earth would be today a vastly different place, and for the better. Many more people would be in the kingdom of God, the kingdom itself would be very effective and the devil would have no resting place. One would think that this problem of ignorance being one of the major issues in the Christian faith, Christian leaders would dedicate much more time to explain who exactly the new creation is. Well, it is rarely happening. Most people and even colleges for training ministers are mostly teaching other far less important things and leaving the most critical subjects barely touched. That is where this book comes in. There was no more immediate time than now to arm ourselves with this accurate and crucial knowledge of who we are and what our inheritance and capability is in Christ Jesus.

This book is for every breathing human being. It is as much for the believer as it is for the non-believer. They both will find it absolutely resourceful. For the believer in Christ, it will take the burden of the law and religion off one's shoulders and usher in an era of unparalleled liberty, righteousness, true holiness, all-round prosperity and victory in Christ. The law is a hindrance to righteous, victorious and holy living. It is also a weigh down to those who want to glorify God with their lives because the way to be dominated by sin is to be under the law; while sin cannot dominate the person who is under grace. This book unveils the awesome beauty of the grace of God in our Lord Jesus Christ by which we reign in life.

This book preaches expressly the unconditional forgiveness

of man's past, present and future sins; and justification (declaring righteous) of the sinner by grace. Only those who believe this report benefit from the immense advantages of the manifold grace of God. The verdict of those who despise the good news is clear from the Bible. Amazingly, the Lord foresaw some people, including professed believers, doubting and even despising the good news of the gospel of grace.

Acts 13: 38 *Be it known unto you therefore, men and brethren, that through this man is preached unto you the forgiveness of sins: 39 And by him all that believe are justified from all things, from which ye could not be justified by the law of Moses. 40 Beware therefore, lest that come upon you, which is spoken of in the prophets; 41 Behold, ye despisers, and wonder, and perish: for I work a work in your days, a work which ye shall in no wise believe, though a man declare it unto you.* (KJV)

Isaiah 53:1 *Who hath believed our report? And to whom is the arm of the LORD revealed?* (KJV)

For non-Christians, there is no better time to believe in Jesus than now. Contrary to religious people, Jesus is not seeking to burden you with the law. He is not asking you to do anything more than just to simply believe that He is the son of God who came to earth, died for our sins and was raised to life by God so that he who believes in Him can be declared righteous and truly holy. Salvation is so simple and free it should be the eighth wonder of the world why everyone is not saved. No one ever lost anything worth having by being born again. Just the contrary is true. Being born again makes available to you everything you ever dreamt of. Paul tells us all things become ours when we become joint-heirs of God with Christ, and that has been my experience.

CHAPTER ONE

THE NEW CREATION: FAR FROM AN ORDINARY HUMAN BEING

2 Corinthians 5: 17 *Therefore if any man be in Christ, he is a new creature: old things are passed away; behold, all things are become new. 18 And all things are of God...* (KJV)

Being born again, which is what produces the new creation or what I have christened the "original superman" is much more than modifying behavior or turning over a new leaf in life. When you believed in Christ, something that could not be noticed by the natural eye actually happened in you; there was a real spiritual birth. Just like you were first naturally born of physical human seed, this second time you were still born of seed but this second seed was the Word of God and the Spirit of God facilitated the birth. That's how come you have the life, nature and character of God in your spirit; it's a completely new life. As new creation, your spirit is a direct offshoot of God, just like your body is a direct offshoot of your parents. Being born again is not a reformation but regeneration. It is a fresh rebirth and just like we could not give birth to ourselves naturally, it follows we cannot do it also spiritually. The Holy Spirit is the one responsible for the birth of these awesome junior brothers of Christ. You cannot be responsible for your own second and spiritual birth any more than a baby can be responsible for its own birth. Some religious people try to merit salvation by their obedience of the law, good works or the many religious exercises and rituals they engage in. The second birth is an invaluable free gift from God courtesy of Christ's completed work at the cross.

Titus 3:5 *he saved us, not because of righteous things we had done, but because of his mercy. He saved us through the washing of rebirth and renewal by the Holy Spirit...* (NIV)

Since the dawn of time, mankind has been obsessed with acquiring supernatural powers with which to reign over all the circumstances that threaten life on earth and even to save humanity. We read of ancient stories of Hercules, the Greek super hero who was the son of Zeus, a god. He supposedly went on many adventures helping people and slaying mythical monsters by use of his half-god strength. That same mentality is still the idea behind all the fascination with the occult. It is also the reason behind the efforts to build supercomputers and other powerful scientific and technological systems. When they discovered nuclear energy, some thought there was a way to ultimately harness it to fix all of humanity's challenges. All these things are geared towards finding the magic bullet that will vaporize all the problems of humanity and create an earthly utopia. For nuclear energy, far from being the boon it was thought to be, it was actually found to be capable of vaporizing entire civilizations in a heartbeat. It created more and deadlier problems than it solved. Instead of most of these inventions bringing men closer to solutions, they have mostly driven existence to the edge of extinction. In fact, most of them have the world in tenterhooks even now.

Many of us are familiar with a fictional character called superman who was invented by Jerry Siegel and Joe Shuster. They depict him as a non-descript beggar who was picked from the streets and given supernatural powers almost by accident. The new found powers gave him new ideas and he set out to rule the whole world. Without being aware of it, many people admire the many fictional superheroes men have invented over the time and even wish they possessed such powers in reality. I have great news for all who have been yearning for these seemingly distant pipe-dreams to come true. The truth is, there is actually one genuine superman in existence, Jesus Christ. There is even better news; that He has given birth to billions of other supermen by His Spirit and those constitute all born again believers better known as the new creation. These super beings are the exact offspring of the original superhero who is Christ. They are born in His exact image and likeness. They have His same capabilities. They can do all He can do and even more. These super beings are absolutely victorious in all situations and under all circumstances because He causes them to triumph always as He spreads the aroma of His knowledge in every place by them-2 Corinthians 2:14. The new creation cannot lose, even if He is in prison. We have many accounts throughout the Bible of God's people who were either imprisoned or in captivity but still thrived superfluously even there. The new creation prospers hand over fist even in the direst of circumstances. There is no known thing that should set back this new, born again man.

This re-born superman who takes after Christ is far from being an ordinary human. Unlike all the past superheroes who are fictional creations of men, this final man who is in Christ is a real and practical supernatural spirit being who actually does supernatural things. He follows in the highway created by the forerunner Jesus and does even greater works. Just like his Father Jesus, this new man can handle any eventuality with ease. There is really no emergency that can successfully overwhelm him just like none can be too much for Jesus. The reason for that is simple; by His Spirit, Jesus lives in and through this new man. He has given him the mandate to rule and dominate the earth till He returns again to earth in the flesh.

Luke 19: 13 *And he called his ten servants, and delivered them ten pounds, and said unto them, Occupy till I come.* (KJV)

This verse means that Jesus has given us the necessary instruments of authority and everything we need for life and godliness so that we can subdue the earth on His behalf and to ensure His will is done on earth as it is in heaven. Knowing very well that there is absolutely nothing we cannot handle and control by faith in Him, He instructed us sternly in very many places to not fear or be anxious for anything- John 14:1, 27: Philippians 4:6-7: Matthew 6:34: 1 Peter 5:6-7. You see, worrying and fear mean you think there is an uncontrollable situation that can arise that Christ in you cannot handle.

A direct son of God cannot be an ordinary human being. Have you heard Christians who say things like: 'I am just an ordinary or common person? I am an average, everyday person. I am not special. I am just an ordinary man or woman trying to do extra ordinary exploits.' I hate that kind of talk when applied to a new creation. The new creation is far from an ordinary human. There is nothing about him that is ordinary or common. How can you be one spirit with Christ and call that ordinary? Are you calling God ordinary? The only thing about me that has a remote semblance of ordinary is my body but that is not me. That is simply my temporary tent or dwelling place. And even that one is not ordinary! My body is not like that of common people who are not in Christ. It is indwelt by the Holy Spirit who quickens it constantly. I can't just fall sick or drop down dead like an ordinary person! Even my body is holy because it is the temple of God, just like the Old Testament Solomon's temple. Could anyone call that temple ordinary? That temple or the earlier tabernacle were in their days the most important buildings in the entire planet. They 'housed' God. They were far from ordinary constructions. The very word holy means set apart, separated, special and consecrated for God's purpose. We are not commoners but the very royalty of God!

1 Peter 2:9 *But you are a chosen people, a royal priesthood, a holy nation, God's special possession, that you may declare the praises of him who called you out of darkness into his wonderful light.* (NIV)

Ephesians 2:10 *For we are God's masterpiece. He has created us anew in Christ Jesus, so we can do the good things he planned for us long ago.* (NLT)

<u>The new creation is not born of man but of God. God gave birth to us by His own word. Our new spirits come from the spirit of God.</u> That is why I usually say we are god-men or Jesus-men. The born again spirit of man didn't come from the dust. Only the body did. The spirit is a direct offspring of God through the word. The natural life we inherit from earthly parents gets completely dissolved and displaced by the divine life of Christ at the point of this new, spiritual and divine birth.

1 Peter 1:23-25 *Your new life is not like your old life. Your old birth came from mortal sperm; your new birth comes from God's living Word. Just think: a life conceived by God himself! That's why the prophet said, the old life is a grass life, its beauty as short-lived as wildflowers; Grass dries up, flowers droop, God's Word goes on and on forever. This is the Word that conceived the new life in you.* (MSG)

John 1:12 *But as many as received him, to them gave he power to become the sons of God, even to them that believe on his name:13 Which were born, not of blood, nor of the will of the flesh, nor of the will of man, but of God.* (KJV)

The Greek rendering of the term "new creation" refers to a new kind, type or quality of life; not a new beginning or fresh start. It is not new life in that it is just beginning a fresh. It is a new kind of creature or species that has never been witnessed again. That is why Peter calls the new creation a peculiar people, holy nation, royal priesthood and a chosen generation. This new creation is far superior to Adam, angels or any Old Testament figure- including Moses, David, Elijah, Elisha and John the Baptist. That is why Jesus said that he who is least of the new creation is greater than John, though John was the greatest man of all time, until Jesus. <u>This new creation is far superior to Satan and all his demons. As a matter of fact, just one among these new creation people has more power at the tip of his little finger than Satan has in his entire dominion.</u> In fact, the new creation will judge the angels!

1 Corinthians 6:3 *Know ye not that we shall judge angels? how much more things that pertain to this life?* (KJV)

At no time did God say to the angels that they own anything or are heirs of Him. To us, He says all things are ours and we are heirs of Him, and joint-heirs with Christ! -Romans 8:17. What a deal! Thank you Jesus! The Bible says at no time did God tell the angels they are His begotten sons and that He is their God like He has said to Jesus and to us.

Hebrews 1: 5 *For unto which of the angels said he at any time, Thou art my Son, this day have I begotten thee? And again, I will be to him a Father, and he shall be to me a Son?* (KJV)

Instead, He says that all angels are ministering spirits sent forth to minister for the new creation. He further says we are sons of God after Christ and it is unto us He has subjected the world to come, not to angels.

Hebrews 2: 5 *For unto the angels hath he not put in subjection the world to come, whereof we speak... 11 For both he that sanctifieth and they who are sanctified are all of one: for which cause he is not ashamed to call them brethren...* (KJV)

That is why it is not a compliment to call a Christian an angel. A Christian is in the league of God. He is a partaker or sharer of divine nature. This new creation does not even operate just on earth or the first or second heavens only. He has surpassed all these three realms and gone to sit in Christ by God's right hand in the third and highest heaven. He has already come to Mt. Zion, the city of the living God, far above all principality, power and any name that is named now or in the ages to come. This new species doesn't need deliverance because he cannot be oppressed. Even sin and bad habits cannot have dominion over him because he's not under the law but under grace. He is not subject to Satan. He is not fighting with Satan. He simply and very easily tells Satan what to do. When I say he is a partaker of divine nature, I mean he belongs to the class of God and he lives in, and together with Him. They share eternal life or *aiónios zóé*.

God no longer lives that special and top-most life all by Himself; He shares it now with His new and beloved sons. Blessed be God!

The new creation is more than a physical being like an ordinary man is. He is an eternal living spirit. He is not just spiritual; he is a spirit just like his Father God. As a new creation, my body cannot define me as it is dead because of sin. What defines me is my spirit (which is one with the Holy Spirit) as it is life because of righteousness.

Romans 8: 10 *And if Christ be in you, the body is dead because of sin; but the Spirit is life because of righteousness.* (KJV)

This verse is more important than most Christians care to know. It is not just saying that our spirit part is alive. It also means that although we are dead in the flesh because of the nature of sin and death in operation therein, our spirit part is a source of life as it is the righteousness of God in Christ Jesus. One thing we need to understand is that our spirit cannot be separated from the Holy Spirit because they are one and they are our life. In our spirits is where we are alive, not in our flesh. Actually, water baptism signifies death of the flesh and newness of life in the spirit. We must also remember that righteousness is the foremost quality or attribute that makes God who He really is. Righteousness cannot be separated from eternal life which is the life of God, or life as God has it. When Adam and Eve lost righteousness through disobedience, they died spiritually.

Jesus makes us alive again by making us eternally righteous by His own righteousness, not ours. Not only does He make us alive again, He makes us fountains or sources of life. He makes us life-giving spirits like Him. In Christ, we are dispensers of both natural and eternal life.

1 Corinthians 15: 45 *And so it is written, The first man Adam was made a living soul; the last Adam was made a quickening spirit... 47 The first man is of the earth, earthy; the second man is the Lord from heaven. 48 As is the earthy, such are they also that are earthy: and as is the heavenly, such are they also that are heavenly.* (KJV)

Ordinary and natural men who are not in Christ are dead spiritually. To be dead spiritually is to be disconnected from God and that is what happened to Adam and Eve after they disobeyed God. You see, God is not only the source of all life, but is life Himself. One of His descriptions is that He is life. Anything that is outside of God is dead and that was our situation before we received new and divine spirits. At that point, we became new creation and that simply means we are living and life-giving spirits. Before you get confused, I am not talking about Jesus here; I am talking about the offspring of Jesus - the born again man. God is spirit and so are His sons and daughters. That is why the new creation cannot die. Spirits don't die. The new creation simply changes residence from the body then to heaven with the Lord. He remains with the Lord in heaven until such a time in future when there shall be a new earth and a new heaven in place where he can reign again after he is united with a new and glorified body. Have you ever heard of the scripture "absent from the body, present with the Lord?" The new creation is the only creature who can absent himself from the body on earth and be present with the Lord in the next moment. That means he was not the body. He was just living there and he can absent himself from it and go to live with the Lord and then the inhabitants of the earth can be left interring that old and tired house. That is why in the kingdom of God, there is no Jew, Greek, male or female, rich or poor and other categories which men invent. To God, what matters are not the attributes of the temporary house we call body which the Bible calls tent, but the resident in there-the new creation.

Galatians 6:15 *For in Christ Jesus neither circumcision availeth anything, nor uncircumcision, but a new creature.* (KJV)

Colossians 3: 10 *And have put on the new man, which is renewed in knowledge after the image of him that created him: 11 Where there is neither Greek nor Jew, circumcision nor uncircumcision, Barbarian, Scythian, bond nor free: but Christ is all, and in all.* (KJV)

Commenting on the stupid, demonic and backward stronghold called racism and all other forms of prejudice, William J. Seymour, he of the Azusa Street revival fame remarked that 'the bloodline has washed away the color line.' He meant that the same blood of Jesus Christ has washed clean every child of God and made them new creation, which is a spiritual person indefinable by any race, gender, class or any other known physical orientation.

Galatians 3: 26 *For ye are all the children of God by faith in Christ Jesus. 27 For as many of you as have been baptized into Christ have put on Christ. 28 There is neither Jew nor Greek, there is neither bond nor free, there is neither male nor female: for ye are all one in Christ Jesus.* (KJV)

Racism, tribalism and all other manifestations of sectionalism and prejudice are at best just stupid. They reveal utter ignorance of God and His word. They dwell on superficial and transient attributes that really don't matter to anyone else beyond the parochial person harboring them. You see, there are only two types of people before the supreme judge of the universe whose verdict is the only one that matters, and that is God. God only sees people as either living or dead. Anybody who is not in Christ is dead while anyone who is in Christ is alive for ever more. For people who are not believers, we can with difficulties excuse them for being racists, tribalistic and prejudicial because they are ignorant and don't know any better. They are incapable of thinking rightly. However, even as they judge and look down upon other people just because they are different from them, they should know they are dead themselves. It is just a silly case of dead people comparing themselves to other dead people and judging themselves to be better. It doesn't make sense. Whether one has been dead for only a few hours and is wearing a good suit, or died decades ago and is in terrible state makes no difference.

They are all dead and without mercy, their destination is the soil. All flesh other than the glorified flesh of Jesus is a product of the soil and is corrupted to the core. All human flesh finds a common ancestry in Adam, including those you don't think are descended from that original man. That is why we will all receive new and glorious bodies upon Jesus' coming. Only blindness can make some people think they are special dead. The only difference between dead people is that they are at different stages of corruption but they are all corrupted. That is why we don't pay attention to spiritually dead people who are basically saying that their flesh is better than their neighbor's.

However, we have a serious problem with people who claim to be new creation and are prejudicial. It is even inconceivable that a born again person can think like that but it does happen and it stinks to the heavens. Those who engage in this foolishness are seriously ignorant believers who have completely refused to renew their minds and instead walk guided by their sensory perceptions. They live based on what their senses pick, not what the word says. In the Old Testament and when people were not spiritually enlightened, you could forgive someone for engaging in prejudice because Jesus had not yet revealed the heart of God toward human beings. Men ignorantly judged others based on physical appearance. After Jesus shed so much light on how God loves all men, it is stupid to still be engaging in the backward practice of bigotry.

2 Corinthians 5: 16 *Wherefore henceforth know we no man after the flesh: yea, though we have known Christ after the flesh, yet now henceforth know we him no more.* (KJV)

When Jesus came to earth, everybody was dead around here. Those who claim that their flesh is better than that of their counterparts (forgetting they did not pay for it or apply to be born as they were) were just as dead as the people they despise and all have a common maker. To kill all this unnecessary madness of prejudice and self-righteousness, God provided one standard of perfection- Jesus. Anyone who is as perfect as Jesus in spirit, soul and body can stand up to be counted and relate to others with an air of superiority. Only a deluded person can think they measure up to Jesus. As a result, every mouth was shut by that sublime benchmark of Jesus.

That is why we say that God concluded us all under sin (and therefore dead) so that He may have mercy on us all. We all sinned and came short of the glory of God and that glory is Jesus.

2 Corinthians 5:14 *For the love of Christ constraineth us; because we thus judge, that if one died for all, then were all dead:* (KJV)

Besides the misfortune of Christians who put pride in the appearance of their flesh, there is an even worse category of faith people who think they are better than other believers either because they perform or conduct themselves better than others or, they think they had fewer sins to be forgiven of in the first place. They think they were already very good people before they were found by Jesus and all He did was to top up the little remaining part so that they can be complete. Sometimes I wonder whether such people are really born again. I actually had one Christian tell me that the apostle Paul suffered so much because before He met Christ, he was very wicked. This person reasoned that Paul was paying for all the sins he was doing before his conversion. This fellow went further to tell me to my face that even before he got born again himself, he was a very good person and didn't have as many sins to be forgiven of as other people. You will be shocked to find out how many Christians think like that. Such people forget that it is the disobedience of one man (Adam) which made them sinners, not their own sinful conduct. What follows automatically where such people are concerned is that they are the very same people who engage in self-righteousness after they are born again because they refuse to understand that it is also by the obedience of one man (Jesus) that those of us who believe in Him are made righteous. Once again, there are no degrees of death and there are no special dead people. Before Jesus came, the rich, the poor, black, white, the coloured, literate and illiterate; all were dead and destined for hell. As a matter of fact, since Adam sinned, every human being who is born of a woman (save for Jesus only) is born dead in sin. If we were all dead, pathetic and bankrupt sinners with nothing to offer to God before Jesus came, why brag and create physical divisions in the body of Christ based on such silly things as physical appearance, performance or one's perceived holiness before the second birth? Those who recognize they are born dead in sin (even if they are the holiest people as far as they know) and look to Jesus for help receive a second birth and become alive again (with eternal life) forever more. Those who cling on to their self-righteousness and don't recognize the need for a savior die in their sins. No bigger sin exists than that of self-righteousness because it dishonors the bitter work of Jesus by treating it as nothing special. For that reason, Jesus told the self-righteous Pharisees that prostitutes and publicans would enter the kingdom of God before them.

Jesus dismantled all physical divisions that men used to create imaginary barriers between them.

Ephesians 2: *12 That at that time ye were without Christ, being aliens from the commonwealth of Israel, and strangers from the covenants of promise, having no hope, and without God in the world: 13 But now in Christ Jesus ye who sometimes were far off are made nigh by the blood of Christ. 14 For he is our peace, who hath made both one, and hath broken down the middle wall of partition between us; 15 Having abolished in his flesh the enmity, even the law of commandments contained in ordinances; for to make in himself of twain one new man, so making peace; 16 And that he might reconcile both unto God in one body by the cross, having slain the enmity thereby... 19 Now therefore ye are no more strangers and foreigners, but fellowcitizens with the saints, and of the household of God;* (KJV)

The children of God are spirits and that is why they have no gender or race or any physical attributes. That is also why because this book is chiefly about the new creation, there will minimal references to female pronouns because all born again people are new creation and therefore spirits, and the Bible simply designates such by male references. So, let not any sister in Christ feel left out when I keep Using the male pronoun and other masculine references because she is totally included in there as a son of God-Romans 8:14,19; Galatians 4:7; Ephesians 1:5; Revelation 21:7. Tragically, many new creation people know more about their physical residence which is their body, than they do about their real and true self. The cardinal rule of reproduction states that like begets like. The Bible itself proves that when it calls God Father of spirits. We who are born again constitute a pretty good chunk of those spirits.

Hebrews 12: 9 *Furthermore we have had fathers of our flesh which corrected us, and we gave them reverence: shall we not much rather be in subjection unto the Father of spirits, and live?* (KJV)

According to Romans 7:15-22 which we will be delving deeper into later, your spirit comes alive to God at the point of the second and spiritual birth, and seeks only to please Him and do His will. That begs the question, why is it then that believers still struggle with some unwelcome issues from the past? The truth is, those things don't come from their new spirit, but from the unrenewed mind and the senses. This doesn't mean a Christian should resign and let those weaknesses from the past reign in his life. There is a way out and this is where the importance of renewing the mind with the word of God comes in. At the point of salvation, the soul and body components of man are not touched. Only the spirit is born anew. If as a Christian you don't renew your mind, it will always be at odds with the new and perfect spirit and it will get in your way of living a life like that of Jesus when He was here on earth. If you are not single minded (synchronized in spirit and mind) your spiritual life will not move forward and you will be stuck for life-James 1:8; James 4:8. Christians who don't renew their minds are stagnant in life. But if you renew your mind, your mind will be reading from the same page with your new spirit which is one with the Spirit of God and both will be able to prevail over your body and you will live an absolutely glorious life just as Jesus did while on earth.

What happened with us at the new birth is not a changed spirit; it's an exchanged or replaced spirit. Our spirit was not improved or changed. The old spirit was replaced with a divine one that is just like God; just as holy, righteous, able and powerful.

Ezekiel 36: 26 *A new heart also will I give you, and a **new spirit will I put within you:** and I will **take away the stony heart** out of your flesh, and I will give you an **heart of flesh.*** (KJV) Emphasis added.

Yes, this new spirit is as righteous and as holy as God Himself. In fact, he is the righteousness of God in Christ. Some people because of their religious conditioning and false humility shudder at the weight of statements like these but I mean every bit of what I say. I repeat again; if you are in Christ, you are not just completely righteous and holy; you are the very righteousness of God in Christ Jesus. You are the embodiment, portrait and personification of God's righteousness. Your life is the very manifestation of God's perfection because Christ is in you and you are in Him.

A.   RIGHTEOUSNESS DEFINED

There is a most common description of righteousness in church circles that has almost become standard. It goes something like; "righteousness is the right standing with God." That is the most prevalent description of righteousness for most people and I have a problem with it. Don't get me wrong, righteousness does lead to right standing with God, but I don't believe that is its description. If it were to be, then, when we say God is righteous, then who is He in right standing with? Right standing with God is the effect of righteousness, not its description. Righteousness is divine nature, or the very nature of God. It is His quintessential composition, character, quality and essence. Righteousness speaks of absolute or perfect godliness, justness, flawlessness, impeccability, faultlessness, spotlessness, perfection, uprightness, exactness, truthfulness, goodness, innocence, divinity, perfect rightness and blamelessness. Righteousness is the height of virtue and the attribute that makes God, God. It is purity of state, the state of being divinely pristine and absolutely unadulterated. Righteousness is God's absolute goodness, which is the extreme opposite of wickedness or evil. It is God's goodness; in contradistinction to the devil's wickedness. God is a good God while the devil is a wicked devil. Righteousness is the supreme glory or weight of God. It is God's absolute and undefiled goodness and holiness that flows out of purity of motive. That is why God can never harbour ulterior motives. There is in Him no darkness because He is the Father of lights. He has no capacity to change and neither does He have any shadow of turning. He is transparently pure. Righteousness is the highest peak, or the pinnacle of morality, and its very standard. Against righteousness, there is no law. Righteousness is the perfect nature and standard of God that no fallen man can ever dream to attain. It can only be imputed as a gift. It is the costliest and most sublime quality. The opposite of righteousness is wickedness.

Psalm 45: 7 **Thou lovest righteousness, and hatest wickedness:** *therefore God, thy God, hath anointed thee with the oil of gladness above thy fellows.* (KJV) Emphasis added.

You can see in this Psalm that wickedness is applied as the antonym to righteousness. Righteousness is God's unadulterated goodness. God is the epitome of goodness. Only He has all the preserve of all goodness. There is no goodness apart from His divine goodness and there is nothing about Him that is not good. There is no single speck of wickedness in Him and He has no ill-motive. If we were to define righteous as good standing with God, then how would you explain a verse like Isaiah 41:10?

Fear thou not; for I am with thee: be not dismayed; for I am thy God: I will strengthen thee; yea, I will help thee; yea, I will uphold thee with the right hand of my righteousness. (KJV)

Does it mean God will uphold you with the right hand of His good standing? No way. This verse is saying that God will uphold you with His goodness, justice and grace. God's goodness has no pretense or hypocrisy; it is only authentic, genuine and 100% dependable. Righteousness is God's integrity. It is His unchanging, enduring, static divine nature that holds everything in place. Righteousness is the nature of God.

Now, God is not only righteous; the very foundation of His throne is righteousness. In other words, the foundation of the kingdom of God and His claim to it is His perfect fairness, flawlessness, justness, perfection, truthfulness, faithfulness, uprightness, purity and His inability to err. God is perfectly capable of running the universe without a single thing going wrong. Those qualities are also His symbols of authority and they are the very instruments He reigns by.

Psalm 89:14 *Righteousness and justice are the foundation of your throne; love and faithfulness go before you.* (NIV)

Hebrews 1:8 *But unto the Son he saith, Thy throne, O God, is for ever and ever: a sceptre of righteousness is the sceptre of thy kingdom.* (KJV)

The Marvel Of The New Creation Superman

Isaiah 9: 7 *Of the greatness of his government and peace there will be no end.* **He will reign on David's throne and over his kingdom, establishing and upholding it with justice and righteousness** *from that time on and forever. The zeal of the LORD Almighty will accomplish this.* (NIV) Emphasis added.

The greatest news here is; God is no longer the only one who is made up of those supreme qualities. Not after Jesus came, died for our sins and was raised from the dead. Now, righteousness is also the very element that makes up the new creation. We are not just righteous (just, godly, perfect, holy, flawless, exact, godly, pure, truthful, excellent and exactly right); we are the very righteousness of God in Christ Jesus. This doesn't mean we are God's right standing as righteousness is commonly defined. It means we are the radiance and express image of His nature and character. It means we give vent to God's excellence, and glory. We shine forth and manifest His perfection. In other words, people of the world should not be asking where God is and how He looks like. They should see His dazzling glory displayed in the life of the new creation person. I like the way Pastor Chris Oyakhilome puts it. He likens the new creation individual to an icon on the desktop of a computer. He says we are the icons of God in Christ. When you click an icon, every resource it represents comes forth. Similarly, Pastor Chris says when they touch you, every blessing of God is supposed to flow from you to them. Virtue is supposed to flow from the new creation person like a river. The bible calls that 'rivers of living water.' That is why, whatever the new creation touches must prosper. Now, this righteousness is in our new spirits. Don't look for that perfection in your soul and body. You will surely miss it. We live in and from the spirit by faith, not in and from the flesh by sight. Righteousness is what and who we are now. As Jesus is, so are we in this world. That means by the force of righteousness, we reign also because we reign with the King of kings.

Romans 5: 17 *For if by one man's offence death reigned by one; much more they which receive abundance of grace and of the gift of righteousness shall reign in life by one, Jesus Christ.)... 21 That as sin hath reigned unto death, even so might grace reign through righteousness unto eternal life by Jesus Christ our Lord.*

(KJV)

You cannot deal with God if you are not righteous. That is why the Old Testament people had hard time relating with Him because there was not yet provision for them to be as righteous as God Himself. We have that privilege now. The good thing is, righteousness is not a wage to be worked for. It is not earned through one's conduct; it is not acquired through payment of any kind, or, by any sacrifice or any act of commission or omission. It is a gift to be received completely freely upon believing in Jesus Christ.

Romans 4: 5 *But to him that worketh not, but believeth on him that justifieth the ungodly, his faith is counted for righteousness. 6 Even as David also describeth the blessedness of the man, unto whom God imputeth righteousness without works...* (KJV)

You are not going to be righteous and holy in some future day; you are righteous this very moment and it is in your spirit, not your body or soul.

Romans 6:6 *Knowing this, that our old man is crucified with him, that the body of sin might be destroyed, that henceforth we should not serve sin.*

The "old man," meaning the life you had before you were reborn in the spirit, or the old spirit with sin nature isn't just kind of suspended; it's totally buried. The moment Jesus died, that sin nature was totally negated and buried with Him because He died not for Himself but in our place. His death was totally vicarious. When Christ went to hell, our old self went to hell in Him too. When He scored victory there over death and the grave, we scored in Him too. When He rose from the dead, we were raised with and in Him to new life. The new spirit being who came up with Christ at resurrection is called new creation or God's first fruits and that is you if you have faith in Christ. This new man is not an improvement of the old man. He is totally new and fresh. He is not the old man who is now trying to sin less and less until he gradually approaches perfection. He is born totally new and completely perfect and sin-free. You see, even if you could somehow stop all sins (which is impossible), you would still be an old creature, dead, and, cut off from God. To acquire eternal life and be reconnected to God, you must be born again and that is not negotiable. If you are born again not through righteous works but by faith in Jesus, you're now a new man as explained in 2 Corinthians 5:17. The Greek rendering of the expression "new creature" is 'new species' of being; one that never existed before—one without a past. In God's scheme of things, who you were and everything you did before you were born again never existed; there's no such record, because you're a new creation, a new being. Believers who are in the dark concerning this are held in bondage and at ransom by their past, which without doubt makes them ineffective in the kingdom of God.

All those things I have shared there are true but not every Christian accepts them. If you have been religiously brainwashed, I don't think I can help you very much other than to pray for the eyes of your understanding to be enlightened so that you may know what are the riches of the glory of God's inheritance in you. I have come to learn that most believers walk around ignorantly wearing false humility. If you try to help them understand that they are the manifestations of the very perfection of God and even quote scriptures, they fight it and never believe it. They would rather remain in a worthless, powerless and oppressive religion than embrace the empowering and liberating truths of God's word. They say outdated things like: "no please, I am not righteous. Only God is righteous. I am neither an angel nor a saint. There is none righteous, no not one. I am only a humble old poor sinner saved by grace. I am a salvaged wreck and a weak vessel. I am an unworthy sinner before God" Those stupid religious things Christians say disappoint God. How can God send Jesus, heaven's best to take your place so that you can take His place and you say degrading things like those about yourself? You are as valuable as the blood that bought you and you must never cheapen that precious and eternal blood by pinning on yourself such derogatory labels. Referring to you as a sinner saved by grace and those other labels is really a mark of ignorance and even pride because Jesus never referred to us by them. That is one of the statements I detest most. It is as blind as a bat. <u>If you are in Christ, you are worth the life of that perfect son of God because that is what God paid for you!</u>

God can't respond to you if you come to him as a sinner saved by grace or as an unworthy fellow pleading for mercy. He had mercy on you already, loved you and that made Him sent Jesus to take away sin for you so that you can boldly fellowship with Him. He is now your Father and does not recognize you as a sinner because He is not the Father of a sinner as that would make Him a sinner too. You can't be both of those two at the same time- a sinner and His son. You have to choose one. God can't respond to something He is not. He is holy. He has integrity. He can't answer to and validate your religious lie. You must understand that you are not saved by your own life. You are not saved by your good actions and works of obedience. You are saved by the life of Christ.

Romans 5: 10 *For if, when we were enemies, we were reconciled to God by the death of his Son, much more, being reconciled, we shall be saved by his life.* (KJV)

That means when God looks at you, He sees the life of Christ in you and is perfectly pleased. <u>There is never a better sacrifice to bring before God than that of His son.</u> Never bring to God the sacrifice of yourself. That simply means you must never purpose to deal or fellowship with God and relate to Him based on your performance. He can never take that.

Ephesians 5:2 *Live a life filled with love, following the example of Christ. He loved us and offered himself as a sacrifice for us, a pleasing aroma to God.* (NLT)

2 Corinthians 2:15 *Our lives are a Christ-like fragrance rising up to God. But this fragrance is perceived differently by those who are being saved and by those who are perishing.* (NLT)

Many people bring many things like money and works of righteousness but God only delights in the offer or praise of His son before Him. How do you offer Christ before God? It is by first recognizing and acknowledging Him as your savior, the lamb who took away all your sins and who also is your very life.

Mention to God also that the only basis you have of fellowshipping with Him and being His son and in His company is because Jesus has made you His (God's) righteousness in Him (Jesus). We need to let God know that we are His sons not alone as individuals but in Christ. We dare not bring to God our works but Christ who is our very life. In judgment day, we will also be saved by Jesus' life in us and our genuine faith in It; not by how successful we were in living holy. So, we deal with God based on the truth and accuracy of His word. That is the true worship in truth and spirit, and the only one that God recognizes and accepts.

We don't start as incomplete and imperfect and try to begin to work towards perfection. God's way is to start from a position of completeness and perfection, then renew our minds and manifest in the natural that which has been worked in us already. We start our Christian walk with where Jesus said "it is finished." That means <u>the redemption work was completed by Jesus. All we do is walk in it, not try to redo it.</u> Religion has got it backwards. It tells its deceived followers to come to God, surrender their lives to Him and begin walking holy and righteously. Peradventure, if they are very holy and righteous, God may be happy with them and grant them perfection and admission to heaven. Until they "finish strong, righteous and holy," nobody can be sure of salvation. All that is absolute religious garbage. God saves us first by perfecting us and giving us the gift of eternal life which is the life of His son, then He tells us to work out that salvation that He graciously worked in us. The apostle John tells us in 1 John 5:13 that he wrote the things he did to us who believe in the name of Jesus that we may know we have eternal life now! It is not coming sometimes in the future; we have it now. We are living eternal life or the God-life now. That is why we are not ordinary human beings. We are supernatural beings, new race and new species. That is why we defy sickness and all other systems of the world set against us. We absolutely overcome them all. We chew them. They are bread to us. That is the transcendent life Christ has afforded us and we are enjoying it now. If that is not what you believe, then you have embraced a religion rather than the gospel and faith of our Lord Jesus.

To label yourself an unworthy sinner is to demean the perfect work of Christ which secured your redemption, righteousness, perfection and sonship in the divine family of God in heaven and earth. As Jesus is, so are you in this world-1 John 4:17. We need to call ourselves what God calls us, not what religious training has taught us. Of course you are not an angel; you are higher than an angel. You are in the class that is immediate after God. That is how high God has placed us. He determined that we are worth the life of His son who is God. He never died for angels although there were some fallen ones who would have required redemption. Some of these deniers of their divine nature are really making a sincere attempt at being humble but they are sincerely and ignorantly wrong! In their pathological desire to steer clear from pride, they give the devil a chance to cage them right in it. To be humble is not to behave in some kind of a cowed manner or to reject privilege and grace even where they are granted out of goodwill and the sovereign will of God. <u>Humility is submitting to, believing in and acting on God's word even when it appears alien to or at odds with one's preconceived and usually religious conditioning.</u> Humility is God-dependency as opposed to self-dependency. In fact, self-righteousness which is common place in religion is the highest form of pride because it disregards the completed work of Jesus and seeks to establish another righteousness born out of self-effort. Humility is relying totally on Jesus' finished work and not trying to help Him save you. If you are in Christ, it is the highest form of humility to declare yourself perfect, righteous, holy and the very excellence of God. Pride is calling yourself a sinner or just a weak believer trying to cope, even after Jesus has washed, justified and perfected you. When the word says you are totally and permanently righteous if you are in Christ; you must forget all those religious platitudes of being a sinner saved by grace or whatever other thing society has ignorantly repeated for so long. If you are humble, you must fully believe and act on what the word has exactly said and not even dare say anything else because it will conflict with God's true position and that is the real pride. Outwardly, you can be the most abased person but still be very proud if you disagree with God or if you reject His word to embrace some contrary religious making of men. Pride is not being too courageous, showy or bold. Pride is simply excessive self-consciousness. Those who are excessively inward or shy are just as equally proud as those who are cocky. None of those extremes is any better or any less ungodly. The reason I say those religious labels we paste on ourselves are symptomatic of pride is because we are not saved by our own lives or by what we do or don't. We are saved by the life of Jesus- Romans 5:10. That means your life is just like the life of Jesus. We died and our lives are hidden with Christ in God. Christ is our very life- Colossians 3:3-4. That is why John tells us that we will have confidence in the Day of Judgment because as Jesus is, so are we in this world! You certainly can't call Jesus imperfect or a sinner saved by grace. <u>To be humble is to have an accurate estimate of yourself derived from the word of God.</u> Don't afford religion and the devil the opportunity to keep you groveling in the mire of false humility.

    Many Christians are not bold enough to state the Word of God as it is. Religion has conditioned them to be timid and to subscribe to false humility which is not humility at all. It is just utter ignorance and even pride. For example someone will come up to you and ask; 'Do you heal?' Many will be afraid to say 'yes I heal.' When somebody else says it, they jump, protest and get startled. That is pure hypocrisy because when you are asked; 'do you preach?' Why don't you say 'No, I don't, it's God who preaches!' The instruction is very clear in Matthew 10:8. *Heal the sick, raise the dead, cleanse the lepers, cast out demons: freely ye received, freely give.* Jesus didn't say we heal the sick through Him. That is what most religious people say. The thing is, He lives in you, don't you get that? He works, sees, touches, walks, blesses in you. If you are in Christ, you are one spirit with Him. Your spirit has mingled with his spirit to become one divine and inseparable being. I heard the true story of a minister who went to work in a very populous country and saw many miracles, signs and wonders. One day as he walked through town, some people noticed him and knowing what he had done, they mobbed him, touching and excitedly talking about him. Instantly he tried to shake himself free and tried to distance himself from the divine works he had been doing by yelling to the people; "it isn't me! It is Jesus. Don't touch me!" He had scarcely blurted out that last statement when God rebuked him. He asked him, "what would you think if the donkey used by Jesus in His entry to Jerusalem suddenly stopped and said; oh please, it is not me, it is the master!" God continued; "It is not you they want to touch. It is me in you! Everybody knows that in yourself, you can't even heal a fly. Let them touch you for as long as they want to!" After that, the man now walked freely and let the people touch him for as much as they wanted to. You see, a lot of Christians are like this man. In an effort to not appear like they are arrogant, they really appear so. Let's take the example God gave this man: if that donkey had really stopped in between the palm branches and exclaimed "it is not me!" The people would have laughed. Of course it was not the donkey but the one riding on it. In fact, by trying to put the disclaimer, she would be working to turn the attention on her and that is the real pride. We all know the power to heal belongs to God but He gave us the authority. We are in charge here and we need to begin taking charge. It is when we try to deny that it is us doing the exploits we do that we really call attention to ourselves. We are healers and life givers. Freely we have received life; freely we dispense life and healing as instructed by Jesus. You can't give what you don't have. When Peter encountered the crippled beggar at the temple gate, he told him; "Silver and gold have I none; but such as **I have give I thee:** In the name of Jesus Christ of Nazareth rise up and walk." - Acts 3:6. Notice he told the man that he did have something to give him and it was healing. Did you know we can use everything God has given us to promote His cause on earth? I mean if you have a great name on earth, you can use it to popularize the name of Jesus also just like He gave us gifts and talents to promote expansion of His kingdom. You can use your money, beauty, strength, intellect, fame, education, success, charisma and general prosperity to make Jesus known. All those are gifts of favor from Him and each must be used for the cause of Christ.

Deuteronomy 8: 18 *But thou shalt remember the LORD thy God: for it is he that giveth thee power to get wealth, that he may establish his covenant which he sware unto thy fathers, as it is this day.* (KJV)

Of course I am not saying we walk around boastfully saying outrageous things like "look at me, I am a healer, I have power and I am great" That would be foolish to not wisely give glory where it is due. All I am saying is that agree with God in everything He has said in His word. Study His word to know everything He has stated concerning you and embrace it fully by saying it boldly and actingon it.

B.   GOD SHARED HIS GLORY!

I have heard it said in religious circles that "God will not share His glory with anybody." People who say that may appear humble and I will admit I sometimes don't know what exactly they mean by that statement; but, I happen to know one or two things about the new creation's relationship with God. If what those people mean is that God is the sole creator of everything that exists; if they mean the Lord alone is the genuine God and He has no competition with all the gods and idols of men; and, if they mean He has no rivals or comparisons and that He alone is to be worshipped, I have absolutely no quarrel with that. By saying that God has shared His glory with the new creation, I don't mean we are to be worshipped. We remain worshippers of God. We are the lesser kings who worship the King of kings and Lord of lords. He remains the only one to be adored and worshipped for eternity and that position will never change. <u>What it means for God to share His glory with us is that He has elevated us to His own class in that we are partakers of His nature, the divine nature. Keep in mind we are also His children. We proceed directly from Him. We are made of what He is made of. We have His nature and character.</u> For example, we are His righteousness in Christ Jesus in that our new man is created after Him; in righteousness and true holiness. That is glory! God has built us just like Himself! He has shared His life with us. He doesn't hide anything from us! He has even given us His mind! We are not only His dearly beloved children but His bosom buddies as well.

John 17:22 *And the glory which thou gavest me I have given them; that they may be one, even as we are one:* (KJV) Emphasis added.

Romans 8: 30 Moreover whom he did predestinate, them he also called: and whom he called, them he also justified: and whom he justified, them he also glorified. (KJV)

2 Thessalonians 2: 14 *Whereunto he called you by our gospel, to the obtaining of the glory of our Lord Jesus Christ.* (KJV)

For those who say God will not share His glory with anybody, if what they mean is that He is alone and highly exalted up there while we all are down here; as insignificant and as small as dust without knowing what He is doing up there, I disagree completely. We are not inconsequential minions in the universe who are far removed from God and without any idea what He is doing. We are not distant servants of God who are totally junior, far below Him and whose function is only to follow His orders and obey His rules like a slave would. God is not interested in distant servants who don't know what He is up to. He has given us His mind. He has allowed us into the core chambers of His divine reasoning. He doesn't hide things from us.

1 Corinthians 2:16 *For who hath known the mind of the Lord, that he may instruct him? But we have the mind of Christ.* (KJV)

Genesis 18:16 *Then the men got up from their meal and looked out toward Sodom. As they left, Abraham went with them to send them on their way. 17* **"Should I hide my plan from Abraham?"** *the LORD asked. 18 "For Abraham will certainly become a great and mighty nation, and all the nations of the earth will be blessed through him.* (KJV) Emphasis added.

Look at how the Lord highly esteems those who receive His favor from these verses! He treats them like mature associates! In another place, He says that He will not do anything without informing His servants the prophets. I repeat here again that God wants associates He can fellowship with, not a bunch of religious, cowering people who are intimidated in His presence and who consider themselves unworthy of His companionship.

There are at least three ways to assess or view oneself: first, you can view yourself through the opinion of other people. This is the riskiest way to arrive at an estimate of yourself because most people are ignorant of spiritual things, are envious of you or have no real incentives to think highly of you. They are not obligated to hold a favorable view of your worth. Many of them also hold very unfavorable and low opinions of themselves and will not hesitate to use the same scale to rate you any way. Secondly, you can see yourself from the perspective of your own opinion. This is also a dangerous route because your opinion may be subject to your cultural upbringing, traditions and beliefs of those around you, what the devil whispers to your ears and what religious people say. The third and only sure-fire way of assessing your worth is through God's eyes. This perspective is found in the word of God and it is the very subject of this book. You need to drop every consideration of yourself which is not sourced from the Bible's position on the true identity of the new creation, and embrace exactly what the word of God says. That word says those of us who believe in Christ are partakers or sharers of divinity (the very nature and life of God). We are not ordinary or natural men but supermen in Christ. We are the offspring of God and God is far from an ordinary or natural being. We are made exactly of the same material (word) as Jesus and we can do what He can do and even more. We are brothers of Jesus the divine. We need to begin taking ourselves seriously and when we do that, such humility will please God. God is not the Father of some pathetic minions who think they are just as ordinary as the unbelievers and are just lucky to be alive because they don't count for much before Him. He wants bold and confident sons who know they carry the DNA of their heavenly Father and are here to transform this entire planet to conform to the standards of heaven.

Daniel 11:32...*but the people that do know their God shall be strong, and do exploits.* (KJV)

God takes no pleasure in all this outrageous and religious false piety where Christians keep mindlessly repeating; "I am nothing; I can do nothing without God and I have nothing that He can desire. I am unworthy of His goodness; I am not good enough to stand before Him; I am unrighteous and unfit to come before the Lord because I am a man of unclean lips and I live among filthy people." Old Testament people could say some of those things but not the new creation.

For a new creation person to make those terribly wrong confessions; it is the highest display of Christian illiteracy, foolishness, ignorance and utter unbelief. God made many classes of creatures and they were for different purposes. Long after the original creation of nature, roughly 4000 years later, God created in Christ a new and superb class of beings called the new creation who are unlike anything that went before them. These supermen are created in Christ Himself. They carry His very genes. They and Christ are all cut from the same stock, which stock is God. They are part and parcel of the God-club; the highest in the universe. They are not cheap and common creation. They are an integral part of

God because they constitute the body of His son. Just like human beings have human life, those who have received eternal life like the new creation supermen can't be called human beings: they can only be referred to as eternal beings. The life they possess is far superior to human life and it is called aiónios zóé or eternal life. This is the life of God Himself and it is far from ordinary or common. Far from this being blasphemy, it is actually a present hour reality. If it were possible for God to lose these eternal, new creation people in some way, He would have lost part of Himself and would actually be incomplete. How can He be complete without His body? I know that is a heavy and revolutionary statement but it is very true. That is how God has designed it to be. Not that He needed us, but that in His love, grace and wisdom, He chose to make us an inseparable and integral part of Him.

John 17:21 *That they all may be one; as thou, Father, art in me, and I in thee, that they also may be one in us: that the world may believe that thou hast sent me. ...23 I in them, and thou in me, that they may be made perfect in one; and that the world may know that thou hast sent me, and hast loved them, as thou hast loved me.* (KJV)

John 14:20 *At that day ye shall know that I am in my Father, and ye in me, and I in you.* (KJV)

Beloved, it is not about God not sharing His glory with anybody. He has glorified us already and there is nothing we can do about it. We can only flow in it and enjoy ourselves thoroughly. He has made us participators in His league of divinity-2 Peter 1:4.

There is no question as to whether God has shared His glory with us. That He has done.

Psalm 84:11 *For the LORD God is a sun and shield: the LORD will give grace and glory: no good thing will he withhold from them that walk uprightly.* (KJV) Emphasis added.

The issue really is whether we can believe it and if after we do, we can still remain grounded in genuine humility. The Lord is not against us boasting in our glorified status. What He detests is pride and arrogance. He even advises that we glory and boast in Christ. What would be tragic is if this glory got into our minds and we began entertaining the thought that by our own achievement, we have merited this glorious and esteemed position. We must remain humble and know we are glorified and glorious, relative to our position in Christ. The other deadly thing that would happen is if we begin to think we are any more special than other people. God loves and blesses us equally and there is never a cause why anyone believer would think of himself more highly than others. We should not even look down on non-believers and people of the religions of the world because Jesus equally died for them and He wants them all to be saved and come home to Him. That is why He stands in heaven with outstretched arms all day long waiting to receive His long lost sons.

Banish false humility from your life by submitting to God's word and you will have clothed yourself with genuine humility. And let me suggest to you that next time you use that unfortunate phrase of "we are all sinners saved by grace," don't include those of us who are not confused about our identity. Just speak for yourself. For my part, I honor the blood of Jesus so much I can never say I am still a sinner after He has washed me with it. I am the righteousness of God in Christ even when I sin. <u>Sinning doesn't mean my identity of righteousness in Christ is erased any more than doing a righteous act before I was born again erased my identity of a sinner in satan.</u> After I have become a new creation, sinning simply means I am a righteous person who has sinned because he has not sufficiently renewed his mind. A beautiful butterfly which falls in a mound of dirt doesn't become a housefly, it is still a butterfly. Likewise, for the person who is not born again, doing one righteous act doesn't make them a righteous person. It only makes them sinners who have done a righteous act. That includes all the unbelieving millionaires and billionaires who give a lot to charity with an inadvertent motive in their minds to court the favor of God or appease their stinging consciences. Christians sin but that's not who they are. Sinning only makes them righteous people who have an old program in that area of life where they are sinning. They simply need to do an upgrade of their software in the area. That sin is not in their spirit but in some areas of the soul and body.

Romans 6: 12 *Let not sin therefore* **reign in your mortal body,** *that ye should obey it in the lusts thereof.* (KJV) Emphasis added.

As can be seen in this scripture, when a believer sins, that sin affects the soul and the body but not the spirit. Sin reigns in the body because it is still not born again but the reason the body becomes a slave of sin is because the soul allows and sides with it. If you sufficiently renew your mind which is in the soul, you will not conform to this world but will be transformed to be able to prove what is that good and acceptable and perfect will of God. That way, sin will not reign in your mortal body but instead, righteousness will. It all depends on the condition of the soul. The soul determines the way your life goes. If it is renewed with the word of God, your whole life goes the direction of righteousness. But if the soul is not renewed and is left to continue in the ways of the world, fulfilling the desires of the flesh and of the mind; then your whole life will be in the way of the prince of the air. It is in our best interests to renew our minds at every opportunity if we want to kiss goodbye to sin. Sin is a terrible master who must be driven out of our lives but the way we do that is not by will power and trying to keep the law but by beholding the glory of Christ in the word of His grace. By that process, we are effortlessly transformed to the same glory we see in the word. That is called grace at work. <u>You see, with increase of the knowledge of God and of Jesus comes multiplied grace and grace is the antidote for sin.</u>

After all is said and done, we have no option but to adopt a lifelong posture of renewing the mind with the word in order to live lives of victory. Sin opens up our lives for destruction and erodes our confidence in our righteousness in Christ. We have no option but to get rid of it. However, whatever stage of mind renewal we are at and no matter how much sin still rules our lives, we must learn to embrace Christ as our righteousness because that is the only way to successfully eventually wipe out sin from our experience. But, to Continue calling ourselves sinners (just because we sin) after we have been washed by the eternal blood of Jesus is like putting the impeccable blood of the son of God in the same class with those Old Testament bloods of animals which were offered continually every year and were mere shadows that could never make the worshippers perfect. In those sacrifices was a remembrance again made of sins every year-Hebrews 10:1-3. Sometimes I wonder whether some people can read and believe the simple word without complicating it. How can any believer read these clear passages and still continue saying they are sinners? Someone is asking; but sir, don't you sin after you are born again? Yes I do but my conduct doesn't any longer define me. What defines me is what Jesus did for me at the cross that made me eternally righteous and holy. My standing before God is now wrapped in Jesus, not in myself. If I still say I am a sinner, then I am saying that Jesus is a sinner because Jesus is my life and my new identity. I no longer live because I am crucified with Christ and therefore I am dead. Jesus now lives in me. He is my very life. The life I now live I live by the faith of the son of God, who loved me and gave Himself for me-Galatians 2:20. I am dead and my life is now hid with Christ in God- Colossians 3:3. The only people who are still sinners are those who are either without Christ or are self-righteous and are banking on their goodness to impress God. They are in trouble already! I have eternal life but this life is not in my physical life. It is in Christ and I am in Him too through my faith in Him. That is how I get to have it.

1 John 5: 11 *And this is the record, that God hath given to us eternal life, and this life is in his Son. 12 He that hath the Son hath life; and he that hath not the Son of God hath not life.* (KJV)

In the history of the Bible, we find four types of people who had the righteousness of God; the righteousness that is not of works. The first was Adam before he fell. He was perfect in His thinking, speech and conduct until he committed sin. The second was Abraham. Just because He believed, God imputed to him eternal righteousness and made him the father of all who would likewise later receive righteousness apart from works. Next came Jesus. His case was unique because he did not have righteousness imputed to Him. It is His nature. He is righteousness, the very fountain and source of it. Lastly, we have the children of Abraham, the new creation. These ones are born righteous and truly holy.

Now, sometimes, the new creation may not manifest the righteousness of God in daily life as per exact expectation. He may have some challenges producing a manifest fruit of righteousness. Don't let that fool you. He is still new creation. A mango tree is still a mango tree even if you don't see mangoes in it. Actually, what makes it a mango tree is not really the fruits themselves but the root. Similarly, our root is righteousness and for those who still have challenges manifesting it, they just need some little time to establish themselves in the right soil of grace and before long, the fruits will be pouring out. The fact is, we are born again righteous and truly holy. There is no process of acquiring righteousness and holiness for the believer. The process is in renewing the mind and manifesting the fruit of holiness and righteousness. It need not be long though and the fruits should intensify in quality and quantity with time. <u>The issue is always that people look at one's external factors to disqualify the person but God looks at the heart to qualify us. We can never fail God's test as long as our faith remains in Christ and never in our strength or holiness.</u>

    The new creation has no past just like a new born baby has none. I will make a very staggering statement here. In fact, the new creation is not even the person who was forgiven. The new creation has never sinned and has no capacity to sin. He is brand new from God and in God. You don't need to be told that in God, there is no sin. The issue is, the new man still possesses an old body in which past sins were committed. Those are the sins that were forgiven but they belonged to the old man who died so that the new creation can be born. That is the first natural man who was born by natural parents and after the nature of Adam and he died in Christ. In his place was born a brand new past-less man whose nature and capabilities match those of his senior brother, Jesus. Besides being a brother of Jesus, this new man is also the son of Jesus. That is why we call him a Jesus-man. You see, the death of Jesus on the cross was akin to Him being planted. Jesus Himself said that unless a grain of wheat falls to the ground, it abides alone. But, if it falls and dies, it brings forth much produce. He meant that if He didn't die on the cross, He would not save us and He would not have offspring. But He died and sowed Himself to the ground and when He resurrected, He gave birth to billions of sons who are exactly like Him-Christians throughout all ages. This is the mighty family of God in heaven and earth named from Jesus. Even genetics teach us that like begets like. That means whatever God planted in the divine seed that is

Jesus is what came up. You don't plant wheat and expect to reap maize. He planted Jesus and He has a rich harvest of Jesus-men. That is why Jesus is the first born from the dead-Colossians 1:18, and the first-begotten-Hebrews 1:6; Revelation 1:5. Because of the foregoing, Jesus is not ashamed to call us His brethren. This truth is too staggering to contain! This new man is not born by man or of the will of man. He is born of God and we know God is spirit. So, this new man is spirit as well.

John 3: 6 *That which is born of the flesh is flesh; and that which is born of the Spirit is spirit.* (KJV)

There it is. The new creation is not a physical entity but a new and perfect spirit being housed in an old body. Just like the old natural man had the capabilities of natural Adam, this new man has the capabilities of God. He is just like Christ and that is why Jesus said this man shall do the same works He did, and greater works even. Religion has reduced many Christians to timid, begging and ineffective people whom the world doesn't take seriously. Imagine this, Jesus expects the people He left behind who carry His hopes of reigning in the world on His behalf to function just like He did and even do greater works. Now, instead of them stepping up to the plate and getting down to that business, they've reduced that mandate to nothing by developing an elaborate and cumbersome religion of rituals, liturgies and traditions and rules of men which insulate the very power of God which is supposed to ooze from these people to heal and preserve the world! Check this out:

Philippians 3: 10 *That I may know him,* **and the power of his resurrection,** *and the fellowship of his sufferings, being made conformable unto his death;* (KJV) Emphasis added.

You see that? I bet you had never seen that verse in that light. That verse is saying that the resurrection of Jesus unleashed an unlimited power which is available to us because the Spirit of God who raised up Jesus from the dead indwells us. We need to understand who we are in Christ and what we have. That realization alone will eliminate all the small and nonsensical prayers which have become the hallmarks and preoccupation of most Christians' lives. These songs and prayers of: "touch me once more Jesus; pass me not o gentle savior; I need your touch; if I may touch the hem of your garment, I can get well" No Christian needs to be found singing or praying ineffective and religious, even stupid things like those. That particular song of "pass me not" must be one of the silliest songs of unbelief ever written in the New Testament era. Christ doesn't visit us, He lives in us. The Christian is not only eternally touched but he is reborn a superman! The new creation is the powerhouse of God on earth. He is supposed to supply life giving power to all who are in need. He is not supposed to be singing small nonsensical lullabies which lack revelation and seriousness. <u>The Christian is the headquarters of Jesus on earth and is supposed to be the light (the solution provider) and salt (the standard setter) of the world. The Christian is the embassy of God on earth. He processes passports of men to the kingdom of God.</u> How can he then begin to beg for a touch from Jesus who indwells him? Jesus didn't want to touch you; Instead, He made His home in you. Which of the two is better? To demonstrate to you how low most Christians have sunk from Jesus' expectation, let me call your attention to one ailing woman in the Bible who had an issue of blood for a dozen years. She hid in a massive crowd of people who were thronging Jesus and touching Him on every side. She also touched Jesus but her touch was different because it was of faith. Many Christians have taken the position of that Old Testament woman in their relationship to Jesus. How many sermons are preached today that tell the listeners to push their way through the crowds to reach Jesus and touch Him in order to obtain solutions to their problems? First of all, what are you doing in the crowds? Haven't you been consecrated as a special species, God's own handiwork, created in Christ Jesus to do *good works*, which God *prepared in advance* for us to walk in them? What are you doing in the religious masses? You are not among the suffering crowds. You have been singled out as the powerhouse of God on earth. Power flows out of you to heal the world. If anyone dying of some terminal disease had sense enough to see Jesus in you the hope of glory and they touched you **by faith**, virtue would flow forth and heal them. Yet, how many teachings out there are designed to place the new creation right in the exact position of that ailing woman, a lowly position of trembling and begging? The new creation is not in the position of that woman. He is in the position of Jesus whom she sought to touch at the risk of her very life. I still hear Christians saying, "if you are in trouble, cry unto the Lord like the blind man, or the bereaved woman, or the sinking disciples, or some suffering person in the Bible who cried unto Jesus." This is not the time to "cry unto Jesus." You cannot now cry unto Jesus. Jesus is in you, not out there in heaven. Heaven moved into you- John 14:23. Which other Jesus are you crying unto? He expects you to manifest Him for all to see what He would have done had He been in your place. You are the one with the authority. You are in the driving seat. Kings don't cry; they decree. Only religious people cry. Kings reign with their word. Even in the Old Testament when Moses tried to cry unto the Lord, He asked him, "why cry unto me Moses? Tell the Israelites to continue moving and exercise the authority in your rod over the waters!" That is an apt paraphrase of Exodus 14:15-16. You need to decree the word of God and tame your situation to line up with the will of God. The most you can do is seek direction from the Holy Spirit if there is some information you can't seem to receive clearly from the written word. After you get the revelation, ultimately, it is your duty to put your authority to work following the revelation that you have. If you have no revelation, then not even God can help you. You are in the category He says perish for lack of knowledge. I see people like those everywhere and all the time. They are good and humble Christians who serve the Lord, keep the law, give and do all manner of religious things but they are broke, sick, suffering, oppressed and depressed and they can never seem to get out of trouble. Let me assure you, these people are not "suffering for the Lord." They are suffering and will continue suffering because they have no revelation. By revelation I don't mean knowing the Bible. You can be a "senior apostle" and read through the Bible a billion times and still be very spiritually illiterate and ignorant because you read it religiously like most Christians do. The Bible has to be read through the lens of grace and it has to be rightly divided. You have to know how the cross of Christ completely changed the way we relate to God. After you receive the revelation, you must command ith the word and make a demand on what has been provided by Jesus' sacrifice. Remember when Jesus put His disciples on a boat and instructed them to cross to the other side? Later in the night when they saw Him, they were in serious trouble but the Bible says He would have by-passed them with their trouble - Mark 6:48. Jesus wasn't about to pass by because He was ignorant, irresponsible or nonchalant. They had to exercise some authority on their part and make a demand on His power to save them or else they would all perish. That is why most of the people who Jesus healed or otherwise touched had to make the initial step and solicit for His help. Then, when they reached Him, He always asked, "what would you have me to do for you?" It is different in our covenant. You can't cry to Jesus like Bartimaeus. You are not in the position of that blind man but of Jesus. You really don't need help because you've been greatly helped. You need to be helping those who are religious, ignorant and unconverted. Jesus has already done everything and all we do is receive with thanks.

Hebrews 5:12 *You have been believers so long now that you ought to be teaching others. Instead, you need someone to teach you again the basic things about God's word. You are like babies who need milk and cannot eat solid food.* (KJV)

The problem is that we usually approach trouble from a position of powerlessness and disadvantage. We need to respond to problems from our born again spirits, not naturally or from the flesh. When we respond to problems supernaturally with strength and authority, supernatural answers are guaranteed. For example, taking the instance I gave above of Jesus' disciples who put a demand on His saving power and were saved; did you know when Jesus came to the boat and saved them they were also translated immediately to the shore? That is supernatural!

John 6:21 *Then they were eager to let him in the boat, and immediately they arrived at their destination!* (KJV)

Anyway, God knows exactly what you are going through. He knows you are passing through a very rough patch. You keep wondering why He can't just save you if indeed He is God and He knows everything. That frustration is shared by the vast majority of Christians. Some even give up on the faith altogether. You must know that although God knows exactly what is happening, He did everything He ever needed to do. He has supplied for everything. The authority to receive what has been provided for or to correct what is going wrong has to be exercised by the bona fide authority-wielders on the earth and that is us. This is where most Christians lose it. Silently, they keep wondering why the word doesn't seem to work for them. The problem is, they are seated doing nothing with the word yet they wait for it to work for them. No wonder many of them die while they wait for the word or for God to heal them. Nothing works in your life until you take the word of God and work it. You must make it work and produce the fruits it talks about in your life. The word is for working, not for memorizing. You can memorize the whole Bible including the maps and still die of something that could have very easily been taken care of by the word. For example, if you are under attack from some sickness, you can't sit there and continue to passively quote scriptures. You must take specific scriptures dealing with healing and sow them in your heart so that they can hatch into healing and wholeness. Then, you must also follow up with decrees from the word to drive out the sickness from your body. You can start with declaring that by the stripes of Jesus, you are healed and must remain so in the name of Jesus. It is not just about mouthing those words. You must believe you are already healed by the completed work of Jesus and see yourself totally as such. The mental image or mind movie you have during this period matters very much. If you say by the stripes of Jesus you are healed but in your mind you imagine yourself becoming sicker and weaker, then what you have is not faith but a religion that will ultimately hurt you. You must see yourself healed as the word declares. After this crucial step, it is important to banish the disease from your body by commanding it to go in the name of Jesus. Once you uproot it with your faith-filled words, you must consider it gone and thank God for it. That is another crucial step of faith. Ultimately, the way your life goes is not dependent on God but on what you decide to do with the word. Will you let it stay idle in your heart as you hurt or will you take it and make it work for you and banish all problems from your life? This is part of what God means when He says He has handed us life and death and that we should choose life. To choose life is make the word work for you while to choose death is to treat the word as a religious talisman by just revering it but never applying it to release its power.

The new creation is the hope of the world and the closest the heathens can ever come to God. The new creation is the effulgence of God's glory and the express image of Christ on earth. Men need not ask where Christ is. Men need never miss Christ because the 'Jesus men' are supposed to represent Him to the fullest, doing even greater works than He did when He was around.

Matthew 5: 13 *Ye are the salt of the earth: but if the salt have lost his savour, wherewith shall it be salted? It is thenceforth good for nothing, but to be cast out, and to be trodden under foot of men. 14 Ye are the light of the world. A city that is set on an hill cannot be hid...16 Let your light so shine before men, that they may see your good works, and glorify your Father which is in heaven.* (KJV)

One of the reasons why religious Christianity is so boring and off-putting is because it likes to identify with everybody else but Jesus. That is how come you hear of all these uncalled-for songs of "these are the days of Elijah, of Ezekiel, of Moses" and other Old Testament characters. We are supposed to stand in the place of Jesus only, not any other character. We are not seeking some help. We are the help the world needs badly. Men are supposed to press into the crowds seeking to just touch us or attempting their luck if peradventure our shadow can just cast upon them and heal them like Peter's. We are the ones who have the anointing which breaks all the yokes of bondage and introduces the glorious light of Christ which shatters to smithereens all the works of the devil. When we are clothed with Christ and we come into contact with suffering men, we can be the end of their long search for solutions of and meaning in life. Remember, God doesn't just want to reveal Jesus to us; He actually wants to reveal His mighty and famous son in us. That is a whole lot of difference.

Galatians 1: 15 *But when it pleased God, who separated me from my mother's womb, and called me by his grace, 16* **To reveal his Son in me,** *that I might preach him among the heathen; immediately I conferred not with flesh and blood:* (KJV) Emphasis added.

This new species of man takes up serpents and doesn't suffer harm; he drinks any deadly thing and it does not hurt him; he lays hands on the sick and they recover; he raises the dead, cleanses lepers and does many other extra-natural exploits. You see, what is born of natural man produces the natural, ordinary results of a natural man. What is born of God gets the supernatural results of God. <u>What is born of natural man fails like man and is limited and handicapped by nature. What is born of God excels like God, triumphs like God, is a mystery and is unlimited just like God.</u> Being a spirit just like his Father, the new creation is capable of operating spiritually even in physical earth. He calls things that are in the spirit world as though they are in the physical, and then they appear in the physical. Now, when we explain this phenomenon called new creation, some people think it is a New Testament only concept. This super being however was prophesied of old:

Psalm 102: 18 *This shall be written for* **the generation to come: and the people which shall be created** *shall praise the LORD.* (KJV) Emphasis added.

Most people have never heard of this verse but it is absolutely mind blowing. Its context is all about God acknowledging that His people were at the time trodden down, hopeless and appointed to death. He however says that a time is coming in the future when He will arise and have mercy upon His people and favor them. That speaks of the dispensation of grace we enjoy now. He then says the people who will enjoy that enviable period will not be ordinary but that He will create a new generation of people. That time is now and that new creation is all of us who believe in Christ Jesus.

Psalm 102: 13 *Thou shalt arise, and have* **mercy upon Zion:** *for the* **time to favour her***, yea, the set time, is come…19 For he hath looked down from the height of his sanctuary; from heaven did the LORD behold the earth; 20 To hear the groaning of the prisoner; to loose those that are appointed to death;* (KJV) Emphasis added.

We need to know that Satan has been controlling the earth through men ever since Adam fell. That is why the Bible calls him the god of this world or of this age. He was riding rough-shod on men for millennia until God said it was enough and sent Jesus. God wanted to return control of the earth to the original beneficiary who is man. Man lost control of the earth when he lost his spiritual authority by sinning. The principle is, whoever controls the spiritual realm in any given area, is also in charge of the physical realm there as well.

Christians have been ignorant of this for far too long. From time to time, some Christians have become fed up with the yoke of satan in their areas of operation and thrown him off. Others have been clueless and only keep wondering why things are the way they are. We are entering a phase in the life of the church where such a huge number of Christians will be so armed with wisdom, knowledge and spiritual understanding that they will rise up to control the spiritual atmosphere in their areas of operation and hence control the physical environment there as well. They will control the politics, the economy, the education, the opinions and the culture of the areas they are in. You see, our problem is not power. That one we have and it can't be contested. But power is nothing without knowledge of the truth. The Bible doesn't say Christians are destroyed for lack of power. It doesn't also say that we shall have power and power shall make us free. It is the truth that makes us free, and not just the truth that is still in the pages of the Bible which is gathering dust in the coffee table. It is the truth we have known, believed and internalized. All Jesus spoke was the truth when He was still interacting with religious people on earth yet most of His hearers weren't made free by His words. Wide eyes and wide ears don't necessarily guarantee a wide and fertile heart for the truth. The devil can make a complete wreckage of your life even if you have a billion Bibles in your pocket. You must transfer that knowledge out of those holy pages, renew your mind with it and act on it. If you are in Christ, you are a new creation in your spirit and when you also renew your mind; your spirit and soul are in sync. That means the only part of you that is not renewed is your residence which is your body. Because your spirit and your mind are now one, they can prevail over the body and align it with them as well.

Seek knowledge of the word of God in order to renew your mind more than you do gold and silver. Here is wise speech: what you put in your head as accurate revelation from the word of God is what puts you ahead. You must let that knowledge transform how you think and what you think about, what you say, where you go, how you talk and ultimately how you act.

Proverbs 11: 9 *An hypocrite with his mouth destroyeth his neighbour:* ***but through knowledge shall the just be delivered.***

(KJV) Emphasis added.

Proverbs 4: 5 *Get wisdom, get understanding: forget it not; neither decline from the words of my mouth. 6 Forsake her not, and she shall preserve thee: love her, and she shall keep thee. 7 Wisdom is the principal thing; therefore get wisdom: and with all thy getting get understanding. 8 Exalt her, and she shall promote thee: she shall bring thee to honour, when thou dost embrace her.* (KJV)

This deliverance is not the one religious people are used to of chasing demons and other satanic influences out of people. The new creation doesn't need any such "deliverance." He has been translated from the dominion of darkness unto the kingdom of God's dear son.

Colossians 1: 13 *Who hath delivered us from the power of darkness, and hath translated us into the kingdom of his dear Son:* (KJV)

Galatians 1: 4 *Who gave himself for our sins, that he might deliver us from this present evil world, according to the will of God and our Father:* (KJV)

The apostle Paul tells believers that God the Father "has delivered us from the power of darkness and has conveyed us into the kingdom of the son of His love." Notice there has been a change of location. You used to be under the power of darkness but the moment you believed in Jesus, you were moved and placed under the blood of Jesus.

The only deliverance the new creation needs is not from the devil but from ignorance for which the people of God are destroyed. Nobody can do this deliverance for the Christian except him. Not even God can. Only the believer can deliver himself by renewing his mind with the word of God. This deliverance depends solely on the individual believer. You certainly don't need some preacher or a professional prophet to deliver you from ignorance of spiritual things. You only need you, the Holy Spirit, your Bible and some time to deepen in the knowledge of the secrets of the kingdom of God. The more you deepen in knowledge of spiritual things, the less the devil will have anything to do with you. Being born again is the first and most critical stage of deliverance from the power of satan. After that, what remains is deliverance of the mind so that the believer ceases to be deceived and taken advantage of by satan through ignorance. This cumbersome and weird charismatic religion of holding deliverance services or conferences is not only unbiblical but is a senseless waste of time and other resources. Instead of attending such, just take your Bible and lock yourself in a quiet room and meditate on the word of God. You will have all the deliverance you will ever need. Hearken to this; you will never have a health, a relationship or a financial problem. You only have a knowledge problem. Where your life is not doing well is the very place where you need to augment your knowledge and wisdom. There is some knowledge you are lacking in that area and when you acquire it, you will then be delivered in the same. The more you renew your mind by the word and acquire the mindset of God, the less the devil will interrupt your life. Every problem in your life is a wisdom problem. In fact, I will venture to say that you should not be afraid of satan and his cohort; be instead afraid of your ignorance. <u>The Bible doesn't say God's people are destroyed because of the devil or demons but due to ignorance. You need to be concerned about where you lack knowledge, not satan coming against you.</u> The reason is because while satan never tires from trying to ruin your life, if you are properly exercising the mind of Christ in you, all dirty spirits will have to give you a wide berth. Satan doesn't go around devouring anybody in sight by will. He moves around looking for the ignorant and least resistant to devour. It means there are those who he cannot devour. It is not that they have any special power or ability but because they have renewed their minds and they cannot be conformed to the thinking and patterns of this world. They rarely have anything to do with the devil because they play in God's league.

    Even the devil when he had exhausted all his temptations, he had to flee from Jesus because he had no more business with Him. You can be like Jesus. You can take the whole armor of God so that you withstand in the evil day and, having done all to stand- Ephesians 6:13. It is through the word of God that we can renew our minds; can be brainwashed after God's counsel and will; and can also be reprogrammed from a carnal worldly way of thinking to a kingdom one. <u>Ignorance cancels the ability to apply power.</u> Come on let's face it, all Christians who are Holy Spirit filled are imbued with divine power because Jesus said we shall receive power after He has come upon us. Yet, how many such Christians are suffering unnecessarily while the Holy Spirit silently inhabits their spirits? Did you know that what Peter could not be and do while walking with Jesus for three and a half years, He did in a few minutes of being with the Holy Spirit? Ignorance is so dangerous that one can be sitting on immense power and not even know what is available to them. One can be ignorantly leaning on a well, and dying of thirst. That is what we need to deliver ourselves from by arming ourselves with knowledge of the truth of the word of God, not just by being religious. I have heard it said and correctly so, that one's area of ignorance is also their area of bondage.

2 Corinthians 2: 11 *Lest Satan should get an advantage of us: for we are not ignorant of his devices.* (KJV)

An army of super-intelligent members of the new creation race is rising up and is increasingly limiting the frontiers of the once formidable enemy called satan. That sinister witch is losing ground left, right and center. He is losing it in the hearts of men, on the face of the earth and even in his own turf- the spirit world. He no longer can rest easy in his wicked abode. He will never have peace and he will never have his way where these light beings from heaven on brief loan to earth are operating. Some people could be wondering what on earth I am talking about. <u>This book is not a religious text. It is God's own special divine tool of revealing to the new creation who he is, whose he is, where he comes from, what he has and what capabilities he has.</u> This is far from religion.

As new creation, we are partakers of the divine nature. That means we are vital participants in the class of God Himself.

2 Peter 1: 4 *Whereby are given unto us exceeding great and precious promises: that by these ye might be partakers of the divine nature, having escaped the corruption that is in the world through lust.* (KJV)

The new creation has already escaped all the corruption, the death, the tragedy that is this brutal life and the decadence that is so rampant in every corner of this world. He has come out unscathed, alive with Jesus and is seated in Him in heavenly places far above all principality and power. The new creation is the born again brother of Christ Jesus. He is a born-again member of an original and first time new spiritual species that existed only in the mind of God before Jesus came. God was all along pregnant in His Spirit with this superman who is created in the image and likeness of Christ. A believer is not a changed person; he is created a fresh as a brand new creature. The new creature is not a successive improvement of the old creature that had the sinful Adamic nature. He is a brand new species with divine nature from God Himself. <u>He doesn't get better every day. He is a final-once-and-for-all made masterpiece who cannot be improved upon either in time or in eternity.</u> The new creature has "arrived". We cannot be made better by any good we do or made worse by any bad we do. We are just new, static and stable. <u>The new creation is not an improvement of the old man. He is not the old creation trying to perform better than he did before salvation. He is a brand new person from a brand new birth in a brand new start for a brand new destiny.</u> The resurrected Jesus is Himself the first born of this new spiritual species.

Colossians 1: 18 *And he is the head of the body, the church: who is the beginning, the firstborn from the dead; that in all things he might have the preeminence.* (KJV)

Revelation 1: 5 *And from Jesus Christ, who is the faithful witness, and the first begotten of the dead, and the prince of the kings of the earth. Unto him that loved us, and washed us from our sins in his own blood,* (KJV)

Jesus suffered, died and resurrected after three days. The Bible calls His resurrection a rebirth. Death has no power over this re-born Jesus. The spiritual forces of darkness cannot understand, affect or handle Him. They cannot predict Him. Here is the million dollar revelation. Those who put their faith for salvation in Jesus also die symbolically. They lay down their old sin nature and receive the new nature of Christ in them. Christ is born in them. They cease to exist and Christ becomes the new person inside them. He lives in them, walks in them and works through them.

Colossians 3: 3 *For ye are dead, and your life is hid with Christ in God. 4 When Christ, who is our life, shall appear, then shall ye also appear with him in glory.* (KJV)

Galatians 2:20 *I am crucified with Christ: nevertheless I live; yet not I, but Christ liveth in me: and the life which I now live in the flesh I live by the faith of the Son of God, who loved me, and gave himself for me.* (KJV)

Romans 8: 10 *And if Christ be in you, the body is dead because of sin; but the Spirit is life because of righteousness.* (KJV)

2 Corinthians 6:16 *And what agreement hath the temple of God with idols? for ye are the temple of the living God; as God hath said, I will dwell in them, and walk in them; and I will be their God, and they shall be my people.* (KJV)

Only the old body and soul are retained of a born again person. The spirit nature becomes one with Christ henceforth. This is a great and deep mystery that carnal people scorn and jeer at. When we come to Jesus, although we don't die physically as yet, God counts our flesh as dead so that Christ can introduce His own new and divine life through our new spirit. The eternal life we talk so much about and which many Christians still don't understand is in the new spirit. Eternal life is the pulsating divine life of God in a human person. It is the vital energy of God at work in a person. Essentially, it is what we loosely call Christianity. It is not a religion of doing rituals, observing laws, reciting litanies and chanting things. In fact, <u>we can define Christianity as a continuation, extension and prolonging of Christ's life in the believer.</u>

Isaiah 53: 8 *He was taken from prison and from judgment: and* **who shall declare his generation?** *for he was cut off out of the land of the living: for the transgression of my people was he stricken...10 Yet it pleased the LORD to bruise him; he hath put him to grief: when thou shalt make his soul an offering for sin,* **he shall see his seed, he shall prolong his days**, *and the pleasure of the LORD shall prosper in his hand.* (KJV)

We are the generation of Jesus as declared so by God and He prolongs His days on earth through us. That is what Christianity is. It is also called eternal life. Eternal life is the divine life of God in the believer unleashed on the environment. Eternal life is the life of God in you which is far superior to challenges, diseases, sicknesses, death and every weapon launched by the devil. It is a life of total success, victory, dominion, peace and prosperity in every sphere. It is what transforms the life of the believer and makes him different from the non-believers. Lives don't change as a result of trying. They change because the nature which caused those evil works is no more and has now been replaced by the life, nature, power and ability of God. There is new nature that knows and does only good. To try to change and also cause change by human effort or will power is not only unacceptable by God but is actually a recipe for guaranteed failure. <u>Religious people think we are called to "live for Jesus." That is not the case. We are instead supposed to let Jesus live in and through us by His Holy Spirit.</u> That is why we don't strive and struggle in life. If you really are anointed, then there is no place for striving because the anointing carries you through life and your only duty is to yield to it. If you are holding on to Jesus, you will soon grow tired and fall by the way side but if it is Jesus holding and carrying you, He never grows tired and you are safe forever. It is not us living for Christ, but He living through us that assures us of victory. The Christian life must be by the Spirit of God, never by might or by power. Religion wants to get us living for Christ by trying hard and that leads to legalism, works of the law, condemnation, burn out and death. That is precisely why a lot of Christians seem so powerless in life. They can't heal themselves or others; they don't have solutions for their problems or for others and generally, their Christianity appears to be of no earthly good. It is just a powerless, irrelevant and unattractive religion. The law is about telling the outer man what to do and how to conduct himself. Grace focuses on telling the soul what is already done through Christ. We keep talking about being under the law and some people wonder what we mean by it. Here is how to know whether you are under the law or grace: <u>if you are focused on what you must do so that God can accept you and bless you, then you are under the law. On the other hand, if you are focused on learning what Christ has done for you so that you can have faith in it, act on it, act it out and relate to God on its basis, then you are under grace.</u> People who don't believe that without doing righteous acts they can be righteous seek to attain righteousness through keeping the Law and are consumed with "doing." On the other hand, those who receive righteousness by faith simply confess what Christ has already done in their lives which they receive by grace through faith and not by works. This is a simple and yet critical difference. If we are still "doing" acts of holiness to get God to accept and bless us, then we are still operating under a "Law" mentality. When we simply believe and confess what has already been provided through Christ, that's faith in grace.

C. RIGHTEOUSNESS BY FAITH ONLY

To symbolize that we have died and resurrected to new life, we undergo complete water immersion or what religion calls baptism. Seeking to be justified by the law automatically leads to falling from grace which further leads to Christ being of no effect in our lives. That is the most tragic progression on earth. You see, when you are sick, you want Christ to be of effect to you so that you can receive your healing. When you are broke, you want Christ to be of effect to you so that you can receive your provision. The last thing you want in life is to be needy and then find out that Christ is of no effect in your life. Yet, if you were to ask many Christian leaders, they would emphatically say that the reason why Christ can be rendered of no effect in a Christian's life is because of sin! There is no where it says sin can make Christ to be of effect to us. We are all against sin and its practice but sin can't block Christ from being of effect in our lives. If sin could make Christ to be of no effect to us, then He would not have come in the first place because He came for lost sinners. When He came, every human being was a lost sinner heading to destruction, including the very religious Pharisees. He Himself said He didn't come for the healthy people who needed no physician. He put it plainly that He came for the sick. Jesus was of much effect to the thieves, adulterers, tax collectors and corrupt individuals. He forgave, saved and healed them all. The only fellows Jesus was of no effect to were the Pharisees, the scribes, Sadducees and other religious, self-righteous groupings. I like the way the message Bible winds up the whole debate sustained by legalistic people who want to remain under the servitude of the law:

Galatians 2:19-21 *What actually took place is this: I tried keeping rules and working my head off to please God, and it didn't work. So I quit being a "law man" so that I could be God's man. Christ's life showed me how, and enabled me to do it. I identified myself completely with him. Indeed, I have been crucified with Christ. My ego is no longer central. It is no longer important that I appear righteous before you or have your good opinion, and I am no longer driven to impress God. Christ lives in me. The life you see me living is not "mine," but it is lived by faith in the Son of God, who loved me and gave himself for me. I am not going to go back on that. Is it not clear to you that to go back to that old rule-keeping, peer-pleasing religion would be an abandonment of everything personal and free in my relationship with God? I refuse to do that, to repudiate God's grace. If a living relationship with God could come by rule-keeping, then Christ died unnecessarily.* (MSG)

Matthew 21: 31 *Whether of them twain did the will of his father? They say unto him, The first. Jesus saith unto them, Verily I say unto you, That the publicans and the harlots go into the kingdom of God before you.* (KJV)

As the name hints, the gift of righteousness is received by faith, not merited by working for it. In fact, it is revealed from the word of gospel of Jesus, not earned through the hard work of holiness.

Romans 1: 16 *For I am not ashamed of the gospel of Christ: for it is the power of God unto salvation to everyone that believeth; to the Jew first, and also to the Greek. 17 For therein is the righteousness of God revealed from faith to faith: as it is written, the just shall live by faith.* (KJV) Emphasis added.

Romans 10:3 *For they being ignorant of God's righteousness, and going about to establish their own righteousness, have not submitted themselves unto the righteousness of God. 4 For Christ is the end of the law for righteousness to everyone that believeth. 5 For Moses describeth the righteousness which is of the law, That the man which doeth those things shall live by them.* (KJV)

A person who is living under the Law by works and a person who lives under grace by faith should have very similar actions of holiness, but their motivations are completely opposite. Yet, the Lord only looks at the motivation of the heart. The law person has their attention on what they must do, while the person living by faith has his attention on what Christ has already done for him. The gospel of the grace of our Lord Jesus Christ is not about what man must do. If that was the case, then it would not be good news at all. It would be terrible news because man can hardly ever get his doing as perfect as God requires. The gospel is about what Christ has done for us already that is available to us on an unearned and unmerited basis. Notice below here the thought process of both the person under law and the one under grace. I will take the example of healing: The Scriptures teach us to confess with our mouths and believe with our hearts, and we will receive from God. Upon reading that, the legalist thinks, "I can get God to heal me by confessing, 'By his stripes I am healed.'" However, the person who understands God's grace will not confess the Word to get healed. They will confess, "By His stripes I am healed" because they really believe it has already been done.

True life is only to be found in union and meaningful fellowship with the one who alone is the way and the life-Jesus Christ. Even the faith we live by is not our own but Jesus'-Galatians 2:20. _**Never have faith in your own faith. Have faith only in the perfect and sufficient faith of Jesus in you.**_ Every Christian has received the same precious and perfect faith of the son of God. The question of having little or not enough faith does not apply to the genuine Christian. The question is always whether or not one is using the faith of Jesus in them. We have the same faith Jesus and the early apostles operated in-2 Peter 1:1. Some use it more and others less and that is what brings about the difference in the results Christians get.

D. THE NEW CREATION: A BRAND NEW SPECIES OF BEING

To symbolize that we have died and resurrected to new life, we undergo complete water immersion or what religion calls baptism.

Colossians 2: 12 *Buried with him in baptism, wherein also ye are risen with him through the faith of the operation of God, who hath raised him from the dead.* (KJV)

This new birth is not like the natural one. This one is done by the Holy Spirit following one's decision to believe in Christ. The Holy Spirit "cuts away" the old nature and introduces a new spirit with the nature of Christ in our lives. That is called spiritual circumcision shadowed by the physical circumcision done during the Old Testament. Now, the new creation is such a superior being that he's not even comparable to Adam even before he sinned. The new creation is the greatest gift from God ever given to mankind in all of human history. We have more going for us than Adam had in his perfect environment in the beginning. Adam was not the brother of God's own son-Jesus. We are! We are hewn from the same rock as Jesus. We and Jesus are chips of the same age-old block, the Lord God Almighty.

Isaiah 51: *Hearken to me, ye that follow after righteousness, ye that seek the LORD: look unto the rock whence ye are hewn, and to the hole of the pit whence ye are digged. 2 Look unto Abraham your father, and unto Sarah that bare you: for I called him alone, and blessed him, and increased him.* (KJV)

Hebrews 2: 11 *For both he that sanctifieth and they who are sanctified are all of one: for which cause he is not ashamed to call them brethren,* (KJV)

Romans 8: 29 *For whom he did foreknow, he also did predestinate to be conformed to the image of his Son, that he might be the firstborn among many brethren. 30Moreover whom he did predestinate, them he also called: and whom he called, them he also justified: and whom he justified, them he also glorified.* (KJV)

Being new creation has nothing to do with any form of human works or human effort. It is a gift of God. <u>It is a creature God begot not from anything visible but from God Himself. This is a spirit super being just like God. The new creation is a direct son of God in the same way Jesus is.</u> That is why this new creature is an enigma.

John 3: 8 *The wind bloweth where it listeth, and thou hearest the sound thereof, but canst not tell whence it cometh, and whither it goeth: so is every one that is born of the Spirit.* (KJV)

1 Corinthians 2:15 *But he that is spiritual judgeth all things,*

yet he himself is judged of no man. (KJV)

This new creation has in him divine nature (God's own life and nature) that God has put absolutely freely in every single one who believes in Jesus Christ as saviour, even in those who resist these words. This new spirit is the one who is united as one spirit with the Holy Spirit. From the seat of our new spirits, the Holy Spirit leads us. The Holy Spirit doesn't speak to us audibly from outside like a natural person would engage us. That is how carnal people would like to have it. The reason God doesn't work that way is because He is a spirit and His sons are spirits as well. Those who seek to relate to God must do it in the spirit, not in the flesh. <u>Communion or fellowship between the new creation and God is a spirit to spirit affair.</u> God cannot now be worshipped with feelings and other sensory instruments. He is pleased with faith. Hearing His voice audibly and externally would not take faith. Being spiritual, God imparts knowledge to us in our spirits. It's a spirit to spirit transaction. After that, we can get that revelation into the mind and consequently, the body will be impacted. We are not old covenant folks. We are spiritual beings. God speaks in our spirits and we catch it as first person. We just find ourselves knowing what to do and how to do it, where to go and what to say in every circumstance.

Romans 8:16 *The Spirit itself beareth witness with our spirit, that we are the children of God:* (KJV) It is impossible for the new creation person to sin. That which is born of God cannot sin because it is divine and the divine seed remains in the offspring.

1 John 3: 9 *Whosoever is born of God doth not commit sin; for his seed remaineth in him: and he cannot sin, because he is born of God.* (KJV)

I know a lot of Christians are shaken and even terrified by this verse but they need not. Many are asking, "But I am a Christian and I still sin! Does that mean I am not properly born again or is there something wrong with me?" Beloved you are very born again and there is absolutely nothing wrong with you. This new creation is the one who is the real you and is certainly the one incapable of sinning. The problem is that he has been put in an old body or container that is not only not yet glorified but was also accustomed to the old wicked ways. Your body is not the real you. The real you is the new creation. That is the part that will not go back to the soil and you should regard yourself not according to your body but your new creation. That is your true nature and identity.

2 Corinthians5: 16 *Wherefore henceforth know we no man after the flesh: yea, though we have known Christ after the flesh, yet now henceforth know we him no more. 17 Therefore if any man be in Christ, he is a new creature: old things are passed away; behold, all things are become new.* (KJV)

Every Christian must learn to live life from the born again spirit and not the flesh. When facing the circumstances of life, learn to face them as the newly recreated superman, not an old unregenerate man. You see, when the unregenerate man is told he has an incurable disease, he is shocked almost out of breathe and his life is altered forever. It is different with you. If they say you have an incurable illness, ask them, "what is that?" In fact, you can put it like Gabriel Mirabeau who quipped, *"Impossible" - never let me hear that foolish word again.*

So, what do you do with the sickness? We are not to be alarmed by things that are easy to deal with as if we were natural men. There is no problem we should ever allow to cause us sleepless night for even a moment. The very power that raised Jesus from the dead resides in us. Nothing is a big deal. Just unleash that fearsome divine power on whatever problem is ailing you and watch it get destroyed. The new creation has so much power working for him that disease is never supposed to kill him. Instead, he kills any illness that tries to attack him. There is no mountain the faith of Jesus at work in you can't easily move. Nothing is impossible to the person who is in Christ. If you live from your new spirit as opposed to from your soul and body, there is never a problem you can't beat. It is only by living from your spirit that you can do the very things Jesus did and greater things. You can't live like Jesus from your body and soul because there is no power in that. If you insist on living from your flesh, the Bible calls that carnal mindedness and inevitably, death-Romans 8:6. If you live from your spirit, I guarantee here that you will never ever be fearful, depressed, not knowing what to do, defeated and limited in any way. This is because you will always attack everything that pits itself against you as Jesus and not as a human being. If you respond to situations from your flesh as a human being, you will only get human results but if you respond as if you are Jesus of which you should, the results will always be glorious. Here is what is I have been able to learn from the Bible: if you find yourself in a fix and meet it not like a non-believer but with a supernatural reaction, you will get a supernatural response. Consider Paul and Silas. The natural and fleshly reaction to people in jail is to sulk, be sullen and sad. Paul and Silas decided not to live from their flesh but from their spirits. In the new born again spirit, we always are full of joy, peace, patience, forgiveness, praise, happiness, love, faith and every other divine virtue. These two knew they were not their flesh and decided to respond based on who they were in the spirit, not what the senses were dictating to them. When they did that, the Bible says immediately, heaven just happened in the earth. The supernatural broke out and they were liberated. Likewise, it is natural to say "I hurt badly" when you are in pain but the word has trained us not to respond naturally or from the flesh. In other words, we are trained not to respond based on what we can gather from our senses. We don't respond based on our experience because we don't live by the senses but by faith. So, when there is hurting, we say: "by His stripes, I am healed. I shall not be afraid of the pestilence that hides in my body. I am indestructible because I have the life of God at work in me. No evil or plague can come near my dwelling." If you follow that pattern in everything and refuse to respond naturally to circumstances, you will get supernatural results.

Turning now to your body, it loves to sin. Your body is made of local earthly material and that is why it loves the things of this world. The body in its pre-glorified state cannot relate to spiritual things. It has no capacity to appreciate heavenly and spiritual realities. But the new creation would never stand sin for a moment. He only delights in righteousness because he is himself perfectly righteous. The new creation loves the things of heaven where Jesus is seated because he is made of spiritual material from there. The body and spirit are in constant jostling within the same space that is you.

Romans 7: 15 *For that which I do I allow not: for what I would, that do I not; but what I hate, that do I. 16 If then I do that which I would not, I consent unto the law that it is good. 17 Now then it is no more I that do it, but sin that dwelleth in me. 18 For I know that in me (that is, in my flesh,) dwelleth no good thing: for to will is present with me; but how to perform that which is good I find not. 19 For the good that I would I do not: but the evil which I would not, that I do. 20 Now if I do that I would not, it is no more I that do it, but sin that dwelleth in me. 21 I find then a law, that, when I would do good, evil is present with me. 22 For I delight in the law of God after the inward man: 23 But I see another law in my members, warring against the law of my mind, and bringing me into captivity to the law of sin which is in my members. 24 O wretched man that I am! who shall deliver me from the body of this death? 25 I thank God through Jesus Christ our Lord. So then with the mind I myself serve the law of God; but with the flesh the law of sin.* (KJV)

Galatians 5: 17 *For the flesh lusteth against the Spirit, and the Spirit against the flesh: and these are contrary the one to the other: so that ye cannot do the things that ye would.* (KJV)

Mark 14:38 *Watch and pray so that you will not fall into temptation. The spirit is willing, but the flesh is weak."* (NIV)

So, don't be alarmed over your seeming inability to shun evil one hundred per cent. There is still sin in your soul and flesh. Your body only houses the new creation, but is not an integral part of it. Just to encourage you, your flesh won't be around for long. It will soon be destroyed and its place taken by a glorified one from heaven which will be as unlimited and as glorious as the one of the resurrected Jesus.

Philippians 3: 21 *Who shall change our vile body, that it may be fashioned like unto his glorious body, according to the working whereby he is able even to subdue all things unto himself.* (KJV)

1 Peter 1: 24 *For all flesh is as grass, and all the glory of man as the flower of grass. The grass withereth, and the flower thereof falleth away:* (KJV)

This sinful body which harbours vile desires and which is only your house and not the real you will soon be replaced by a divine, spiritual and glorious body in which there is no more sin, corruption and mortality.

1 Corinthians 15: 44 *It is sown a natural body; it is raised a spiritual body. There is a natural body, and there is a spiritual body* (KJV)

Does that mean it is okay to continue in sin because the flesh is ever present with us? Am I excusing sin? That is impossible! Those who understand and embrace grace will find they start with a willingness to hate sin and love that which is good. Soon enough, that willingness will be followed by power to overcome that sin and triumph over evil. Those who embrace the law and the commandments will continue to be servants of sin - every single one of them. Those who fail to understand that it's the new creation who is their new person that was perfected and not their body will continue to seek to attain perfection in the flesh. Consequently, they will inevitably all fall into self-righteousness, legalism and earn a curse.

Then, there is a third faculty in the composition of man- the soul. The soul is neither the body nor the new creation. It is an intermediary or interface in between. That is where the will, emotions and intellect reside. We cannot say that the soul was left entirely untouched by the new birth. It was somewhat affected and it is the reason you developed faith to get born again. If the soul is well trained and educated by the new creation through the word of God, then it will choose to do the will of God. If it is in the dark regarding the will of God, it will join forces with the body and head to sin. Upon believing in Jesus Christ, God gives us as a gift of the new creation at once and throws away the old Adamic sin-laden spirit. That procedure is the new circumcision.

Colossians 2: 11 *In whom also ye are circumcised with the circumcision made without hands, in putting off the body of the sins of the flesh by the circumcision of Christ:* (KJV)

That is God's part solely. We have no input there other than our response of faith to God upon hearing the gospel. After that, it is our job to renew our souls by God's word. God still helps us even at that but the initiative is first ours. So, to the extent you embrace grace and renew your soul, you will be triumphant over sin which wars against your spirit. Now, not only will the body pass away, but the soul also. This soul that is contaminated with sin and ignorance will be no more when Christ returns. We will be so renewed in the soul (intellect, will and emotions) that we will not even remember how corrupted this earth was.

Isaiah 65: 17 *For, behold, I create new heavens and a new earth: and the former shall not be remembered, nor come into mind.* (KJV)

Just like our born again spirit, that soul will be perfect in comprehension, knowledge, wisdom and every other function. Then we will know everything in the soul just as God knows us and nothing will be hidden from us. The soul will then have been saved. Soul salvation can also entail renewing the soul to where it is in greater tune and harmony with the word of God and the new spirit. At that point, all the components of the soul are greatly synchronized with the new spirit. The believer's will or chooser will be highly responsive and positively inclined to the will of God. His intellect or thinker will be greatly renewed and affected by God's word. He will think like God and respond to everything just like God would. He will have the mindset of God. His intellectual capacity will be enhanced and he will make proper use of the mind of Christ in all his endeavors. He will have his emotions in check and they will not get out of control and rule him. Just like money, emotions are good servants if kept in control but if they are let to go wild, they can be terrible masters and destroy their holder.

1 Peter 1: 7 *That the trial of your faith, being much more precious than of gold that perisheth, though it be tried with fire, might be found unto praise and honour and glory at the appearing of Jesus Christ: 8 Whom having not seen, ye love; in whom, though now ye see him not, yet believing, ye rejoice with joy unspeakable and full of glory: 9* **Receiving the end of your faith, even the salvation of your souls.** (KJV) Emphasis added.

Right now, we still know all things and have the mind of Christ but those are still restricted in the new spirit and we never seem able to completely ever renew our minds so that what is in the spirit can also be transferred to the soul as well. But, when the new and glorified soul is revealed upon Jesus' return, the soul and the spirit will now become one integral, synchronized and undivided entity with the body. There will be perfect harmony between the three faculties of man just as there is between God the Father, the son and Holy Spirit.

What makes us so superior to Adam is that while Adam was natural and from the earth, we, the new creation are spiritual and from Heaven-1 Corinthians 15:47-49. We have not taken the nature of Adam, but of Christ who has sired us by His own seed. Just like the Holy Spirit spoke Jesus into being in the womb of Virgin Mary without involvement of the seed of man, He again speaks Jesus to be born today in the hearts of those who believe. This is the revelation that made me christen myself "God's own offspring." Jesus is the word of God. When that word which is the seed of life is preached by the power of the Holy Ghost, it germinates into Christ in the lives of the hearers who believe. That is the deep mystery of the new creation. That is why this new spirit being is not an ordinary, earthly creature. He is seated in Christ by God's right hand; a place of power and dominion. It is important to stress here that the phrase is not that we are 'seated with Christ,' as a lot of people mistakenly quote it. Instead; it reads that we are 'seated in Christ.' We are the body of Christ. We are not beside Him but one with Him and in Him. A lot of people quote it as if it says Christ is seated by God's right hand and we are also seated beside Him. We are in Him, one with Him and reigning together with Him. That means that because the earth is His footstool, it is our footstool as well. That is why we are not of this world although we are in it. The little things men fight over here like gold and other elements constitute our footstool. That is why no Christian worth his salt should ever be caught up in these squabbles over transient earthly things. Hearken to this, we are the body of Christ and because the feet are part of the body, we are His feet and hands. That means we should be controlling this world underneath our feet. The implication of that is that we should be the ones calling the shots here. The world should be like a play thing in our hands and under our feet, directing it to go the way of our master and head, Jesus Christ. The body doesn't do its own bidding but the will of the head. We operate far above the operations of the devil and his miserable demons. We are not trying to fight the devil. A king doesn't fight his subjects; he orders them to do His bidding. We are kings in the universe 'in and with Christ' and the devil is our subject. He is under our feet. If we want to pass a message to him, we scribble it under the sole of our feet because that is what his current estate is - chewing dust. We operate so far above that the devil cannot even decode or intercept our frequency of communication. That is what speaking with tongues affords us but if you are still praying in local languages of men, you are not even a threat to the devil because he can hear everything you say and therefore plan a counterattack against you. That is why some people pray for the same thing for a long time and never seem to see any shift. The truth is, the thing was released long time ago but satan can delay or frustrate your efforts to receive it. That is where tongues come in to elevate the whole affair to a realm where if the devil tried to poke his dirty nose, he would sink and drown. Just like Jesus, we also are not ordinary men. We are born of God and so we come from above. As is the rule, he who is from above is above all. We are above all the universe because we are in Christ Jesus. We are above the earth and all the operations of men and devils. We are masters in the game of life, not helpless victims. We don't participate when ordinary men are crying because they are being beaten down by the systems of the enemy. When men are cast down, we say there is a lifting up-Job 22-29. Arm yourself with this extra ordinary mind-set of the righteous and you will see yourself reigning in life in a way that will both shock and fascinate you big time.

    At salvation, the very vital life of Christ starts throbbing in our hearts. You see, the unsaved (natural) man lives by or is powered by blood, but a Christian lives by the Spirit. The life of the Christian is not in the blood but in the spirit. Adam's life was in his blood and that also applies to all those who are born once. But, the life of the new creation is in the spirit, although he still has blood running through his veins. The knowledgeable new creation person should not contract diseases and other curses passed down through the blood like an ordinary man. The divine blood of Jesus has cancelled all of those generational and genetic disadvantages for the new creation.

    Romans 8: 1-2 *With the arrival of Jesus, the Messiah, that fateful dilemma is resolved. Those who enter into Christ's being-here-for-us no longer have to live under a continuous, low-lying* black cloud. A new power is in operation. The Spirit of life in Christ, like a strong wind, has magnificently cleared the air, freeing you from a fated lifetime of brutal tyranny at the hands of sin and death.* (MSG)

Romans 8:11 *But if the Spirit of him that raised up Jesus from the dead dwell in you, he that raised up Christ from the dead shall also quicken your mortal bodies by his Spirit that dwelleth in you.* (KJV)

We live in Heaven on earth and therefore we are subject to the laws of Heaven, not of earth, though we are still on earth. Consider carefully the following verses and tell me whether they are not referring to a special species of invincible people who are not subject to the things that affect ordinary men:

Mark 16:18 *They shall take up serpents; and if they drink any deadly thing, it shall not hurt them; they shall lay hands on the sick, and they shall recover.* (KJV)

Psalm 91: 5 *Thou shalt not be afraid for the terror by night; nor for the arrow that flieth by day; 6 Nor for the pestilence that walketh in darkness; nor for the destruction that wasteth at noonday. 7 A thousand shall fall at thy side, and ten thousand at thy right hand; but it shall not come nigh thee. 8 Only with thine eyes shalt thou behold and see the reward of the wicked.* (KJV)

Do you see that God has a special breed of people who are exempted from the things that common men dread most in life?

There is no disease, disaster, or any evil sufficiently potent to ravage our lives. Diseases assault the body and blood cells leading to destruction; but our lives are not dependent on blood. We are dependent on the Holy Spirit who quickens (makes alive) our mortal bodies. We are no longer sons of men but sons of God.

John 1:12 *But as many as received him, to them gave he power to become the sons of God, even to them that believe on his name:* (KJV)

The new creation has for him the same exceeding, great and abundant power which raised Jesus from the dead. Whenever he is challenged by any disease or any other thing, he just summons that power to work and set things straight again. Nothing is ever too hard for the superman.

Ephesians 1: 19 *And what is the exceeding greatness of his power to us-ward who believe, according to the working of his mighty power, 20 Which he wrought in Christ, when he raised him from the dead, and set him at his own right hand in the heavenly places...* (KJV)

CHAPTER TWO

MAN: GOD'S STRATEGIC CREATION

Man is a tripartite being.
He is a spirit, has a soul and lives in a body.

1 Thessalonians 5: 23 *And the very God of peace sanctify you wholly; and I pray God your whole spirit and soul and body be preserved blameless unto the coming of our Lord Jesus Christ.* (KJV)

We now have some people especially in sections of the science and environmentalists' camps who think man is no different from other animals and is in fact, not special at all. We know who is behind this wicked campaign. It is the same age-old foe fuelling the atheistic, evolution, agnostic and similar movements across the globe. These people are being influenced from dark quarters without their awareness and the chief aim is to lower the status of man to where he is not made in the image of God but is actually just a common product of an accident called evolution. In fact, they classify man under evolved animals, in complete rebellion against the Bible established order that we indeed are masterpieces of God; fearfully and wonderfully made. Once they succeed in degrading man, we can then just murder unborn babies with abandon and treat fellow humans with recklessness. I remember one atheist, a lizard specialist who quipped that people were too many in the world and there needed to be a plan to reduce them so that "mother-earth" could breathe. You will know them by their characteristics, one of which is that they like terms and slogans like, "mother earth, earth first" and other similar coined phrases. It is no coincidence. They have spiritual connections to ancient pagan religions which worshipped creation. Make no mistake, this is a religion. The latest twist in the evolution of this dark conspiracy is radical environmentalism and of course their favorite object of worship is the environment. If they can convince everybody, and especially people in power that man is the enemy of the environment and is totally responsible for climate change, then population control can become the new song. Lest you forget, many of them are also racists and some of them advocate for more population control in some places of the earth than in others. They also seek to line up their pockets from their activities and that reveals the ugly underbelly of their dishonesty and greed. As pointed out earlier, they are hiding behind pseudo-science to convince the world that their fundamentalist and twisted version of environmental protection should override every human concern on the earth. They have succeeded in fooling a lot of world leaders and governments and for that they are reaping big, money wise. They now even have an ally in the Vatican who subscribes to this new global warming religion whose high priests are condemnable God-deniers donning cloaks of scientists. This Vatican occupant has even gone further to swallow their other pet baits of big bang and evolution. You can see how this elaborate and diabolical scheme is working towards the hope and eventuality that matters of faith in God will be disregarded, kept in the back-burner and eventually forgotten altogether. If that happens to a significant degree, schools can also begin to shun the creation account of the Bible (as is happening in America) and then we can all hide our heads in the sand and pretend that God doesn't exist. In fact, when the pope made the remarks that "evolution and the big bang are real," at the Pontifical Academy of Sciences, experts said he put an end to the "pseudo theories" of creationism and intelligent design that some argue were encouraged by his predecessor, Pope Benedict XVI. I still grapple to understand why people who claim to know God are so predisposed to bend over backwards to please (by adopting their fallacies) a confused bunch of pagans who are working overtime to discredit God. Here is newsflash: we have gathered from these so-called scientists that they actually don't respect Christians who try to reconcile creationism with these atheistic assertions of evolution, big bang and billions of years old earth. Instead, they despise them.

Please don't get me wrong. We do have very many credible

Christian scientists who are working very hard swimming against this putrid deluge of deception to set the record straight and we need to support them fully. They have been able to disapprove all this garbage of evolution, big bang, an extremely old earth and the global warming hoax. There is no question that we need to take care of our environment as a gift from God. Life is richer, better and fuller for all of us if we live in healthy surroundings as humans, but, global warming is a totally different matter. There really are *no* "climate change deniers." Nobody denies that the climate changes; it does so all the time, for totally natural reasons. Real science has established that the climate changes on multiple different time scales: annually, on an 11-year sunspot cycle, on a scale of 2/3 century due to the Pacific Decadal Oscillation, the Roman and Medieval Warm Periods, and so on to hundreds of thousands of years. The climate is changing due to reasons beyond human activities and we should not listen to these leeches who seek to control people and milk them dry by claiming that our few and far-between industries and small cars are responsible for climate change. Isn't it common sense that it is the sun which drives the earth's climate and weather? How do solar flares for example, which occur 150 million kilometers away and are partly responsible for changes in temperatures on earth connected with human activity on earth?

    This wide scheme of deception also serves another purpose: it deadens the screaming and truth-witnessing conscience and temporarily, we can assume we are not accountable to God. We can also take it that man evolved over billions of years and was not created, has no links with an "imaginary" God, did not sin and doesn't need a savior and that when he dies, life is over and there is no God to face on the other side. It is a well-orchestrated diabolical scheme and conspiracy of rebellion against God. These rebels are advocating what they call "free-thought" and basically what that means is that man should be unshackled from the chains of religious "superstition" to think freely and not give any regard to some God who according to them is only a pie in the sky. God saw these dissidents ahead of time and He lets us know what He thinks of them.

    Psalm 2:1 *Why do the heathen rage, and the people imagine*

a vain thing? 2 The kings of the earth set themselves, and the rulers take counsel together, against the LORD, and against his anointed, saying, 3 Let us break their bands asunder, and cast away their cords from us. 4 He that sitteth in the heavens shall laugh: the LORD shall have them in derision. 5 Then shall he speak unto them in his wrath, and vex them in his sore displeasure. (KJV)

Romans 1: 20 *For ever since the world was created, people have seen the earth and sky. Through everything God made, they can clearly see his invisible qualities—his eternal power and divine nature. So they have no excuse for not knowing God. 21 Yes, they knew God, but they wouldn't worship him as God or even give him thanks. And they began to think up foolish ideas of what God was like. As a result, their minds became dark and confused. 22 Claiming to be wise, they instead became utter fools. 23 And instead of worshiping the glorious, ever-living God, they worshiped idols made to look like mere people and birds and animals and reptiles. 24 So God abandoned them to do whatever shameful things their hearts desired. As a result, they did vile and degrading things with each other's bodies. 25 They traded the truth about God for a lie. So they worshiped and served the things God created instead of the Creator himself, who is worthy of eternal praise! Amen... 28 Since they thought it foolish to acknowledge God, he abandoned them to their foolish thinking and let them do things that should never be done.* (KJV)

I like the way God is not baffled by these so-called intellectuals. I like the way He lets them create their own little imaginary world without Him out of incredible ignorance. He still gives them ample time to reform and turn to Him before the door of grace is shut and these people who have chosen ignorance instead of revelation have no more chance. The truth is, man is no ordinary creature. Man is not to be categorized among animals. <u>Man was created as the last and most awesome masterpiece in day six of the creation week roughly 6000 years ago and he was the crown of all that God made.</u> In fact, the rest of the creation was made for man, not the other way round. After that brief introduction, I would like us to delve into more details about this wonder called man. In total, man was made in three interesting phases. In Genesis 1:27, we see

God creating man, both male and female in the sixth day of the creation week. As we will see later, it was the spirit of man which was created by God in this day and man still remained inside God. We know it was the spirit man because he was made in God's own image and likeness and we know God is spirit. So, when God spoke of man as being made in His image and likeness, He certainly was not referring to man's body which is simply an earthly suit and we know God was not physical until Jesus gave Him a body. He was not released by God to begin operating on his own yet. So, by evening of day six, man was still not on the physical land. Genesis 2:5 confirms that later after the seventh day, there was still no man on the ground to work it. In Genesis 2:7, God fabricated the body of man from the soil and He released Adam the spirit into it whereupon the body was put to motion. It is important to note that up to this point, Adam was standing on wet (because God had been watering it using a mist from underneath the earth) and completely bare ground. There was no single vegetation growing on the earth even by the time Adam got his body. God had simply created them but they were still in the spiritual realm, ready to be released to the physical earth. There was also no single animal on the planet. They were all still inside God. There is a revelation here to be grasped in that God continued to prepare the ground for the plants before any of them was on the surface. If we are incubating something, it is important we prepare the capacity for it. An even bigger revelation is for us to be operating like God. We must always conceive our projects in the spirit almost to readiness at the same time as we prepare capacity on the ground for their soft landing. We have the capability like God to visualize projects clearly in our spirits even before none of it is visible to the eye.

Romans 4:17 *As it is written: "I have made you a father of many nations." He is our father in the sight of God, in whom he believed--the God who gives life to the dead and calls into being things that were not.* (NIV)

After Adam had a body and was already moving around, God then planted the garden in Eden. After the garden was set, God released all the plants that He had created and the rest of the earth was populated with all manner of trees and herbs. God then put man in the garden to work it and enjoy it. He also gave him firm instructions on what to eat and what not to eat and it was all herbs. No animal was ever supposed to eat another. Even lions were all herbivorous before the curse and corruption. All this while, Eve was still inside God as a spirit. Thereafter, God formed all the animals and birds and brought them to Adam for naming. Then, there came the third and final phase of the making of man. This time, it was Eve. God took a rib from Adam and with it made a body for Eve and just like Adam, He released Eve into it and she too was launched into the planet. Briefly, that is how man came to be. He was spirit first before a body was given to him. Man is not his body but his spirit. God never was very concerned with the body at any given time. That is why He told man that in the day he ate of the forbidden fruit, he would die. When Adam and Eve ate of that tree they didn't drop down dead in the flesh. According to God's word, they died but it was a spiritual disconnection from God who was their source. Their bodies remained alive for many centuries later. They were basically empty shells walking on the face of the earth, not very different from animals. That was to continue until Jesus came and gave us new spirits after His death and resurrection. Without a living spirit, the body is basically almost a useless mound of dirt. When they were stoning Stephen, he released his spirit and dropped down dead. So did Jesus. We are spirits; we have a soul and live in a body.

Here is the truth: God made us spirits to relate to Him because He is spirit Himself. We were created to fellowship with God, not to do the many other useless things we've come to heap upon ourselves. Then, God gave us a body to relate to the physical environment with.

He also gave us a soul to act as a bridge or interface between the spirit man and the spiritual world on one side; and the body and physical environment on the other. Now, after Adam sinned he died and after his version, we all are born with dead spirits. You can call it a dull, hard and unresponsive spirit. Death of the spirit simply means a spirit which cannot contact God.

Ephesians 2:1 *And you hath he quickened, who were dead in trespasses and sins;* (KJV)

After Adam's fall and with his spirit dead, man has been

trying to contact God and relate to Him from his soul. You will realize man can still do a lot with his soul even with the spirit dead. He can still advance scientifically and intellectually and achieve many other mind-boggling feats. The question is, how much more do you suppose the regenerated man with a perfect and godly spirit can do? We who are born again are sitting on so much potential. The problem with relating to God from the soul is that we can only do so based on knowledge sourced from the environment through the senses and such information is very faulty and even deadly. That is how all these dead religions came about, including some many Christian based religious cults, some of which are enormous and worldwide. They are not based on knowledge of God's revealed word but on man's faulty thinking. God is spirit and He has to be contacted from man's spirit based strictly on His revealed word. That is why a man's physical orientation during worship doesn't matter very much. Before man could be born again, there was a lot of emphasis on the physical location from where man had to be in order to worship. There were rules on which direction to face and which body posture to assume amongst many other physical considerations. That is not the case with the new creation. God is now only interested in the spiritual orientation of man. If you are born again, you have a new and a perfect spirit and you are good to fellowship with God no matter how you are faring in the body and soul.

 1 Samuel 16: 7 *But the LORD said to Samuel, "Do not consider his appearance or his height, for I have rejected him. The LORD does not look at the things people look at. People look at the outward appearance, but the LORD looks at the heart."* (NIV)

 In the Old Testament, no one could serve God as a priest if they had even a minor defect in their bodies. Only perfect males from the tribe of Levi served in that critical capacity.

 Leviticus 21: 16 *Then the LORD said to Moses, 17 "Give the following instructions to Aaron: In all future generations, none of your descendants who has any defect will qualify to offer food to his God. 18 No one who has a defect qualifies, whether he is blind, lame, disfigured, deformed, 19 or has a broken foot or arm, 20 or is hunchbacked or dwarfed, or has a defective eye, or skin sores or scabs, or damaged testicles. 21 No descendant of Aaron who has a defect may approach the altar to present special gifts to the LORD. Since he has a defect, he may not approach the altar to offer food to his God.* (NLT)

If that law or standard was still in force today, it would virtually eliminate everybody from the possibility of ever approaching God to worship or praise. Thank God for Jesus and this era of pure grace. In the New Testament where men have perfect spirits, every Christian without considerations of race, tribe, gender, education, condition of body and any other physical attribute is a priest, king and a prophet. Don't you just love the New Testament? Jesus removed every limit which stood in the way of people becoming vital sons of God and today, everybody and anybody can become a child of God without any conditions. God was not giving those instructions regarding priests so that we in the New Testament can try to measure up to them. The thing is, priests were an Old Testament shadow of Jesus who is the perfect man without blemish. So, because we are all priests in this testament, does it mean we go for reconstructive surgery so that we look physically perfect like Jesus? If a Christian is a dwarf, does it mean they climb on top of something to appear taller or approach medical science for help? Religious people who support works of the law and force their victims to observe the law in a bid to appear righteous like Jesus are actually trying to do reconstructive surgery. God's lofty standards and demands of the law are not for us to try to attain. They are put there for us to realize they are so high that no man can attain them and therefore everyone except the religious people is forced to look only to Jesus, the only perfect man. That is what we call faith in Jesus. Jesus came down as a perfect man not for Himself but for us. He didn't need perfection because He is perfection Himself; we are the ones who needed it. Those of us who believe in Him have His perfection imputed unto us without breaking a sweat for one moment. That is called effortless transformation. I get shocked when I see sane people fighting to remain under law. I still don't understand what it is with these legalists. The only explanation I can offer is that they have no clue how high the standard of the law was. Back then, just being a non-Jew knocked you out of the congregation of God. Never mind no body applies to be born where they are born. When we keep talking about the law, some people who are held in bondage by it without their knowledge refute that they are victims. They claim not to be under the ceremonial law of Jews. To be under the law is to have any conditions that you must fulfill before you are acceptable to God, blessed by Him or counted as righteous. Religion has expanded that law and it differs from one person to another depending on who you ask. Basically, the law now is that you must keep all the Ten Commandments; you must repent and confess all sins; you must pray, fast and read the Bible; you must tithe; you must give; you must attend church service; you must wear a garment this long; you must do this and no do that; you must fulfill these many requirements and, you must not wear make-up. The list is long and endless depending on the denomination. If in your mind you must do any or several of these things plus many others I have not mentioned for you to be saved, counted righteous, blessed, accepted with God or even in order to sustain your salvation, then you are a victim of the law! Jesus removed all the formidable obstacles that stood in the way of belonging to the family of God and now the only qualification is to trust in Jesus for salvation. Blessed be God! Jesus told the Samaritan woman that a time was coming when those who worship God must do so in truth and in the spirit. He was referring to the time after His resurrection when men who believe would receive new and living spirits. The truth is God's revealed word. What does the word say about the believer? It says he is perfectly righteous, holy, accepted and worthy before God. So, the believer must never feel unworthy before God because he fellowships with God based on the perfection of Jesus Christ our High Priest; not his own. The only time he can feel unworthy to worship is if Jesus just became unworthy Himself, and that can never take place. We are completely cleansed and perfected once and for all through Jesus' offering of His body once, so that we should never be ashamed or fear again communing with our heavenly Father. Hebrews 10: 10 *By the which will* **we are sanctified through the offering of the body of Jesus Christ once for all... 14 For by one offering he hath perfected forever them that are sanctified.** (KJV) Emphasis added.

1 Corinthians 2: 6 *Howbeit we speak wisdom among them that are perfect: yet not the wisdom of this world, nor of the princes*

of this world, that come to nought: (KJV)

Hebrews 12: 23 *To the general assembly and church of the firstborn, which are written in heaven, and to God the Judge of all, and to the spirits of just men made perfect,* (KJV)

It is sad how many Christians have let their lives to constantly revolve around that which Jesus took away. Jesus took away sin yet a lot of our sermons are still about sin. A lot of the preaching coming from our pulpits is mostly responsible for the rampant sin-consciousness in the body of Christ. In fact, many preachers have almost no other message. If it is not to glorify sin by making it appear too powerful, it is to dwell on how to defeat it. A lot of our preaching is centered on sin and not on Christ. That has led to the common belief in the body of Christ that Christianity is about identifying sin, meditating on it, trying to defeat it or confessing it and repenting. Bear in mind religion has given repentance a new definition which is to be sorry for sin, beat oneself over it, do penance and try to pay for it. Religion has rejected the true meaning of repentance which is to change one's mind from wrong thinking which leads to wrong actions, to godly thinking which leads to a godly way of life. *Repentance is simply turning away from a wrong way of thinking which leads to wrong believing and wrong actions; to an accurate and biblical way of thinking which leads to right believing and consequently right actions.* You see, if you receive faulty information, you will believe wrong and then you will: reason wrong, pray wrong, speak wrong and ultimately live wrong. My slogan is, what you believe is what you live. If you receive untruths and therefore believe wrong, you will live according to the faith derived from that wrong information and your life will undoubtedly go wrong. Likewise, if you receive true revelation from God, your faith in God will work and produce results or fruits of righteousness. So, it behooves every serious Christian to ensure they first receive the truth and believe in it so that their lives can takeoff on the journey of glory.

Most Christians are ever learning the Ten Commandments, trying to keep them, examining where they may have sinned by breaking the law, confessing all known and unknown sins and some even doing penance. We keep occupying ourselves with that which was taken care of eternally by Jesus, and never spend time with Jesus Himself. Our prayer life is full of confessions for sin. We keep reminding God that which He said He took away, shall not remember any more and is not imputing unto us. If God said He will be merciful to our unrighteousness, that our sins and lawless deeds He will remember no more and will not impute them unto us; then what sins are religious people afraid God will punish them for? That simply means they don't believe anything He says. What is wrong with such people? If we were to get our worship correct, there would be no place for sin and sin-consciousness in our lives. Where there is genuine and rich fellowship with Jesus, sin is consumed and Jesus exalted. *I want you to know that Jesus is not standing in heaven daily atoning for sins. He did one sacrifice for all sins, for all men and for all time.* Unlike the Old Testament priests who offered sacrifices for sins daily and were still never able to perfect the worshippers, Jesus did a one-time job and is now seated in His Father's right hand. Jesus' one supreme sacrifice forever perfected those who put faith in Him.

Hebrews 9: 24 For Christ is not entered into the holy places made with hands, which are the figures of the true; but into heaven itself, now to appear in the presence of God for us: 25 Nor yet that he should offer himself often, as the high priest entereth into the holy place every year with blood of others; 26 For then must he often have suffered since the foundation of the world: but now once in the end of the world hath he appeared to put away sin by the sacrifice of himself...28 So Christ was once offered to bear the sins of many; and unto them that look for him shall he appear the second time without sin unto salvation. (KJV)

Hebrews 10: 1 For the law having a shadow of good things to come, and not the very image of the things, can never with those sacrifices which they offered year by year continually make the comers thereunto perfect. 2 For then would they not have ceased to be offered? because that the worshippers once purged should have had no more conscience of sins. 3 But in those sacrifices there is a remembrance again made of sins every year. 4 For it is not possible that the blood of bulls and of goats should take away sins... 6 In burnt offerings and sacrifices for sin thou hast had no pleasure... 8

Above when he said, Sacrifice and offering and burnt offerings and offering for sin thou wouldest not, neither hadst pleasure therein; which are offered by the law; 9 Then said he, Lo, I come to do thy will, O God. He taketh away the first, that he may establish the second. 10 By the which will we are sanctified through the offering of the body of Jesus Christ once for all. 11 And every priest standeth daily ministering and offering oftentimes the same sacrifices, which can never take away sins: 12 But this man, after he had offered one sacrifice for sins forever, sat down on the right hand of God...14 For by one offering he hath perfected forever them that are sanctified. (KJV)

You can rest assured God is not looking at your conduct to determine your standing before Him, He is only looking at your representative before Him-Jesus Christ. God is interested in whether or not you have a new spirit. If you are born again, you are alive and if you are not born again, you are spiritually dead and even if you have the best conduct and character on earth, you are still eternally damned. If you are a Christian, your new spirit is every bit and every inch like Jesus. As He is, so are you now! So, where does the fear come in now? Our confidence and boldness before God does not come from our own goodness or righteousness but Christ's. We are wrapped up in Christ before God and that is why He accepts us.

Ephesians 3: 11 *According to the eternal purpose which he purposed in Christ Jesus our Lord: 12* **In whom we have boldness and access with confidence by the faith of him.** (KJV) Emphasis added.

Romans 5:1 *Therefore being justified by faith, we have peace with God through our Lord Jesus Christ: 2 By whom also we have access by faith into this grace wherein we stand, and rejoice in hope of the glory of God.* (KJV)

Few Christians remember seeing Ephesians 3:12 above. That verse needs to be pasted in the first place you see when you wake up in the morning. It is so critical that to keep it out of view will cost you a huge part of your confidence and boldness before God.

That is the truth of God's word and on that basis, we must worship God. Some people think worshipping God in truth and in spirit means whipping up emotions until one feels transported to an imaginary sensational world to where they cease to be themselves. That is superstition and not true spirituality. The context in which Jesus made that statement of worshipping God in truth and in spirit was when the woman tried lecturing Him on how the Jews worshipped in the temple in Jerusalem while the Samaritans worshipped on some mountain. Jesus didn't entertain those carnal arguments of religion further. He straight away told the woman that God is spirit and worship must be from spirit to Spirit, not from soul or body and the physical environment to God. He meant that God is Spirit and He can only be contacted from and by the spirit of man, not the physical body or the soul. The flesh can never contact the spiritual or the spirit. Ideally, the spirit is supposed to be in charge in man but we have reversed that order to where most men have the soul in charge. In other words, most men are carnal and only have a human understanding of God. They don't know God based on His revealed word. That is why even many so-called Christians in large denominational congregations are stuck in religion. They have rejected the word of God. Instead, they read other funny and satanic worship guides authored by equally lost and blind clergy. So, they light candles, walk slowly and meekly, bow before idols, offer some strange smoke and assume a humble posture during church service. God recognizes none of those practices because they can never be found in His word. These people no matter how humble they may like to appear, they make a joke of real humility. They are actually very arrogant and rude because they have rejected God's truth and proceeded to establish their own religious order. Humility is to read God's word and do it. But I know some stubborn men use their own Bibles and other religious texts authored by mere men. For others, their services are so dry, so formal and so dead the Holy Spirit cannot minister. They are stuck in strict and rigid worship services where the Holy Spirit cannot get a word in edgeways, yet they claim to be worshipping a living God. They have rejected the simple and straight forward way to worship prescribed by the Bible and gone to elaborate and complicated rituals devised by men which make the word of God of none effect.

Matthew 15: 9 *But in vain they do worship me, teaching for doctrines the commandments of men.* (KJV)

Mark 7: 13 *Making the word of God of none effect through your tradition, which ye have delivered: and many such like things do ye.* (KJV)

Before you engage in any worship practice or before your religious leader asks you to do something in worship or in church, always settle these questions first: "can I find the thing they are asking me to do in the Bible? And if I can find it, is the context correct or are they quoting scriptures out of context to fit their preconceived motives? Are they applying it accurately or have they distorted the meaning of scriptures? Is the thing suitable to be done by a New Testament person? How does it square with the cross of Jesus Christ?" If you can't find whatever you are engaged in within the pages of the Bible, then stop it and move church or better still start your own that is wholly Bible-based! If they threaten to curse you tell them the curse will land on them because no man and no one can curse what the Lord has blessed and the Lord never revokes His blessing. While at it, tell them also that you are not resisting the Lord but their vain, baseless and worthless religion. Always remember that the fight is for your soul which is too precious to be gambled with. Some Christian denominational religions have established extra-biblical materials full of traditions that have taken over the true Bible-based worship. We are talking about rebellious and impudent men who usurp the place of God to convene councils where they disregard the Bible and establish their own laws of worship which they in turn shove down the throats of poor congregations. If you are in such a denomination, flee for your dear life no matter how gigantic, how wealthy, how flashy and even how organized the religious movement is. As a matter of fact, some of these religious organizations are some of the best run and organized. You will not be judged based on what some man or a group of religious men sat down and passed. The only criteria for judging people will be the gospel of grace. No man or group of men have any right to sit down in some phony council and come up with a religious and worship order apart from that put in place by Jesus, the apostle Paul and his other original peers. And by the way, they have no parallels today. No man can claim to be acting in the capacity of those original pillars of the church or even boast of having the sole prerogative of exclusively speaking for Christ. Christ doesn't have any particular person sitting in His office today. Any born again person can act on behalf of Christ. No person or group of people has any authority to add to or subtract from the word of God. Any such pretender is an antichrist no matter which religious office he thinks he occupies, and all his followers are in serious jeopardy no matter how many they are. Some people are stuck in these massive denominations and when asked they say, "Even if the others are wrong, I know what I am doing. Everybody will carry their own cross. As for me, I am in it but my worship is totally Bible-based" I beg to differ with such people who think their fate can be any different from that of fellow worshippers in these erroneous congregations.

Revelation 18: 4 *And I heard another voice from heaven, saying, Come out of her, my people, that ye be not partakers of her sins, and that ye receive not of her plagues. 5 For her sins have reached unto heaven, and God hath remembered her iniquities.* (KJV)

2 Corinthians 6: 14*Be ye not unequally yoked together with unbelievers: for what fellowship hath righteousness with unrighteousness? And what communion hath light with darkness? 17Wherefore come out from among them, and be ye separate, saith the Lord, and touch not the unclean thing; and I will receive you,* (KJV)

The scripture we have quoted from Revelation above is talking about Babylon, a fallen church system which has abandoned the Bible and established its own man-made religion. God is warning the congregants (who He refers to as His people) to come out this corrupt organization or else they will also be party to the wrath He will pour on her.

Some people have heard me speak along these lines and asked me: "do you mean all these denominations with some of them so huge, can be wrong?" let me ask you, since when did the masses get it right? Where you see the masses flocking, you will almost always find them wrong because most people cannot resist the urge of being victims of what psychologists call herd-mentality. In fact, sharp investors will tell you that finding what stock to buy is most times a no-brainer. All you need to do is check out where the masses are headed and invest in the opposite stock. Does that mean there are no large churches that are right? The answer is that there are. You just need to go with the Bible and find out which of them sticks to the biblical guidelines of worship and doesn't have superfluous and heretical practices that can't be traced anywhere in the word of God.

The unregenerate soul of man can't understand and appreciate spiritual reality because it is carnal. All it knows is what can be picked up by the senses unless it is renewed with the living word of grace. We must relate to God from our born again spirits which always agree with the written word of God. If you want to know whether you are worshipping in truth and in spirit, just look at whether you are following the laid down truths revealed in the Bible. If you follow the simple and easy way of the Bible, then your spirit will be in charge in your life and your worship and you will be able to contact God.

A. THE MAKE-UP OF MAN

Now that we have been able to describe and comprehend the new creation or the born again spirit of man, we need also to discuss his other two components-the soul and body. We begin by breaking down the next crucial component, the soul. Part of the reason why understanding the soul is critical is because for the born again believer, the soul is where the problem lies. This is the theatre of conflict and spiritual warfare. It is where victory is either secured or lost. We don't have trouble with the new spirit. For the body, well it follows where the soul goes. If the soul sides with the spirit and therefore the word, the body has no alternative because it is a slave of the soul. Just like the spirit, the soul is also misunderstood and unappreciated and hence its potential goes largely untapped. In the soul are four important components: the will, the conscience, emotions and the intellect (logic, thinker, imagination, and the reasoning).

The soul is also called the mind and it sits between the spirit and the body as an interface. It is a spiritual component of man, not a physical one. You can't touch it but can only see its work and effects. According to the Bible, not psychology, the soul is part of the heart of man with the spirit but the two are separate and distinct. Only the word of God can tell between that which is soulish and what is purely spiritual.

Hebrews 4:12 *For the word of God is quick, and powerful, and sharper than any two edged sword,* **piercing even to the dividing asunder of soul and spirit,** *and of the joints and marrow, and is a discerner of the thoughts and intents of the heart.* (KJV) Emphasis added.

When I say the heart, I don't mean the physical muscle in the chest that pumps blood. Actually, I believe the heart of man is located in the head. That is where all the intellectual, will and emotional functions of man are carried out. The heart is really at the heart of the human person. It is when the heart departs during death that the remaining part which is the physical fleshly container drops down dead and is corrupted immediately. The real person is the heart. It is the entity that survives after what we call death. The verse above demonstrates that the spirit and soul are closely linked and live together.

We can deduce from this verse that the soul is so close to the spirit that it takes the extremely sharp sword of the word to tell their difference. That means we must go by the word to tell whether what we think is God speaking is really Him and not just suggestions emanating from the soul. The Bible lets us know that the spirit is the perfect and incorruptible part of the heart which shares space in there with the soul.

1 Peter 3: 4 *But let it be the hidden man of the heart, in that which is not corruptible, even the ornament of a meek and quiet spirit, which is in the sight of God of great price.* (KJV)

Between the soul and spirit, each has its own mind.

Romans 8:27 *And he that searcheth the hearts knoweth what is* ***the mind of the Spirit,*** *because he maketh intercession for the saints according to the will of God.* (KJV) Emphasis added.

The mind of the spirit is the mind of Christ in the Christian and it knows all things because it has unction from the Holy One who abides there. The mind of the soul is the mind of fallen man and it needs to be renewed with the word of God so as to transfer what is in the mind of the spirit to the mind of the soul. That means a Christian who has not renewed his mind can then have two minds:

James 4: 8 *Draw nigh to God, and he will draw nigh to you. Cleanse your hands, ye sinners; and purify your hearts, ye* **double minded.** (KJV) Emphasis added.

That is why the Bible instructs us to believe with all our heart or to have singleness of heart.

Acts 8: 37 *And Philip said, If thou believest with* **all thine heart,** *thou mayest. And he answered and said, I believe that Jesus Christ is the Son of God.* (KJV) Emphasis added.

Colossians 3: 22 *Servants, obey in all things your masters according to the flesh; not with eye service, as men pleasers; but in* **singleness of heart,** *fearing God;* (KJV) Emphasis added.

Romans 7: 21 *I find then a law, that, when I would do good, evil is present with me. 22 For* **I delight in the law of God after the inward man: 23 But I see another law in my members, warring against the law of my mind,** *and bringing me into captivity to the law of sin which is in my members.* (KJV)

Jeremiah 29: 13 *And ye shall seek me, and find me, when ye shall search for me with* **all your heart.** (KJV) Emphasis added.

If you carefully observe these scriptures, you will notice that a person who has not renewed his mind has a heart that is divided and self-contradictory. The spirit is siding with God but the soul is in cahoots with the world. That is why the mind of the soul has to be renewed so that it is in agreement with the mind of the spirit which is the mind of Christ. Such a person will be very spiritual and highly effective in life because his entire being is pulling towards the same direction of the things of God and is focused. Remember, in focus is effectiveness.

All of us know that the soul consists of the will, emotions and the intellect. What most of us don't know is that the born again spirit too has a will and emotions. The emotions of the new and recreated spirit are joy, peace, love and others related to these. Unlike the fickle emotions of the soul, these ones are stable and constant through all circumstances. That is why if we walk by the spirit, we will never be without joy and peace no matter what we are going through. The trouble is when we walk by the flesh and therefore subject ourselves under the unstable emotions of the soul that are dependent on prevailing circumstances. When God instructs us to rejoice in Him always and to give thanks in everything, He knows we have the capacity in our spirits to do that if we choose to walk in the spirit. You will notice that these emotions of the spirit are the very same emotions of God Himself and that is no surprise because our born again spirits are directly born of God. As God is, so are we in our spirits here and now. Likewise, the will of the spirit is the very same will of God. The spirit is joined to the spirit of God and always chooses God's will.

Romans 7: 21 *I find then a law, that, when I would do good, evil is present with me. 22 For I delight in the law of God after the inward man:* (KJV)

Again, the number one job of the believer is to renew the soul totally so that its will, emotions and intellect are synchronized with their counterpart components in the spirit for guaranteed prosperity.

In the Old Testament, man was fallen and his spirit was just as ungodly as his soul. That is why we say he was dead spiritually. He could not contact God with such a wicked spirit which still is operational in those who are not born again.

Ephesians 2: 2 *Wherein in time past ye walked according to the course of this world, according to the prince of the power of the air, the spirit that now worketh in the children of disobedience:* (KJV)

Because man was dead spiritually, that is why God's verdict was that man's heart was deceitful above all things and desperately wicked. We still have Christians who quote that scripture and apply it on themselves. That is not right. God has now given us by grace a new heart of flesh. We have a new spirit. We still don't have a new soul but we can renew it with the word of God so that it reflects the spirit. So, Jeremiah 17:9 is not for the believer but the heathen. Likewise, we cannot tell God to create in us a clean heart and to renew a right spirit within us. As a matter of fact, a believer cannot pray the entire Psalm 51. All those things David was telling God to do, He has done for us in Christ and much more even. God has had mercy on us. We are now trophies of His mercy, love and grace. We now have eternal forgiveness of sins. We have a new and perfect heart. We can't tell God to hide His face from our sins because He is merciful to our unrighteousness and our sins and lawless deeds He remembers no more. Furthermore, He does not impute sins unto us. For any believer to pray according to this Old Testament psalm is to display massive ignorance and unbelief. That would also be a needless waste of time because it is a futile effort. God can only receive such a prayer from a non-believer. When we talk of eternal forgiveness of sins, some people ask; "if we tell people their past, present and future sins are forgiven, will they not go crazy and sin more? What will motivate them to live righteously? Isn't that license to sin?" Well, what do you think? If your earthly parents reassure you of their lifelong love for you and guarantee that you will forever remain their beloved child no matter what happens and that nothing will ever separate you from them, how does that make you feel? Do you feel like going out to deliberately offend them or does it make you so grateful and loving that you never want to wrong them? If Adam being a mere man put in force the sin nature in every man who would ever be born, what is so hard about the God-man Jesus, putting in force righteousness in every man who would ever be born again? If sin came, it means it was not there in the beginning. It came by a man. That means also that sin can go or be taken away through a higher man and that man is Jesus and He did take away for good the sin of the world. <u>Had Jesus not taken care of all our sins, past, present and future, God could not raise Him from the dead and He certainly would not allow Him to sit by His right hand.</u> By Virtue of God raising Him from the dead, it meant He had purged all sins for all men of all time. It was the same sins He had carried on the cross. If one of them had remained unpurged, Jesus would remain in hell because there would still be lingering sin You can trust Jesus to do a perfect work, can't you?

Romans 4:25 *who was delivered up because of our offences, and was raised up because of our being declared righteous.* (Young's Literal Translation)

The problem with most Christians is that they don't relate with God as a real Father but as a religious abstract figure who has no real feelings and who has no capacity to relate to us like a perfect loving father would. God is a real person and we need to relate to Him like so. Here is a sobering truth from which we can learn a lot: Do you remember that when we were young, we used to be almost forced to obey and love our parents? At that time, they had capacity to whip us if we disobeyed them and they did indeed whip us. Yet, even when there was threat of punishment, we grabbed every available opportunity to disobey and even hurt them. We only obeyed for as long as we were being watched closely but immediately we were left alone, we resulted to all manner of foolish behavior. Fast forward to when we grow up and our parents are in a position where they cannot beat us even if they wanted because we are stronger than them. I have noticed that with the vast majority of people, their relationship with their parents improves tremendously when they grow up. They love their parents, visit them, support them in every way and generally obey and would do anything to keep from hurting them. What has changed? It is maturity that has taken place. They now obey their parents not out of obligation but out of love. <u>Love is by far a greater motivation than fear.</u> If you seek to obey the Lord because you fear rather than love Him, then what you have with Him is not fellowship but servitude. You are still a spiritual baby.

B. THE SOUL EXPLAINED

(i) THE THINKER (INTELLECT, IMAGINATION AND MEMORY)

The intellect is the central thought processing unit of man and together with the imagination and memory, they are central to the functioning of the individual as a whole. The memory is the spiritual storage and archive device that holds all the past and present ideas and events in the life of the person. It also has all the future aspirations of that person. In fact, the memory contains the raw materials which the intellect processes in its operations. Just like a computer, we can divide the memory into short-term (current) and long-term memory. The short-term memory holds the raw materials for current thought processes while the long-term one holds both past and current information required for the long run. The imagination is the womb of thought. This is where the grand ideas of life are incubated and hatched. Imagination takes the collective effort of the memory and intellect. All these are very sophisticated spiritual components that we can never understand fully. The intellect, imagination and memory are not the brain. They are spiritual in nature in the sense that you can't touch or even see them. You only see their effects. The brain is the hardware that the intellect, imagination and memory employ so that they can function. The brain is also the physical tool employed by the spirit and the soul to contact the external environment through the body. Thinking, imagination and memory work are a spiritual exercises and yet they are done by a physical brain. The line between the spiritual processes of the intellect, imagination and memory on one hand, and the physical brain on the other is thin and hard to follow. Suffice it to say, the thinking, imagination and memory work are done in the mind of man. In the Old Testament, it was not uncommon for the soul and spirit to be put together and summarily referred to as the heart or even the mind. Nevertheless, even some Old Testament scriptures make a distinction between the spirit and the soul.

Deuteronomy 10:12 *And now, Israel, what doth the LORD thy God require of thee, but to fear the LORD thy God, to walk in all his ways, and to love him, and to serve the LORD thy God with all thy heart and with all thy soul,* (KJV)

The word heart in that verse means the spirit. In the New Testament, the word heart can also be applied to mean the soul. When Jesus told His disciples not to let their hearts be troubled, He was basically telling them to not let their minds be disturbed. That included not letting their emotions to be worked up because that would affect their will and they would end up making terrible decisions. David also instructed his soul not to be disquieted within him but to hope in God. He was actually telling his soul to not be run by emotions but by faith in God. These three parts of the soul are intricately interwoven and the functioning of one affects the other. That is why they are all clustered under the soul. Back then, the spirit was just as dull as the soul itself. None of them could contact God because the spirit was dead towards God and the soul was alive to the world. It is different for the new creation who has a born again spirit. Through the word, the new creation's spirit can renew the mind and affect the individual so that the new man can think, choose and have emotions in line with the word of God. That means if this man takes time and the word to renew his mind, he can no longer say his heart is deceitful above all things, and desperately wicked. That is not a verse for the new creation. The new creature has a new spirit and if with a renewed mind as well, he then thinks on, and chooses God's will, and his emotions are not world-based but word-based.

Romans 12: 2 *Do not conform to the pattern of this world, but be transformed by the renewing of your mind. Then you will be able to test and approve what God's will is—his good, pleasing and perfect will.* (NIV)

Speaking specifically of the mind, the Bible expressly makes it clear that we have no alternative but to renew our minds. Renewing the mind is the process of taking the word of God and enlightening the dumb mind on spiritual matters. It is also the vital process of replacing the memory of sin of the old dead man with the memory of righteous things in heaven.

Colossians 3:1 *If ye then be risen with Christ, seek those things which are above, where Christ sitteth on the right hand of God. 2 Set your affection on things above, not on things on the earth.* (KJV)

The new creation is supposed to be so tuned to the word of God that he sheds all the memory of when he was a sinner. He should make himself also a new creation in his mind. When that happens, his mind and the new spirit are synchronized to agree on everything. For example, the memory is supposed to be so emptied of the old materials that were from the devil and so refilled with righteous stock from the word that it only supplies the intellect and imagination with fresh and pure resources to process. All the materials of prejudice, selfishness, superiority or inferiority complex, rebellion, disobedience, anger, adultery, fornication, gossip, lying and other such wicked substances of satanic origin ought to be discarded and their place taken by the word only. That way, the intellect and imagination will only process clean materials and produce the fruit of righteousness.

Contrary to what many people think, the mind does not come automatically educated on spiritual matters, but the born again spirit does. The new spirit is fully enlightened on spiritual matters and he is full of the light of the revelation of the word of God. That is where the mind of Christ rests. The spirit knows all things because He has the anointing and he doesn't need to be taught anything. The trouble is getting all that spiritual education to the slow mind, or what the Bible calls putting on the new man which after God is renewed in righteousness and true holiness-Ephesians 4:23-24. What all these things mean is that you can have a born again spirit who has the mind of Christ but a mind which is still in the dark. But, a renewed mind is no longer dull in spiritual matters but knows the will of God. It agrees with the new spirit to the degree it is renewed. If you renew your mind with the word for up to 50%, it will only agree with the spirit to that same extent. That is why, it advisable to cultivate the habit of studying through the whole Bible every so often. It should not just be done religiously to satisfy a condemning conscience or to brag to others. It should be done slowly, distilling all the revelation in every verse, letting it settle and giving it the room to change the way we think, feel, act and make choices in life. Such a renewed mind is no longer a burden to its bearer but is actually the guaranteed starting point of success and prosperity. Always remember that <u>a transformed life follows a transformed mind.</u> Your mind is like a valve that if turned on by renewal allows for life to flow from the spirit to the body and the environment. Every Christian has faith, love, joy, healing, wealth, peace and all manner of good things in their spirit. The new spirit is a treasure chest of everything God has given us for life and godliness. We are blessed with all spiritual blessings in heavenly places in Christ. That is simply talking about the new spirit. However, for it to flow from the spirit to the body and to the environment, it must pass through the soul which must be renewed first or it will stay turned off and block the flow of life. You cannot have faith for what you don't know or don't acknowledge. Even with every believer having a spirit full of health, power and wholeness, they are still dying with all of that treasure inside because there is no passage in the soul.

Joshua 1: 8 *This book of the law shall not depart out of thy mouth; but thou shalt meditate therein day and night, that thou* *mayest observe to do according to all that is written therein: **for then** thou shalt make thy way prosperous, and then thou shalt have good success.* (KJV) Emphasis added.

Proverbs 4: 7 *Wisdom is the principal thing; therefore get wisdom: and with all thy getting get understanding. 8 Exalt her, and she shall promote thee: she shall bring thee to honour, when thou dost embrace her. 9 She shall give to thine head an ornament of grace: a crown of glory shall she deliver to thee. 10 Hear, O my son, and receive my sayings; and the years of thy life shall be many.* (KJV)

Proverbs 1: 28 *"When they cry for help, I will not answer. Though they anxiously search for me, they will not find me. 29 For they hated knowledge and chose not to fear the LORD. 30 They rejected my advice and paid no attention when I corrected them. 31 Therefore, they must eat the bitter fruit of living their own way, choking on their own schemes. 32 For simpletons turn away from me—to death. Fools are destroyed by their own complacency. 33 But all who listen to me will live in peace, untroubled by fear of harm."* (NLT)

Psalm 19: 7 *The law of the LORD is perfect, converting the soul: the testimony of the LORD is sure, making wise the simple. 8 The statutes of the LORD are right, rejoicing the heart: the commandment of the LORD is pure, enlightening the eyes. 9 The fear of the LORD is clean, enduring forever: the judgments of the LORD are true and righteous altogether. 10 More to be desired are they than gold, yea, than much fine gold: sweeter also than honey and the honeycomb. 11 Moreover by them is thy servant warned: and in keeping of them there is great reward.* (KJV)

(ii) THE CONSCIENCE

I know in a lot places, the conscience is understood as part of the intellect but I am of a contrary opinion. The conscience is a slightly separate faculty from the thinker (although they have to work together). The thinker is mostly just a thought processor while the conscience is much more than that. It is another inner spiritual facility in the mind. The Strong's concordance defines conscience as "an innate discernment or self-judging consciousness" –Strong's 4893. Strong's goes further with this same definition to put it that "accordingly, all people have this God-given capacity to know right from wrong because each is a free moral agent"

Although all men come with conscience, God had not designed us to function from the conscience initially. Adam walked by the Spirit before the fall. That is why he could not even remember that He and his wife were both naked. In fact, it was after the fall that his conscience (knowledge of good and evil) kicked in and became active. I know there are some Christians who think the conscience is an accurate guide in matters of the truth but that is not true. The conscience can be either worldly or it can agree with the Holy Spirit. It can be conditioned, seared, silenced, deceived, manipulated and deadened; or, it can be educated and renewed with the word of God. The conscience can be affected by culture and other human activities. The conscience can be conditioned by the teaching and information one receives. That means if one receives the wrong information, with time, the conscience will be tuned to lead in that direction of error. That tells you it is not necessarily bible based and hence, cannot be reliable. When man died spiritually, he lost the Holy Spirit and became dull. He could not be guided by God. The conscience became the new tool of guidance but it came with many burdens.

If one is exposed to teachings of the law, the conscience will be set to judge and it will oppress the victim and bring them under condemnation and bondage. Alternatively, if one meditates on the good news of the grace of Jesus, the conscience will be conditioned by grace to build up and liberate and far from being an oppressor to its possessor, it will be a saving force. Hence, depending on the teachings one receives, they can either become sin conscious or righteousness-by-faith conscious. One can have a perfect conscience or sin conscience. Because they were under the law, the Old Testament people had a continual sin-consciousness that could not be purged by animal sacrifices.

Hebrews 9:9 *Which was a figure for the time then present, in which were offered both gifts and sacrifices, that could not make him that did the service perfect, as pertaining to the conscience.*

Hebrews 10:1 *For the law having a shadow of good things to come, and not the very image of the things, can never with those sacrifices which they offered year by year continually make the comers thereunto perfect. 2 For then would they not have ceased to be offered? because that the worshippers once purged should have had no more conscience of sins.* (KJV)

In the New Testament and after Jesus has died for us, we cannot continue to harbor a Sin stained conscience because by His perfect and sinless blood, He has purified our conscience from the harmful effects of the law because we are now beneficiaries of God's manifold grace. We now have no fear whatsoever before God. With a perfect conscience, we can now fellowship with Him boldly and walk confidently before His throne of grace.

Hebrews 9:13 *For if the blood of bulls and of goats, and the ashes of an heifer sprinkling the unclean, sanctifieth to the purifying of the flesh: 14 How much more shall the blood of Christ, who through the eternal Spirit offered himself without spot to God, purge your conscience from dead works to serve the living God?* (KJV)

Hebrews 10: 22 *Let us draw near with a true heart in full assurance of faith, having our hearts sprinkled from an evil conscience, and our bodies washed with pure water.* (KJV)

The bible instructs that if our hearts (conscience) condemn us, we should point them to the Lord who justifies the ungodly. We must learn to be at peace with our conscience if we will have meaningful fellowship with the Lord. Two cannot walk together if they don't agree. That simply means you cannot commune with the Lord meaningfully if He says your life-time of sins is wiped out, dead and buried; but you insist on going by your law-conditioned conscience which screams that God is angry with you over your sins. That is where most religious and legalistic people who are under the law live. They lead tormented lives and are constantly haunted by an unrelenting condemnation occasioned by sin consciousness.

1 John 3:20 *For if our heart condemn us, God is greater than our heart, and knoweth all things. 21 Beloved, if our heart condemn us not, then have we confidence toward God.* (KJV)

This verse makes it clear that it is not God who is responsible for making you miserable over your sins. The Holy Spirit's work is not to remind you of your sins. His work is to reveal to you your righteousness by faith in Christ. He administers God's grace, not condemnation. Nowhere did Jesus say the Holy Spirit is the accuser of brethren. We know which crook takes advantage of the law to nail people over their sins and make a living hell of their lives. The Holy Spirit is not your second conscience. He does not nag you. Jesus said His work would be to teach us all things; comfort us; help us in our weaknesses, and, remind us everything He said. Do you see in that list anything to do with the Holy Spirit being responsible for condemning and judging us over sins? You see, the law activates sin conscience while the Holy Spirit activates righteousness conscience in those who walk by faith. The tree Adam was forbidden from partaking of was called the tree of the knowledge of good and evil. That is the very basic definition we give to the conscience. That tree is represented today by the law because in the law is knowledge of sin –Romans 3:20. It is therefore safe to say the conscience and the law are very related. That is why we must be led by the Spirit and not by the law or the conscience.

Briefly, the conscience is a component in the soul that used to be mute before Adam sinned. Like many other things that existed in potential only, it was actually activated by sin and the quality of one's life now depends on what they choose to do with it. If you choose to renew your mind with the word of God's grace, you will be at perfect peace with your conscience. If you choose to stay under the law which the bible calls ministry of condemnation and of death, you will never know peace. Like money, conscience can be a wonderful servant for the person who is under grace but a very terrible master for both those under the law and those who live in rebellion against God. The conscience still serves a purpose for all of us. For those outside Christ, it is their only guide in matters morality and it could eventually be the homing device which points them to Christ. It is actually their constant reminder that they need to make their ways right before God and that includes all the atheists who yell that they don't believe there is a God. Their conscience is still active and whenever they are quiet, it goes to work reminding them that despite their burying their heads in the sand, God is still there. That is why they constantly fill their lives with empty activities to escape its biting pangs.

For those in Christ but are not led by the Spirit, the conscience similarly serves the same purpose as in non-believers. Because they don't listen to the Holy Spirit and don't study the word, they result to being led by the conscience and that is risky. The devil is known to hijack the consciences of ignorant believers and give them nightmares for life. For those in Christ and who walk in the Spirit rather than in the flesh, the conscience plays a very secondary role in their lives. Spiritual believers ought to walk by faith or by the spirit and not by the conscience. The Holy Spirit is the only accurate and perfect guide. At the end of the day, we all will need the conscience in one way or the other because even for the most spiritual, they are not always tuned to the frequency of the Holy Spirit or studying the word. The second best option remains to be the conscience in such circumstances.

(iii) THE EMOTIONS

Emotions are the next aspect of the soul or mind we will examine. They are closely linked to the thinker and they also affect the will (chooser). Those who are deep in psychology can give several meanings of emotions but by simple definition, an emotion is a state of feeling. Emotions are inner feelings that drive you into a particular direction. Emotions include: desires, love, hate, happiness, liking, fear, courage, lust and enthusiasm among many others. Obviously, some emotions are good and productive while others are bad and destructive. Some of them like love also double up as fruits of the spirit and they are even divine. A special caution here is that a mind that is not renewed has really no capacity for love and faith. What people of the world call love is mostly lust, liking or such other fleeting worldly emotions. What the world calls faith is simply carnal optimism and positivity which is promoted widely by motivational speakers but which is not backed by God. These emotions are not backed by the word of God like charity and faith are and so they have no real force. Love is a very sublime virtue and there is still a debate as to whether it is really an emotion. According to me, we should not classify love as an emotion, although there is an emotional part of love. Love is much more than an emotion. I would venture to say that love is a holy emotion. The Christian life is not to be lived based on emotions but on faith. We live by faith not by sensory perception. <u>Christians are instructed firmly not to live by how they feel but by what they know from the word of God.</u> In fact, that is what is called faith. *<u>Faith comes from acquiring and acting on information provided by God</u>*. Emotions are usually produced by processing external stimuli. For example, if someone tells you there are terrorists intending to strike your city, if you are not strong in faith, you may end up fearing exceedingly even if the report was a hoax. The reason why we should live by faith and not by emotions is because emotions are mostly not based on the truth but on information derived from the environment by the senses, most of which has no basis in the Bible. Now watch faith: if that report of terrorists comes to spiritual person (one who has renewed his mind and functions on faith, not on senses), he will first take his time to process it without fear. He will be aware the report may be true or not. If not true, there is no cause to worry. If true, there is still no cause to worry because those of us who dwell in the secret place of the Most High are covered from these marauding and rabid gangs called terrorists.

Psalms 91: 3 *surely he will save you from the fowler's snare and from the deadly pestilence 4 He will cover you with his feathers, and under his wings you will find refuge; his faithfulness will be your shield and rampart. 5 You will not fear the terror of night, nor the arrow that flies by day, 6 nor the pestilence that stalks in the darkness, nor the plague that destroys at midday. 7 A thousand may fall at your side, ten thousand at your right hand, but it will not come near you... 10 no harm will overtake you, no disaster will come near your tent. 11 For he will command his angels concerning you to guard you in all your ways;* (KJV)

The surest way to wreck your life is to let it be driven by emotions that reside in the soul. Those can sometimes be useful servants but they make a very terrible master. Our lives must still be run by emotions, but those that reside in the new spirit. We are talking about love, joy, peace, faith and other holy emotions like them. Jesus did not "feel" like going to the cross and suffering to death. In fact, He agonized and did not want to be that costly sacrifice at all. He prayed to God to let the cup pass yet He still left plenty of room for God's will, not His, to be done. He subjected His soul to the will of God and denied it the pleasure it was asking for. He was still led by emotions but the divine ones of love, faith, patience and humility. That is the exercise the Bible refers to as presenting our bodies a living sacrifice, holy and acceptable unto God because that is our reasonable service. You don't need to feel good about doing anything yet you must still do it if it is clearly the will of God. Emotions of the world are unstable, fickle and subject to change depending on the prevailing circumstances. <u>Living life based on worldly emotions is like building a skyscraper on a foundation of quick sand by the beach; it will be gone as soon as the first water wave comes.</u> Faith is based on the solid knowledge of God's word, not on feelings. Feelings come and go but the word of God which is the raw material for our faith is forever established in heaven. For example, fear as an emotion can prevent you from stepping out and doing what you need to do to fulfill your God-given purpose in life. That way, you will have wasted your whole life. On the other hand, faith which produces courage produces just the opposite of that. Hate can produce anger and even cause death through illnesses or violent actions. Let me show how counterproductive negative emotions like fear, unbelief and negativity are on the one side; and how prolific faith is on the other. Two investors have just received the same report from the day's financial news. The experts predict the economy will tumble in a few months to levels not witnessed in recent history. One is a carnal Christian who has no time for the word and the other has extensively renewed his mind with the word. The carnal one believes the report of the so-called experts. He anticipates stock prices will dip and he will suffer loss. As a result, he disposes of all his holdings and saves the money in the bank. Because those faithless people are many, others also stampede to sell off their stocks and the prices tumble and most suffer scorching losses. They all converge at the banks which in turn lower the interests they pay on deposits because of the superfluous cash. So, these fearful fellows lose twice. The prophecy of the experts becomes a reality for them, even if it was untrue. The spiritual Christian on his part receives the report not with fear but faith. He doesn't panic. Instead, he refers from his Bible and finds out that he is blessed because he trusts in the LORD and has made the LORD his hope and confidence. He finds that he is like a tree planted along a riverbank, with roots that reach deep into the water so that such a tree is not bothered by the heat or worried by long months of drought. The leaves ever green and it never stops producing fruit. So, he reasons that it is not the time to shy away from the market but to sow big. He withdraws all his savings from low-interest paying banks and buys 'greedily' from all those fearful people who are selling off their fortunes for a song. He knows the masses almost never get it right. Therefore, he has learnt to be "greedy" when the masses are fearful and "fearful" when they are greedy. In no time, he has plenty of cheaply acquired stocks. He then goes to rest as money works for him. It turns out the reports were actually false alarms and erroneous predictions and never materialize apart from only pockets of usual slight setbacks here and there in the economy which are inconsequential anyway. The stocks rebound and the Christian who is full of the word and revelation is laughing all the way to the bank while his carnal counterpart is broke. I will offer you another live example: a few weeks ago I was commuting to the city centre from my estate. On the way, the battery of the bus developed some complications and started producing sparks. Full of fear and panic, passengers went wild and started doing all manner of crazy things. There was a stampede at the door and people were hurting others as they competed to exit the troubled vehicle. Some people, including women, were jumping through the window and hitting the hard unpaved road and bruising themselves. The road was under construction and it was very rough. All the while, I was just watching the drama; completely unperturbed. The only scripture that came to mind was "fear not." I had so much peace and composure that if I had thought about it at that time, I would probably be surprised, even shocked. A little while later, I saw people preparing to do very stupid things and I tried urging them to stop until the driver could stop the vehicle and turn off the ignition, after which we could then alight safely. Fear took the better part of them. One woman who was clearly unable to jump because she had on a very short and tight skirt tried to do it. She only escaped disaster by a whisker because there was a gentleman on the ground who offered to catch her just before she made the deadly plunge. In a few seconds, the bus stopped and the driver was alerted to switch off the ignition. The remaining people alighted safely and at their own pleasure. The mishap was also corrected. It is possible there are people who sustained back injuries that intensified later causing problems, all based on unfounded fears. From the beginning, there was never a need to scramble to get out the bus so hastily because that almost guaranteed someone would be hurt. But, if people tarried for a little while, there was a pretty decent chance that we would all vacate the bus totally safely. The few of us who took everything by our stride did make it out orderly and without placing ourselves in harm's way. The thing is, although a lie or an unconfirmed report is really not true and should therefore not negatively affect anyone, these two tend to become reality for the person who believes them. After that, they foster fear and destroy the life of the victim. <u>Fear and worry are useless and needless emotions because most of the things people worry about never occur and even when they occur, worry can't solve them.</u> Embrace the truth today and smash the bondage that satan and men have caged you in. Be moved only by what the word of God says. For example, when they forecast that the economy of the world will be going through a rough patch, cross-check with your Bible whether those are the sentiments of God. If you have a real Bible, you will find that if you are in Christ, God supplies for you according to His riches in glory, not according to the economies of men. You will also find that you are like an evergreen tree planted by the river which doesn't see when heat comes nor, should you notice when drought approaches- Jeremiah 17:7-8.

    There was also another very sad occasion in a university where there was a power fault and electricity began to explode. There was a group of students in a room who mistook it for a terrorist attack. They panicked, lost their minds and began running helter-skelter. Some jumped off tall buildings, sustained injuries and unfortunately, one even died. For what? What a needless loss? It is very tragic that a life was lost but why act on impulses based on unconfirmed suspicions? In yet another university, they were conducting what they call security drills. Ordinarily, when such drills are carried out in an organization, only the top echelon of leadership is in the know. The rest of the population in there has no clue what is happening. So, these clueless "experts" of security were doing their clandestine business of "security preparedness." The masses again stampeded and people were injured and unfortunately, another life was lost. The question I kept asking myself was, how can people prepare for 'how to be attacked?' Who told them they would be attacked? What were the chances that university would ever be attacked? Even if it were to be attacked, what are the chances that the attack would be fatal? You see, all these are things driven by the terrible and deadly emotion of fear. The administration in that university was afraid they would be attacked and because they were mere human beings and knew nothing about Psalm 91, they were acting on those fears and even without the real terrorist attack ever happening (and chances are ultra-high it will never happen), acting on their fears proved very deadly and injurious. Carnal mindedness or living based on emotional feelings is death on any day. It is always far dangerous, costly and deadly to live by emotions than to live by faith. I never run without knowing why I am running. Instead, I always keep out of the way of those who are running in case they make me a victim of their carnality because I guarantee you unless you live in a war-torn country, there is almost never a need to run because of an emergency. The few emergencies that do happen can be forestalled by constant fellowship with heaven so that you will almost never need to react fast and dangerously to situations because the Lord will always be about your business. He orders your steps and He can't lead you to danger. Even if you were to find yourself in danger, His angels are always at hand to deliver you. That is the meaning of Him keeping you in perfect peace because your mind is stayed on Him. I repeat here that if you were to find yourself facing an emergency, He is ever present to take you through it in a way that only He can. I only run when I am doing exercises and it is always voluntary and I do it in a safe environment. Let me say something that is very important here: even if it was true the terrorist had struck and were attacking a particular place, the answer is not to lose your mind and run heedlessly. I can hear natural and carnal men who have never read their Bibles for ages saying; "have you ever been attacked? Do you know what it is to fall into the hands of those religious beasts? Do you mean terrorists can be attacking and I sit there not reacting at all?" I never put it that you should not react. You have to. But the reaction is not to panic and to allow fear to take over your life. I just narrated above how I kept my cool when a bus was threatening to explode and all the while, fearful people were jumping almost to their deaths. I am not telling you something I have not done myself. The first and foremost reaction of a believer is always to compose yourself and not panic at all. Why panic when Christ is in you, around you, and you are in Him? Do you mean the terrorists can also catch Christ in you and around you unawares? Do you mean He doesn't care about you and He can't deliver you from harm? Do you mean Psalm 91 has been all of a sudden suspended? <u>When there is an emergency, that is not the time to turn to fear but to faith. One clear thing is that you can't have fear and faith at the same time. The two are mutually exclusive. When one is on duty, the other is on vacation.</u> Panic casts any reason out of the window and leaves you vulnerable. The Bible says to not be anxious for anything. But, "being anxious is a normal human reaction to threatening stimuli! How can I keep from hitting the panic button when worrying things are taking place?" Jesus could not have instructed us no to give place to worry and anxiety if we couldn't.

John 14:1 *Let not your heart be troubled: ye believe in God, believe also in me.* (KJV)

Jesus never asks us to do anything He has not equipped us to do. He made us and He knows us more than we can ever know ourselves in this side of life. When He says something that seems a little challenging for a human being, it is because in His mind, we are not ordinary men. We are supermen and His divine power is at work in us.

Ephesians 3: 20 *Now unto him that is able to do exceeding abundantly above all that we ask or think, according to the power that worketh in us,* (KJV)

Instead of rushing to say that His instructions are not feasible, we should always ask how they should be done because they are all doable. If you just reason naturally and straightaway judge that what the Bible asks to be done is not possible, you shut out the power of the one by whom you can do all things with such unbelief. Fear or unbelief is the act of believing something or someone other than God. That something or someone may be the media, relatives, so-called experts, traditions of men or even satan himself or his direct agents.

We must ever be in a position to quiet our souls and prevent them from bolting out like a wild horse that is out of control.

Psalm 131: 2 *Surely I have behaved and quieted myself, as a child that is weaned of his mother: my soul is even as a weaned child.* (KJV)

If you sense there could be an emergency, just let heaven know your hope is there and you are not afraid. Tell Jesus immediately that your hope is in Him. At the same time, be aware that the Lord's angels are where you are in their sufficient numbers and they excel in might and are on top of things. Did you know angels can take the hand of a shooter who is aiming at you and break it and push him violently out of your way? Take also time to calmly study the whole situation to understand what is happening and why there is unrest. You could run ignorantly and now face the danger head on. Don't run like a commoner. You are a king. King's don't run unless they are exercising and even then, they still do it with dignity. Realize you have the Holy Spirit and the entire heaven inside you. Don't you remember when you got born again Jesus said He and God would make you their home? That being the case, why are you running to hide Jesus and where? Can you imagine you and Jesus running away like terrified chickens? What kind of Jesus are you carrying? So, depending on how much time you have, there are several things you can do. You can pray in tongues but please don't do it out of fright. Depending on the nature of the situation, you can carry on praying with tongues until you feel you has have sufficiently taken care of business. Learn to always put yourself together in the face of an emergency and you will be surprised at how much time you have to formulate a plan of action. A worried man who is panicky cannot think straight and he is guaranteed to make deadly blunders.

There were some people who were handling Mephibosheth, the son of Jonathan and a grandson of Saul, the first king of Israel. They acted on false assumptions that David would murder them all and ran hastily, accidentally dropped the young lad and caused him paralysis. The truth was that David was not after anybody and if anything, he would have been very kind to any seed of Jonathan, his covenant brother. It is the same thing satan does even today. He lies to us that God is angry with us and so the ignorant among us spend their lives anxious, fearful, worried and trying to run away from God. In that story, we are represented by Mephibosheth, Jesus by Jonathan and God by David. We are those who have been paralysed by sin. The devil is the religion and its high priests who preach the fear that God is angry with us and could judge us at any time. If we are ignorant of the truth that God is not angry with us, that He has forgiven us eternally of all sins and given us eternal righteousness, and, is not imputing our sins unto us; then, we will be swayed into erroneous thinking and get into fear. We will not be bold to approach and fellowship with God. We will be like Mephibosheth, living in constant fear that God may be after us. If someone had armed Mephibosheth and his handlers with the truth that David had nothing but peace and goodwill towards the house of Saul, they would have confidence in him instead of dread and they would all live well. As it were, they had the wrong information and they acted on it and the result was death and life-long misery. Coming closer home, Jesus already cut a covenant of peace with God on our behalf and we need never fear God or anything else. That covenant is called a covenant of peace, not of judgment, condemnation and revenge.

Isaiah 54:7 For a brief moment I deserted you, but with great compassion I will gather you.

8 In overflowing anger for a moment I hid my face from you, but with everlasting love I will have compassion on you," says the LORD, your Redeemer. 9 "This is like the days of Noah[a] to me: as I swore that the waters of Noah should no more go over the earth, so I have sworn that I will not be angry with you, and will not rebuke you. 10 For the mountains may depart and the hills be removed, but my steadfast love shall not depart from you, and my covenant of peace shall not be removed," says the LORD, who has compassion on you. (ESV)

Ezekiel 37:26 Moreover I will make a covenant of peace with them; it shall be an everlasting covenant with them; and I will place them, and multiply them, and will set my sanctuary in the midst of them for evermore. (ASV)

Today, no matter how lame we are from sin and other effects of the world, we are invited forever to the Lord's Table to feast with the king who is also our Father, and His servants the angels minister for us all the days of our lives. There is never a reason to shun the Lord no matter what we have done because even when we are in bad shape, He is still the only person who can help us. It is therefore in our best interests to run to Him, rather than from Him so that He can fix us. The devil and the world will not help us but will in fact, condemn, judge, kill and destroy us if we fall into their hands. Our enemy is working day and night to condemn us from inside and he knows that if he can drive a wedge between us and God in our reasoning, then he can move in to create an illusion of disappointment, wrath and impending judgment from God and keep us in a constant state of fright. Fear is a debilitating emotion and it is caused by three things: ignorance of the truth, misinformation or misrepresentation of the truth, and refusal to believe the truth which we can call unbelief. Without a doubt, the antidote for deadly emotions like fear is to possess the truth and believe it. That is the sure solution for the miserable emotions led life. At apprehensive times, you can also turn to Psalm 91 and take solace in the warm assurance of those awesome lines:

2 I will say of the LORD, He is my refuge and my fortress: my God; in him will I trust. 3 Surely he shall deliver thee from the snare of the fowler, and from the noisome pestilence. 4 He shall cover thee with his feathers, and under his wings shalt thou trust: his truth shall be thy shield and buckler. 5 Thou shalt not be afraid for the terror by night; nor for the arrow that flieth by day; 6 Nor for the pestilence that walketh in darkness; nor for the destruction that wasteth at noonday. 7 A thousand shall fall at thy side, and ten thousand at thy right hand; but it shall not come nigh thee...9 Because thou hast made the LORD, which is my refuge, even the most High, thy habitation; 10 There shall no evil befall thee, neither shall any plague come nigh thy dwelling. 11 For he shall give his angels charge over thee, to keep thee in all thy ways.

Let me ask you, with scriptures like those, why would

anyone ever be afraid of anything at all? That awesome Psalm covers everything from accidents, disease outbreaks, terrorist attacks, criminal activities, violent upheavals of the weather and any other conceivable danger. Nothing was left out. The fact that even terrorist attacks are well defined in verses 5, 6 and 10 in a Psalm that was penned thousands of years ago is sufficient to let you know the Bible is accurate. God saw those things way before they became reality and He put in place for His children adequate measures to mitigate the disasters. Check out below what the net effect of the covenant of peace will do for us who believe:

Isaiah 54: 14 *In righteousness shalt thou be established: thou shalt be far from oppression; for thou shalt not fear: and from terror; for it shall not come near thee.* (KJV)

This is the critical information the devil prays earnestly that you will not come across and even if you do, that you will not believe it. Unless you are simply ignorant or in unbelief, why would you be afraid of anything? Being afraid is your statement that you either don't know God or His word,, or, you simply don't trust Him. It shows that if you know His word at all, then you don't think it has any real and practical value and you don't take Him seriously. That is terrible. I will tell you the problem with most Christians: many of them are like oil and water with their Bibles. They never read the word. Don't be surprised to find someone who calls themselves a Christian, born again for years and they will be shocked to learn that Psalm 91 exists and that it has such mind-blowing assurances. The rest of the fearful types are those who read their Bibles but don't believe what they read. They say things like: "well, I know Psalm 91 exists but you know the Bible is spiritual and this is reality and I have to take practical and real steps to ensure I am covered" whenever I hear people talk like that, it's all I can do to contain myself from obeying the spirit of slap. How dumb is that? What do you mean the Bible is spiritual? Basically, what you are saying is that the Bible is a useless piece of publication that is irrelevant on earth and you even have no clue why God gave it to us. He should have as well waited to hand it to us once we get to heaven. That is a deadly mentality and a recipe for tragedy. The Bible is for here and now. It is a book of instructions on how to run this life successfully.

No one will require a Bible in the other side of eternity. Life will be perfect like it was in the Garden of Eden. Adam didn't need a Bible. <u>The Bible is a real word for real life on a real earth.</u> There are no terrorists, plagues, bad weather and accidents in heaven. Why would Psalm 91 be applicable there? The Bible is only applicable where the things it promises to guard us against happen and that is earth. It has also instructions on how to be successful in business, finances, health, safety and security, family life and above all relationship with God. Those are the only main and important aspects of life and the Bible is chockablock with instructions on how to go about all of these categories of life. That being the case, how can someone say that the Bible is for spiritual life? That means you don't even know what "spiritual life" is. What you ignorantly refer to as spiritual life is actually the supernatural realm that runs this natural realm we are in right now. So, if you are ignorant of the dynamics in that realm of which are the contents of the Bible, then this life you are calling practical will beat you hands down. The spiritual realm gave birth to the physical and in order to run the physical successfully, you cannot afford to be ignorant of the supernatural. The Bible is the only text for that critical education.

This is the length and short of it; never allow your life to be run by fears, negative feelings and baseless emotions, rumors, hearsays, prophecies of people not ordained to be prophets, predictions and other such like ridiculous things. In fact, fear alone has killed more people that the real things they were afraid of because the truth is, those things themselves mostly never occur. Always carry yourself with dignity and never do rushed things for which you cannot explain why you are doing them, especially if there is danger involved. <u>Fear is the most prohibited negative emotion in the Bible, yet it is also the most favorite among carnal believers and the heathen.</u> Fear occurs when one is not made perfect in love. The Bible says he who fears is not made perfect in love as perfect love casts out fear. In other words, the person who fears does not understand and have faith in God's love. If they did, that love and the confidence it espouses would completely drive out fear from their lives. And, don't think fear doesn't also have connection with sin-consciousness. You see, when you think you have sinned and

God is mad at you, you will not be confident of His love for you. You will think He has temporarily shelved His love until that sin is cleared out of the way. So, when you need to receive something from the Lord, you will most probably not hope in Him because in your mind, you are at odds with Him. You understand now how it works? Because you will not be sure of God's love working for you, your faith will be affected because faith is anchored on God and His unfailing love. Faith works by love. Faith works when you have confidence in God's love, not your love for God and people. When you don't have confidence in God's love, you will therefore not be settled in the face of trouble because you cannot bank on God being on your side. In fact, if religion has really messed you up with condemnation, you will expect God to be working against you and that will further compound your problems. Many people have ended up in the hospital that way. That is called self-destruction and the process happens between the ears of a Bible-ignorant person or one in unbelief.

On the other hand, faith always produces peace, victory, prosperity and success. Faith is nothing more than simply banking fully on God's love and His word. Our faith is the force that overcomes the world and every circumstance that sets itself against us.

Isaiah 26:3 *Thou wilt keep him in perfect peace, whose mind is stayed on thee: because he trusteth in thee.* (KJV)

1 John 5:4 *For whatsoever is born of God overcometh the world: and this is the victory that overcometh the world, even our faith.* (KJV)

Emotions are mostly purely sense-based and living by the senses produces tyranny, loss, misery, enslavement and death. Emotions are usually mostly carnal and they amount to death while faith is spiritual. That simply means it is word based and it produces life and peace. When we live life based on faith, hope and love, we are guaranteed to succeed and prosper because only those three will remain of all the other things people base their lives on. We all have emotions but we should not let them have us because that would spell disaster. An emotion-led person is out of control and sometimes out of his mind because emotions are now running him. We must always be in charge of our emotions and direct them. Just like money, if well harnessed and directed, emotions can make a wonderful servant but if we allow them to rule us, they make a very terrible master.

Psalm 32:9 *Be ye not as the horse, or as the mule, which have no understanding: whose mouth must be held in with bit and bridle, lest they come near unto thee.* (KJV)

Colossians 3: 5 *So put to death the sinful, earthly things lurking within you. Have nothing to do with sexual immorality, impurity, lust, and evil desires. Don't be greedy, for a greedy person is an idolater, worshiping the things of this world.* (NLT)

Let me demonstrate how interconnected the thinker, will and emotions are. Wrong emotions are caused by wrong thinking which is brought about by the wrong input or simply what we allow to into our system to be processed. That is the province of the will. You can see in that one brief example all the three faculties of the mind involved intricately. Wrong input and subsequent wrong thinking automatically leads to a lot of undesirable things all of which eventually sink the person to despair, disease and death. <u>Feeding on junk food for thought leads to depression, repression, fear, hopelessness, defeat, diseases and death.</u> Some people wonder why they are so stressed, defeated, negative, depressed, sickly, weak and in general bad shape. The only reason is because they kick off the whole chain reaction of events that culminate in their deplorable condition. Some may say, "but, I didn't wish for all these, where did they come from?" if you have depression, it came from inside you; it wasn't imposed on you. None of those things come from outside. As a man thinks, so is the he and the Bible is never known to ever lie. <u>Your life is drifting towards the direction of your most dominant thought or thoughts.</u> Emotions don't follow outside circumstances; they follow your thinking. It is not what happens to you which determines how your life goes. It is how, and with what you process what happens to you. Terrible things happen to all of us but not all of us are depressed or even in a foul mood. It is because some of us process everything the God way and with the word of God. So, when the word says to rejoice always in the Lord and to always give thanks, we take it literally and realize God didn't try to qualify that directive with exceptions. Instead of being a slave of your emotions, you can choose to turn things around and be in charge. You can decide to begin controlling your life from your born again spirit, not from your poorly renewed soul which is in constant touch with a depressing physical environment. Carnal mindedness always breeds death but living from the born again spirit which is full of the word of God is life and peace. If you focus on what is happening in this fallen world, you will abnormal not to be depressed or at least bored almost to death. It will show clearly in your emotions. But, if you choose to constantly focus and meditate on the word of God, you will only know what the word produces and that is life, peace, joy, hope, faith, happiness and strength. I don't need to have been with you when you sowed your seeds. I just need to check out your harvest and I will tell exactly what you planted. No one plants oranges and harvests apples. You harvest what you plant. Let me explain how it happens. It begins with your chooser, although that beginning is itself the product of previous processes. The will is influenced by our thinking and emotional parts, yet it also influences those two. For example, if you choose to listen to bad, less than sublime news and place value on them, you will find yourself thinking negatively and your emotions will be messed up. For our understanding, let's just start at the point of choosing the raw material for thought. In our information technology advanced world today, we can have two kinds of sources. One source can be the world; which speaks of the media, street talk, hearsays, idle chatter at the work place, rumors and opinions or forecasts from so-called "experts" from a variety of fields. All that is carnal information based on man's experience and limited observation of the environment. Then, you can also get information from the word of God. Mainly, the former source says the economies of the world are in trouble, poverty is increasing, diseases are becoming a threat to existence, danger and calamity is heightening and there is nothing we can do, climate change threatens our survival and insecurity is at an all-time high. If all that terrible diet finds a mind that is not renewed with the word of God, the person begins to amplify each piece further. He sees all the world economies weakening further until they are doomed. He also gets the sense that uncontrollable diseases will continue to multiply until no one will be safe from the deadly maladies. In the insecurity front, such a person imagines terrorism, wars, crime, genocides, holocausts and other such evils increasing and becoming so terrible that no one will be spared ultimately. The same person also sees increasing trends of droughts, famines, shortages of all manner of essential commodities and other effects of climate change like the new hoax and religion called "global warming." He sees the world headed to a very uncertain future. This person spends all his days stewing on these bad reports and receives even more bad news every day all which further complicate the situation. Inevitably, the result of all that is a very fearful person who is also stressed, confused, discouraged, depressed, less confident, sick, hopeless and defeated. Thinking over those things can never produce any positive thing. Garbage taken in automatically leads to garbage discharged out. All these disturbances and fears don't do good to the body system. They begin degrading it and compromising its immune system. Diseases become a permanent companion of that person. A lot of deaths and health complications are now caused by stress and fear related reasons and many such victims end up paying the ultimate price.

Now consider the spiritual man in the same environment who is full of the word of God and faith. To begin, he doesn't give as much time to all those negative and terrible reports and forecasts as the carnal fellow. He cannot afford so much time. He is a man pursuing a divine destiny. He is not earthly minded but heaven focused though still being grounded on earth. He dare not concern himself with civilian matters.

2 Timothy 2: 4 *No one serving as a soldier gets entangled in civilian affairs, but rather tries to please his commanding officer.* (NIV)

Spiritual people feed on a very special diet and that is why their results are very superior although we all live in this same space. They are in the world but not of the world. They come from heaven and play by a different set of rules. They are not subject to the things that affect natural men and they are never perturbed by them.

Philippians 4: 8 *Finally, brothers and sisters, whatever is true, whatever is noble, whatever is right, whatever is pure, whatever is lovely, whatever is admirable—if anything is excellent or praiseworthy-think about such things.* (NIV)

The Marvel Of The New Creation Superman

There is nothing true, noble, right, pure, lovely and admirable about insecurity, escalating, diseases becoming more vicious, economies collapsing, climate becoming more hostile and everything getting worse in the world. When they pick up some of those reports, the spiritual people don't take them to heart. They rush to the only text which contains the truth and confirm the position from there. They find that we who are in Christ are well supplied according to God's riches in glory land, not according to the troubled economies of fallen men. The Lord is our shepherd, we shall not want and no good thing shall He withhold from us. We also find that no disease and no evil will come near us because we dwell in the secret place of the Most High. Even if they discover newer ways of committing evil, we stay ahead of the game because we have made the LORD, which is our refuge, even the most High, our habitation. We know no one can ever be smarter and stronger than God's angels who excel in strength and are ever present to minister for us. We do not even fear climatic upheavals because our Father is the commander of all creation and even the waves, storms and winds obey when we direct them in His name.

Psalm 46: 1 *God is our refuge and strength, an ever-present help in trouble. 2 Therefore we will not fear, though the earth give way and the mountains fall into the heart of the sea, 3 though its waters roar and foam and the mountains quake with their surging... 7 The LORD Almighty is with us; the God of Jacob is our fortress.*

Wrong choice of food for thought causes wrong and counterproductive thinking which in turn causes wrong words and wrong actions both of which further cause a terrible life. That is why they say watch what you allow yourself to see, hear, read, or perceive with any of your senses for it becomes your thoughts. Watch your thoughts for they become your words. Watch your words for they become your actions and your actions become your habits and then habits form your character which then determines your destiny. Be careful to notice that the first thing to watch is what we allow in to our minds because that is what determines the final output. Godly and balanced emotions stem from a renewed mind. Emotions are a direct product of what we allow in and consequently process in our minds.

(iv) THE WILL (CHOOSER)

The will is the fourth component of the mind we will examine; it is very critical but is also one of the least understood and appreciated. This is the seat of all the decisions made by the individual. We all know how decision making is at the heart of the human person. One of the biggest factors that differentiate us from animals is because we can make rational decisions-although that is no longer very obvious. In fact, we are products of the aggregate of our decisions. We choose our careers, spouses, where to live, how to live, what faith to profess, who to regard as our role models and mentors, what to eat, whether to be successful or failures, what time to wake up, how much money to make, whether to be healthy or ill, whether to love or hate, and whether to forgive or hold grudges. We even choose our emotions (yes, we literally choose whether to feel fearful, courageous, happy, sad, depressed, upbeat and many more). Ultimately, we choose between death and life, eternal life and eternal damnation.

Your choice of what to listen to and place value on affects your thinking and emotions. However, your decision or judgment to choose to listen to bad news for example is also influenced by your wrong thinking to begin with because you should know better. You should know that negative news causes negative thinking and causes you to make the wrong decisions and hence you find yourself in trouble. Or, you may decide to marry a very beautiful girl whose character you know very well rivals that of an alley cat. Still, because you are under the influence of negative emotions like lust and raging hormones so that all reason is thrown out of the window, you still decide to go by your feelings. You just let your emotions sway your chooser. So, both the thinker and the feeler sway the chooser as much as the chooser also sways those two. It is a chicken and egg case.

To stop the whole cycle of wrong thinking, wrong choosing and wrong feeling, you can decide to start somewhere. Everything always starts by a decision. Start by making your chooser do you a favor and work for you, instead of against you. You can decide to start by changing what you allow into your mind because it will put to an end the whole unfortunate cycle of carnage. Begin with the word of God and reject all these other worldly sources which fill you with fear, negativity and hopelessness. Be careful what you allow yourself to hear or see because those two avenues of receiving information affect your thinking, talking and ultimately acting. Begin by sticking your nose on the word until it completely occupies your mind, drives out those toxic thoughts and changes the way you reason. If you completely fill up your mind with the word, when these negative reports try to have you, they will have no space. <u>When you take care of your chooser, your thinker and emotions will line up with the will of God. As I always say, if you don't control your thinking, you won't control your actions.</u> Someone said that when you are alone, mind your thoughts. Whoever said that was very right because I will tell you what that translates to. It follows that if you can rein in your thoughts, then, when you are with other people, you can manage to be in charge of your tongue and your behavior as well. Not only so, when you are angry, you can mind your temper. When you are in not so good circumstances, you can mind your emotions and of course when you are on top of the world, you can mind your ego.

Romans 12: 2 *And be not conformed to this world: but **be ye transformed by the renewing of your mind, that ye may prove what is that good, and acceptable, and perfect, will of God**.* (KJV) Emphasis added.

Nothing changes until you begin transforming yourself by renewing your mind. You see, to be able to think right and make right choices, you need the raw materials of sound information (basically the truth of God's word), faith in that word and right thinking. That is what the word of God and faith in it produces in your mind. If you have armed yourself with the mind of God from His word, when the occasion to decide on a particular matter comes up, you will not be lost and agonizing over what to do. You will just know what to do. For example, if you get a disturbing report regarding your health, you can make several decisions that have far reaching ramifications. You can decide to start by being shocked, which has an instant negative effect on the health of your heart. You can follow that with worrying for days on end. You can proceed to tell it to all who care that the doctors confirmed you are a walking corpse. You can waste your life away thinking about how you will continue growing weaker and weaker until you die a slow excruciating death. You can even begin to picture yourself lying in the morgue and people planning your funeral. You can also shrink in to your private cocoon and spend the rest of your days full of darkness, sorrow and just waiting to die. I guarantee you in that case, death will cruise towards you speedily. You can also decide to seek medical solutions and that also has its own fair share of problems. All those are decisions you can make. Tragically, most people react according to that pattern. They think naturally. They think the doctor has the last word concerning their health. They don't pause to consider the God-factor. Notice that because you have no God's mind regarding that area of your life, all the decisions you take are wrong and deadly. Lets now turn to the guy who has read the will of God and is rich in the word. Immediately he gets the upsetting report, he first turns to these two scriptures:

1 Thessalonians 5: 18 *In everything give thanks:* ***for this is the will of God*** *in Christ Jesus concerning you.* (KJV) Emphasis added.

Ephesians 5: 20 *Giving thanks always for all things unto God and the Father in the name of our Lord Jesus Christ;* (KJV)

As you can see, this time, you start by thanking God. You don't thank Him because of the bad report but in spite of it. You thank Him because it is His will to thank Him in everything. Thanking Him also includes letting Him know that you are aware the illness is not from Him but an attack from the enemy which must be resisted. Thanking God even in the midst of the attack is the first step in combating the hardship. It is the very first decision and it is also the will of God. By the way, thanking God in all things is a decision. Sadly, most people choose to do the exact opposite. They complain, grumble, become saddened and begin losing hope in the face of a difficulty. At the same time as you thank God in the face of a challenge, because you are spiritual (word-filled), you also guard your mind from anxiety, panic and sorrow. All of those negative emotions usually further complicate the situation, far from helping it. The scripture that constantly rings in the mind of a spiritual person is, "be anxious for nothing." "Do you mean the doctor has just told me I have a terminal condition and I burst out in joy?" Precisely! Did you know even just a mere scriptural reaction of joy to a dark situation can turn it on its head?

Proverbs 17: 22 *A merry heart doeth good like a medicine: but a broken spirit drieth the bones.* (KJV)

A lot of good things are going on in the mind of this spiritual person even in the midst of the bad news. He is thinking; "the Lord has given me the power to choose whether to take my healing which was purchased by Jesus or not. If I choose to take it, I remain on earth and continue with kingdom work. If I decide not to take it, I go to be with the Lord. Both prospects are very enticing and in both, I win and rub the devil's nose very badly." After that, you can choose whether to leave or remain like Paul but it is always good to elect to remain so that you can be of good to brethren for a little longer. You also don't want to appear like you are in a hurry to check out of earth. You don't want to be seen as if trying to escape hardships. You are a winner and a victor forever. You can choose to hang around for as long as you want and for as long as there is work for you. You choose when you die, not God or satan. Some people find that hard to swallow because religion has brainwashed them to think, "people go when God calls them and when He 'calls,' nobody can resist" pardon me but I think that is a very silly way of looking at things. What about the fellow who commits suicide? Did God also 'call' them? Even governments know better than that because if the attempt is not successful, the person is charged for attempted murder! What about the terrorists who murder months old children? Did God also 'call' such? If God's call cannot be resisted, why then, attempt to resist it by seeking medical attention? You see how confused and hypocritical religion is? Religion likes to heap on God things that are so nasty it always appears ridiculous. It paints God as responsible for perpetrating things He judged and punished people in the Old Testament for doing. God does not determine when people die. It is the people themselves. This is how it works: God wants people to have a long and satisfying life. Jesus came so that we can have life to overflowing. If we cooperate with Him in faith and correct use of our tongues, we live. Satan is also around seeking whom he may devour. If someone is foolish enough to cooperate with him through unbelief and faithless talk, they get devoured. Satan is also at work stealing, killing and destroying and we must resist him and not give him as much as a foothold. What happens in your life is the will of who you choose to cooperate with- God or satan. At the end of the day, death and life are not in the hands of God or satan but in your tongue. God has already offered to us life and death and He doesn't say He will choose any of them for us. He lets us know we need to choose life. One man of God gave an account of how God told him that He (God) had the power to take his life but not the authority. I like that. It is very consistent with scriptures. <u>Life is a personal choice, and so is death.</u>

      It is the same thing with sickness. I have already pointed out that we choose whether we get healed or not. It is always smart to choose healing. God has done everything He would ever need to do to make our healing available. All that remains is to take it. If you think you have tried receiving it and done everything you needed to do but still you don't have it manifested, the problem is not God's. I don't know why when things don't seem to work, we always rush to blame it on He who can never fail. If your life is not working, then you are not working it right. Don't rush to blame God for the non-performance because He has nothing to do with it. That is the sure way to never have it because you are not addressing the real issue. God is not a failure and neither does He do trial and error. Find out where the loophole is and seal it. There is never a time when God is to be blamed. Your healing is sure and ready and so is everything else. By grace through faith, just receive today whatever you need because it is on deposit. It is that easy. That is what we call being in control of your life. Nothing shakes you in life. You are constant and composed in all circumstances. Someone could be asking, "what have you been smoking young man? You live in a make-believe world! What you are suggesting here are fantasies." Well, <u>I have been smoking the word of God and it has given me the mindset of the righteous. I am larger than life. It is also true I am in this world but not of this world. I live in two parallel worlds contemporarily. Life doesn't tell me what will happen, I tell it what will. I am not a victim of life, I 'king' (reign) in it.</u> The reason why I have a different mindset that blows you away is because I have and believe in some information you either do not have or have chosen to disregard. That is what makes us different. We are like day and night. For as long as you reject as foolishness and wishful thinking the information I have, you will never get the results I have. So, don't worry, it will not work for you. Notice how the condition of the mind determines the choices one makes and brings out two radically varied outcomes from the same dark situation? That is the power of a renewed mind. <u>A renewed mind puts its holder in control of his own life while a carnal or natural mind makes one a victim.</u> while a natural one leads to wrong and deadly ones. A renewed mind leads to joy, happiness, positivity, peace and life while a non-renewed one leads to sadness, heaviness, negativity and death. If you submit to God by renewing your mind with the curriculum of His word, You will automatically find yourself willing His will.

Philippians 2: 13 *For it is God which worketh in you both to will and to do of his good pleasure.* (KJV)

God doesn't want you to be obstinate, always choosing your own way. He knows you are not that smart. So, He reveals another way in His word which makes choosing His will an automatic function and that is the way of renewing your mind with His word.

Proverbs 14:12 There is a way which seemeth right unto a man, but the end thereof are the ways of death. (KJV)

CHAPTER THREE

ATTRIBUTES OF THE NEW CREATION

1. THE NEW CREATION: A BRAND NEW AND PERFECT SPIRIT

THE NEW CREATION IS MADE A PERFECT SPIRIT AFTER THE IMAGE OF HIS FATHER GOD.

The new creation man is a spirit and he is born perfect and complete in Christ. That perfection is not in the flesh or in the soul but in the spirit. The redemption of those two (body and soul) is in the near future. They are ready and perfectly set but still kept in Heaven. They will be united with the perfect spirit in the twinkling of an eye upon Jesus' return. When that is done, we will be complete in all our three parts; just like Jesus is after resurrection. For now, we are perfect spirits who are joined inseparably with Jesus. When I say we are perfect in the spirit already, some people may not understand. What I mean by that is that in the spirit, we are righteous and truly holy. We are every bit exactly as He is.

Ephesians 4: 23 *And be renewed in the spirit of your mind; 24 And that ye put on the new man, which after God is created in righteousness and true holiness.* (KJV)

This scripture stands opposed to the many people who don't think we are now completely holy. They do admit we are righteous but they don't agree that we are also holy. Basically what they mean is that we don't work for our righteousness but we do work for our holiness. I want to submit here that we are every bit as holy as we are righteous. For Mount Sinai to be called holy, it didn't do anything. The Lord just came upon it and it was declared holy. It is the same thing with us. The Lord has cleansed us to indwell us. He would never dwell in a corrupted vessel in the first place.

Some other people say that we can't be more righteous but we can be more holy. Besides leading to needless oppression, performance and works of the law, this is also not true at all and the verse above bears it all. It says we are born again righteous and truly holy. Here is another witness;

1 Corinthians 1:30 *It is because of Him that you are in Christ Jesus, who has become for us wisdom from God: our righteousness, holiness, and redemption.* (Berean Study Bible)

This invaluable verse says that the same Christ who is our righteousness is also our holiness. We don't work for our holiness any more than we work for our righteousness. Holiness is a gift from God. Holiness is in our DNA just like righteousness. It is richly in us. We can't be more holy than Jesus has made us, what we can do is manifest more of that gift of holiness in us just like we can manifest more of the gift of righteousness in us.

2 Thessalonians 2: 13 *But we are bound to give thanks always to God for you, brethren beloved of the Lord,* **because God hath from the beginning chosen you to salvation through sanctification of the Spirit** *and belief of the truth:* (KJV) Emphasis added.

Holiness is not something we do; it is a gift of God we are given in Christ. As the scripture above points out, holiness is an operation the Holy Spirit does in our lives to qualify us for salvation. Some people misunderstand Hebrews 12:14 which says to follow peace with all men, and holiness, *without which no man* shall *see the Lord.* They think it means we must strive to be holy and to keep the law more so that we can be holy because if we don't, we will then not be holy and we will not see God. If that were to be so, that would not be good news but bad news because it would take us to performance of the law again. That verse is saying we're created righteous and truly holy, we now need to work it outwards and manifest it because if we don't, then people will not see God in us. This verse simply explains the words of Jesus in Matthew chapter 5.

Ye are the light of the world. A city that is set on an hill cannot be hid. 15 Neither do men light a candle, and put it under a bushel, but on a candlestick; and it giveth light unto all that are in the house. 16 Let your light so shine before men, that they may see your good works, and glorify your Father which is in heaven.

Holiness comes from the Greek word *hagiasmós* and it simply means sacred, dedicated, set apart or special. It is not even a religious word but when it is used in the Bible, it means dedicated for God's use. Religion defines holiness as the absence of sin or the state of being sin-free. If that is true, then how about the children of righteous parents of whom the Bible says are born holy? Those day-old babies are declared holy by the Holy Spirit straight from the uterus before they do anything good or bad. Does it mean they have been acting right and avoiding sin? No! It simply means they are marked for the Lord or dedicated to God. They belong to Him and not to the world. Still in that same verse of 1 Corinthians 7:14, it says the unbelieving spouse is sanctified or made holy by the believing one. Does it mean the unbelieving one has all of a sudden stopped sinning and is now sin-free? The Holy Spirit is not really called so because He is a spirit who does not sin. He is Holy because He is the spirit of the living God and in many places the Bible does christen Him so. The opposite of holiness is common or secular. That is why in many places where it is used in the Bible, it is usually followed by the phrase "unto the Lord." One of Bible's best definitions of holiness is to be found in this awesome verse:

1 Peter 2:9 *But ye are a **chosen generation, a royal priesthood, an holy nation, a peculiar people;** that ye should shew forth the praises of him who hath **called you out of darkness into his marvelous light;*** (KJV) Emphasis added.

No one can argue with that definition because the best way to explain the word of God is to always let the Bible interpret or explain itself. Peter is telling us here that we are not common people but God's own selected, special and set apart people dedicated for the Lord's purpose of manifesting the glory of God who has set us apart from darkness unto His light. When the Bible says without holiness no man will see the Lord, it means that if we don't act like God's special people but behave like commoners or Gentiles, then no one will know we are the Lord's and His reputation will be soiled in the eyes of men.

We don't, and can't make ourselves holy just like we don't make ourselves righteous. It is the work of the Holy Spirit in us. What we can do is to cooperate with the Holy Spirit to manifest more of the divine purpose for which we are set apart to accomplish.

Let's not invent ways to keep people under the bondage of performance when Christ finished all the work for them. The best way to honor what He did for us is to accept it, acknowledge it, believe it, embrace it and then and only then can we live it out. That order must be observed or else we will remain held up in legalism and religious performance.

(i) THE NEW CREATION IS NOT A "SINNER SAVED BY GRACE"

I am not a sinner saved by grace. I was a sinner but that sinner man died with and in Christ at the cross. In his place, I was raised with and in Christ and seated in Him in Heaven at God's right hand, a place of authority and power. That is where my newly created spirit is, as well as being in this bodily house. My old self died and my life is now hidden with Christ in God. I cannot still be a sinner because I am the righteousness of God in Christ Jesus. All that Christ is to God, I am. For example, Christ is God's beloved son in whom He is well pleased; so am I in Him. Christ is the radiance of God's glory and the exact representation of His being; so am I in him. Christ is the measure and expression of God's righteousness and holiness; so am I in Him. I cannot be a sinner and righteous at the same time. Something would be terribly wrong with that picture. Again, I cannot be in Christ and seated in Him by God's right hand and still be a sinner. No sinner makes it inside of Christ and certainly no sinner can be allowed by God's side in heaven. So do I still sin? Certainly yes. Then, if I am God's own righteousness, why do I still fall short of His glory? You see, I am not confused about my identity. My newly created spirit is a tree of righteousness, a planting of the Lord. It has fruit of love, peace, faith, joy, patience, gentleness and goodness. Naturally, we were born dead already after the nature of fallen Adam; but we are born again alive forever more in Christ.

However, at new birth, my soul was not recreated. My soul was used to the ways of the long dead man, who died in Jesus at the cross. My Soul was used to working together with that old dead nature. Therefore, I see another tree in my soul which also has fruit but this other fruit is of hatred, selfishness, evil, despair, unbelief and lust. After the new birth which is my heavenly Father's sole responsibility, I am responsible for uprooting and casting away this tree of evil that grows in my soul and bears these unwelcome fruits. How do I do it? Romans Chapter 12 tells me how. Verse one and two tells me to not be conformed to my old ways of doing things, but to renew my soul and be transformed. Verse 21 tells me to overcome the tree of evil with the tree of righteousness. So, by the grace of God, I supplant hatred with love. I displace pride with humility. I overthrow unbelief with faith. I replace heaviness with joy. I substitute bitterness, jealousy and envy for love. I conquer unforgiveness with forgiveness.

Still how do I do that practically without it coming out as a work of the flesh or my own personal effort? The Bible is not silent again. I collect abundance of grace and the gift of righteousness to reign over every ungodly tendency in my life. Secondly, Colossians 3:1-2 tells me to focus on Heaven and the things of heaven where my life is hidden with Christ in God. Heaven here doesn't necessarily just mean the celestial location where God dwells. It can also mean inside the newly created spirit. God dwells there too and from there we draw the force of grace and righteousness which supplants the vestiges of evil in our souls. It just depends on what we are focused on. If we are focused on Christ and our newly perfected spirits in which dwells righteousness, goodness and divinity; a godly fruit will manifest. You see, we are transformed into Christ's likeness not by striving and trying, but just by beholding Christ who is our life. Beholding Christ is not a mysterious exercise. It is simply spending time in the word and receiving the revelation of Christ. Once we find from the word how Christ is right now, we find ourselves too because we are in Him. As He is, so are we in this world. But, if we focus on ourselves and the everyday things in this life and world, then we will duly see an unholy fruit manifesting. The lord tells us to put off these characteristics from our past nature:

Ephesians 4: 22 *That ye put off concerning the former conversation the old man, which is corrupt according to the deceitful lusts; 23 And be renewed in the spirit of your mind;* (KJV)

Colossians 3:5 *Put to death, therefore, whatever belongs to your earthly nature: sexual immorality, impurity, lust, evil desires and greed, which is idolatry.* (NIV)

It's possible to do and it must be done, otherwise the Lord would not ask us to do it. The Lord never requires of us anything He has not equipped us adequately to do. The first effective way of practically achieving this is by believing and speaking. You must acknowledge and say every good thing you have in Christ Jesus. Your mouth is the rudder which determines the direction of your life. Death and life reside in your tongue. Chart your way in life by biblical use of your tongue. Say what you have in Christ, not what you see with your physical eyes. <u>State the word of God emphatically over your life, don't merely repeat your experiences.</u> We walk by the word not by sight. Believe and declare you have love and not hatred, anger, jealousy and envy. Believe and declare you have faith and not unbelief, worry, anxiety and fear. Believe and declare you are the righteousness of God in Christ, not a sinner saved by grace-a term God never applies to any Christian. Believe and declare that the real you is not those shortcomings that still reside in your flesh, but the pure, holy, precious, majestic and magnificent spirit that's hidden with Christ in God; in whom there is no unrighteousness at all. When you believe those things and declare them with your mouth, your life will immediately start going that direction effortlessly. It is called effortless transformation. The real <u>Christian movers and shakers are those who clearly understand their identity in Christ, and the significance of Christ in them.</u> Just be always conscious of the realities in your born again spirit and let your words and actions be consistent with that new and perfect nature of yours. Call it like God does. We must learn to imitate our everlasting Father in every way, but especially in speech. God works not with His hands but His word. He speaks, it is done. That is how kings operate. You will never find a king digging hard and toiling. They just send the word and their bidding happens because where the word of the king is, there is power.

Hebrews 11:3 *Through faith we understand that the worlds were framed by the word of God, so that things which are seen were not made of things which do appear.*

God uses words to create and sustain. He used His Word to

"frame" the worlds. You just need to scan through the first chapter of Genesis to notice how many times you see the phrase, "And God said." God acts by His word. If you're smart and care about results, you'll adopt that same system too. You'll take His word and speak it out until it takes on form and substance and becomes a reality in your life. Did you know even Jesus is a product of God's word? He was simply spoken into the womb of Mary. How cool is that? God spoke Jesus into being all through the Old Testament, over and over again. God's word was literally made flesh, and dwelt among us- John 1:14. Do you want to play in God's league, operate in God's power and make something impressive out of your life? Then speak out His word and let it frame a life full of glory and blessing for you. God reigns with His word and we have no option but to do the same. Speak only what God speaks and how He says it and while at it, put faith behind that word. Just repeating the word without faith will not avail you anything. The word must be mixed with faith for it to prosper. One could be asking, "But, how do I know how God speaks?" You do. For that reason, God has equipped us with His word. That is why <u>no Christian can afford the luxury of being ignorant of God's word. It the only tool for reigning we have.</u> The word of God must always be in your mouth. One of the top priority duties of a Christian is to learn to replace the words of men and words of the traditions and cultures we grew up in with the word of God. The reason why speaking the word of God is very different from any other speech is because it is power-Hebrews 4:12. That means when you are studying the word, you are actually taking in or ingesting divine power which is then released in your system. That is why you can just lay your hands on a sick person and that power will flow to heal them. One of the best things with the word of God is that all you need to do is lift it from the pages of the Bible and sow it in your heart. The word of God is potent seed. You just need to ensure your heart is well prepared with faith. Faith is the fertile ground on which the word grows and bears much fruit. Remember the parable of the farmer who sowed seeds that fell in different grounds? The different grounds were the different conditions of hearts of men. Some hearts are shallow, some are hard with unbelief, others are distracted with the careers, pleasures and businesses of the world and; some well cultivated ones are rich in faith and therefore fertile grounds of the word. One encouraging thing is that in all these types of hearts, it is not the word that determines the nature and level of yield; it is the soil type. The word of God is the same and has the same effect on all who receive it. It doesn't work for some people and fail to work for others. The word is not personal in its working but it follows laid down divine principles, chief of which is faith. <u>Exposed to the same nature and level of faith, the word bears the exact same nature and quantity of fruit over the same period of time</u>. So, two things need to be done by every believer: first, prepare your heart to be a conducive ground for the word and then work to pump in there as much word as possible. How do you prepare your heart? There are several things to do. Amazingly, to prepare your heart, you still need the word. You just need to know where to start in the Bible. My suggestion is to start building faith in your mind by studying the revolutionary scriptures found in Romans, Galatians and Hebrews. Those are the best ones in shifting the mind from the old covenant way of thinking to the New Testament system. Once your mind is shifted and completely tuned to the New Testament frequency, everything you study in the Bible through the lenses of grace will stick and bear fruit in your life. Nothing begins to work in your life until you tune into the grace frequency and abandon legalism totally. God moved mountains from Mt. Sinai to Mt. Zion and we must move with Him. We can't remain stuck in old Sinai where Moses was. Moses who gave the law is a dead man but Christ who came full of grace and truth is alive forever more. If you still have a law mentality, even if you read through the Bible a million times, you will never understand scriptures and the soil of your heart will remain to be one or several of the three that could not sustain the seed of the word for it to grow and yield fruit. The other thing to do in order to prepare your heart is to pray, and especially do so with new tongues. Praying with tongues opens up one's mind and makes understanding of the word easy because it illuminates the mind with revelation. If you ever read a scripture and fail to understand, just take time to repeat the studying prayerfully by speaking with other tongues and listening to the Holy Spirit and it will become clear to you. Whatever you do when studying the word, you need to directly engage the Holy Spirit to explain to you everything; just the way you would personally and closely engage a friendly teacher in school.

John 14:26 *But the Comforter, which is the Holy Ghost, whom the Father will send in my name, he shall teach you all things, and bring all things to your remembrance, whatsoever I have said unto you.* (KJV)

John 16:13 *Howbeit when he, the Spirit of truth, is come, he will guide you into all truth: for he shall not speak of himself; but whatsoever he shall hear, that shall he speak: and he will shew you things to come.* (KJV)

1 John 2:27 *But the anointing which ye have received of him abideth in you, and ye need not that any man teach you: but as the same anointing teacheth you of all things, and is truth, and is no lie, and even as it hath taught you, ye shall abide in him.* (KJV)

We must strive to eliminate from our everyday vocabulary any humanly or even satanic speech that is not in line with the word of God. It doesn't necessarily need to be obscene speech. As long as it is not of faith, abandon it in a hurry because it will ruin your life. Don't repeat what the unbelievers and ignorant and ungodly governments of men are saying. You are different. Your citizenship is in heaven, not in the earth. So, like Noah, the same storm in which ordinary men are perishing is promoting you to safety because you dwell in the secret place of the Most High and that place is Christ in whom you live and dwell and have your being. Don't be perturbed by sinking economies and systems of men. Their lot is not yours unless you group yourself with them and choose to participate in their faithless talk. You are like an evergreen tree that grows by the ever flowing river which doesn't see when heat comes and is never careful in the year of drought.

Proverbs 6: 2 *Thou art snared with the words of thy mouth, thou art taken with the words of thy mouth.* (KJV)

Colossians 3:17 *And whatsoever ye do in word or deed, do all in the name of the Lord Jesus, giving thanks to God and the Father by him.* (KJV)

I am aware there is a lot of emphasis on the speaking part. It has been drilled in us even by motivational speakers to speak positive words. This approach of the matter from a secular standpoint is equally dangerous. Positive words are not anywhere near enough. If all you speak are positive words, they still remain words of men and you will still sink even with your positive talk. The reason is; positive talk is not backed by anyone. It is simply man's natural way of solving a spiritual problem. So, what words are we to speak? Words of God of course! Our work is the easiest. We are to find out what God has said about a particular issue and simply believe it and then parrot the same. That is the only available formula of dominion. The reason the word of God is a powerful tool for dominion is because it is backed by the owner. God stands behind His word if it is spoken in faith to back it and make it come to pass. Unlike positive words of men, the word of God is powerful and active. <u>The word of God is a prolific instrument of releasing power.</u>

Jeremiah 1: 12 *The LORD said to me, "You have seen correctly, for I am watching[b] to see that my word is fulfilled."* (KJV)

Isaiah 55: 11 *So shall my word be that goeth forth out of my mouth: it shall not return unto me void, but it shall accomplish that which I please, and it shall prosper in the thing whereto I sent it.* (KJV)

If you speak words that God is not specifically backing, then any spiritual power out there will take them and wreck your life with it.

Psalm 39: 1 I said, *"I will watch my ways and keep my tongue from sin; I will put a muzzle on my mouth while in the presence of the wicked."* (NIV)

Reform your ways now and begin to make your words count. Desist completely from speaking idle words that ruin your life. Make God's words your own and let them form the only content in your heart. <u>Your tongue is a small organ which is vested with massive power. Arm it with godly ammunition for it to work for you, rather than against you. There is a miracle in your mouth, let it work the miracles for you, not blunders.</u>

Psalm 141: 3 *Set a guard over my mouth, LORD; keep watch over the door of my lips.* (KJV)

In the Old Testament, David and people of his age could

pray a prayer like Psalm 141:3 above. In our dispensation, the Lord has equipped us with the Holy Spirit to walk in Him and we will not suffer a misstep. To walk in the Spirit is to walk according to the word because the word of God is not just a print on paper, it is spirit and life. This does not rule out the need for us to listen keenly to the Holy Spirit who speaks in our born again spirit to direct and enlighten us even on current issues.

To correct our speech so that we can also set our lives on good course, we must know what God has said. This emphasis on speech only is not enough. The mouth doesn't just speak. What comes out of it is what the heart is full of. So, the emphasis should actually be to fill the heart with the right content which is the word of God. When we are squeezed, the only thing that should come out is that stored word and we will have no option but to be winners in life. Stressing on positive speech without addressing what goes to our mind is futile because even if we were to train ourselves to speak well and speak the word but don't believe our words, they will still not avail us anything. The way to tame our tongues as instructed by the Bible is to get rid of all human and cultural thinking in our minds and replacing or reprogramming it with the mind of Christ. That way, when the tongue begins to run, it will have no option but to repeat the will of God. It is the word we have believed and hidden in our hearts that comes in handy in times of trouble. It's not just a matter of speaking forth words; it pays to speak out of faith as well for us to be able to build our lives with our speech.

The only words we speak that work positively for us are those that we speak in faith and which agree with God's word. For example, did you know most people say only what they see and desist from saying what they don't see to avoid appearing foolish? Now watch God, He operates just in the opposite;

Romans 4: 17 *(As it is written, I have made thee a father of many nations,) before him whom he believed, even God, who quickeneth the dead, and calleth those things which be not as though they were.* (KJV)

God told Abraham he would beget a son when he was way past ordinary child bearing age. His wife Sarah was also many decades past menopause and any doctor would have dissuaded her from carrying such a pregnancy to term-that is if there would ever be any remote chance of any pregnancy happening at that age.

When Jesus saw Peter in the first instance, He immediately changed his name from Simon to Cephas, meaning Rock, or at least a small stone. Yet, Peter continued to be as unstable as a reed for a long time. He tried to prevent Jesus from going to the cross, struck off the ear of the high priest's servant and denied Jesus three times. After Jesus was crucified and buried, Peter even thought their deal with Jesus was over and he persuaded the rest of the disciples to revert to their original career of fishing. But, after Jesus ascended, we see in Peter what He had seen back in their first meeting, a hardened and bold man who with a handful of other apostles turned the then known world upside down. In the very first crusade in history which it was he who presided over, about three thousand people came to Christ. Any other human, including Peter's own mother would have dismissed him as unstable and inconsequential. We must learn to only talk like God talks. Negative talk must be put far away from our mouths. If you are a husband and you think you have reasons to say your wife is not as virtuous as the Proverbs chapter 31 woman, don't call her what you are imagining she is especially if it is negative. Find some good attributes to accord to her. Say of her: "she is diligent and business minded. She rises while it is yet night, and prepares food for her household. She is not an idler. Strength and honor are her clothing; and she shall rejoice in time to come. She opens her mouth with wisdom." Out of all these attributes, you will find there are several that apply to her. Dwell on those ones and the rest will also fall in place. Always look for ways to speak well of those you love and never put them down. Rather than curse, bless your children. Talk well of them. Command over them words of life. Say over them that they shall be great in the land and that they are delivered. <u>Always speak what you want to see, not what you see because you are a king and a priest and your words are anointed with power so that what you say comes to pass.</u>

If you are in business and every other business person you meet is talking about how there is no money in the economy, or how clients are broke, or how times are tough, or how all projections by "experts" are pointing south and how business is bad of late:

THE MARVEL OF THE NEW CREATION SUPERMAN

You cannot participate in such a talk of unbelief. You are too big and too high for that. You know better. You can't curse your future like those other foolish and simple talkers. You bless only and never curse. Just like your heavenly Father, you don't even know how to talk negative. You see no evil and say no evil. When people talk like that in your presence, first of all, ensure they don't continue. One of three things must happen at once: they either vacate your presence, or you vacate yourself or stop them from continuing to pour out that negative garbage. You can do that by introducing immediately what the word of God says or changing the topic of discussion. You must let them know that you never know such tough times. The Lord is your shepherd and you shall never be in lack. You are like a tree planted by many waters which never withers or even takes notice when heat comes. Your path as a righteous man is as a shining light that grows brighter and brighter unto the perfect day. Whatsoever you touch to do is blessed. No matter how tough times may be, no matter how bleak and frightening the future may appear, all things remain yours. You are never afraid because the Lord is your shepherd, you will never lack and He will never leave you nor forsake you. That is God's verdict concerning you in all circumstances. You cannot afford to say anything else. And it is not just a matter of mouthing words mechanically to please yourself or God. You must believe in your heart every bit of those words and then speak them out with your mouth. That is how salvation comes. That is also how you reign in business. It applies to every area of your life. Don't allow people to say that a season for a particular disease or pandemic has come and everyone must brace themselves to be affected. Don't even allow doctors to tell you that you have attained a particular age and therefore you can expect some medical conditions to begin showing up in your body. Cancel all those deadly prophecies from faithless men by a simple "there is no time in life when the word of God doesn't work in all my circumstances." If you don't confront those men because you are afraid to appear different or weird or because you want to please them; their words will be a snare to you. Remember their words of unbelief are weapons of carnage formed against you. Part of your heritage is to condemn every tongue or weapon that rises against you.

Isaiah 54: 17 *No weapon that is formed against thee shall prosper; and every tongue that shall rise against thee in judgment thou shalt condemn. This is the heritage of the servants of the LORD, and their righteousness is of me, saith the LORD.* (KJV)

Apply that in every area of your life and the results will be miraculous. Search the word and get to know what the Lord says about any particular area of your life and reign in that area with that word. If you are ignorant of the word, not even God Himself will help you and satan will destroy you for lack of knowledge.

(ii) THE NEW CREATION HAS NO PAST

A lot of Christians still think Christianity is a life-long exercise of modifying one's behavior from bad to good. Some think it is about making promises to God to be a better person and trying to keep them. Still, others think it is "fighting" the devil throughout life and trying to defeat him. In fact, there are many people who think Christianity is synonymous with fighting the devil (what they call spiritual warfare) or even fighting off bad influences and habits in their lives. Yet, others take Christianity to mean a religion of doing things like performing some rituals, reciting liturgies or conducting litanies. Some say Christianity is a particular lifestyle, or that Christianity is one of the religions of reaching God. Some even group Christianity together with Judaism and Islam as one of the Abrahamic religions. All these perceptions are dead wrong!

None of them is Bible-based but they all are in fact, devices designed in the pit of hell to neutralize the powerful life of Christianity. Muslims say Islam is a lifestyle. Christianity is not a lifestyle, although it produces a particular lifestyle and culture. Christianity is life. It is the only life there is. All else is death. <u>Christianity is basically eternal life which translates to the powerful and active life of God at work in a human person.</u> It goes without saying that Christianity does produce a certain lifestyle and a culture which is compatible with the culture of heaven, but it is not a lifestyle; it is the original, divine life.

Now, Christianity is the life of the person we are calling the new creation. There is a vast difference between the former unregenerate person that was you and the new, born again you. The difference between the two persons is as darkness and light. The former had the nature of Satan. It was an old spirit inherited from Adam that was naturally evil and sinned at will-Ephesians 2:1-3. This old person was an enemy of God because He could not be subject to His will-Romans 8:7

That old nature could not be salvaged. It was beyond redemption. So, what was God to do to save man? Well, God is never short of options. He had a water-tight program prepared before the foundation of the world. He took this old nature called sin and everything it had produced like diseases, curses, judgment, death and poverty, and put them all in His righteous son- Jesus Christ. Jesus bore them all for us so that when we believe in Him, all His attributes of righteousness, purity, wisdom, knowledge, wealth and glory come on us. That is how come we are the righteousness of God in Christ Jesus.

The sin spirit came upon Adam at the fall. When Adam fell, he switched fathers from God to Satan and all who are born naturally only and not of the Spirit also, have the devil as their father too- John 8:42-44. Everyone who is born of woman automatically acquires that spirit called sin. That is why we don't become sinners because we sin. We sin because we are sinners by nature. No one trains babies to be mean and selfish. They come with it. So, sin is a spirit that came upon man after the fall. Now, at the cross, God took this sin, put it in Jesus, judged it in the flesh of Jesus and took it away for good-Romans 8:3.

Now, for those who choose to believe in Christ, God accounts for them as if they were in Christ when He was crucified. In God's mind, their old nature was judged fully in Christ and they have no penalty of sin to pay. Their old nature was crucified and it no longer exists. They now partake of divine nature.

Romans 6: 3 *Know ye not, that so many of us as were baptized into Jesus Christ were baptized into his death?...6 Knowing this, that our old man is crucified with him, that the body of sin might be destroyed, that henceforth we should not serve sin... 11 Likewise reckon ye also yourselves to be dead indeed unto sin, but alive unto God through Jesus Christ our Lord.* (KJV)

Colossians 3: 3 *For ye are dead, and your life is hid with Christ in God.* (KJV)

What is the implication of this? It means that God knew and took all who would believe in His son, put them in Christ together with their filthy Adamic nature and then condemned and destroyed that nature in the flesh of Jesus. I like to call it death of the old self at the cross. God killed the old man in Christ for those who choose to believe. So, what next after that? After having been dead with Christ for three days, God raised us up with and in Him, not with the old nature now, but in newness of life. That is why this unfortunate religious phrase of a sinner saved by grace must be dropped. It's a manifestation of utter ignorance of the true nature of the new creation.

Romans 6: 4 *Therefore we are buried with him by baptism into death: that like as Christ was raised up from the dead by the glory of the Father, even so we also should walk in newness of life. 5 For if we have been planted together in the likeness of his death, we shall be also in the likeness of his resurrection:* (KJV)

Ephesians 2: 5 *Even when we were dead in sins, hath quickened us together with Christ, (by grace ye are saved;) 6 And hath raised us up together, and made us sit together in heavenly places in Christ Jesus:* (KJV)

Colossians 2: 11 *In whom also ye are circumcised with the circumcision made without hands, in putting off the body of the sins of the flesh by the circumcision of Christ: 12 Buried with him in baptism, wherein also ye are risen with him through the faith of the operation of God, who hath raised him from the dead. 13 And you, being dead in your sins and the uncircumcision of your flesh, hath he quickened together with him, having forgiven you all trespasses;* (KJV)

Being raised together with Christ into the newness of life is what we call the second birth, or born again. The Bible says that if we are born so, we are now the first fruits of all of God's creatures, the same term applied on Jesus as well-1 Corinthians 15:23.

James 1:18 *Of his own will begat he us with the word of truth, that we should be a kind of firstfruits of his creatures.* (KJV)

Let me invite you to think critically with me: if God begat

us with the word of truth or by the word of truth; then, who or what are we? The word of truth of course! We are right now the very word of truth. We are the manifestation of the word of God in human flesh. We are made of the word. That is why in this era of the new creation, we don't really obey the word; we do it; we express it and when we are doing the word, we are only acting out who we are. We are the word of God housed or encased in a human body. As Jesus is the word of God, we too are. That is why as He is, so are we in this world! But, when we say we are the word of God, what exactly do we mean? Well, how is Jesus the word of God? Jesus was not conceived by way of physical or tangible seed of man. He is not the product of the flesh. He was spoken into the womb of Mary by God through an angel. Likewise, the new creation is not the product of carnal activity. He is a spirit being born of God. He is a direct offshoot of God's spirit. When you imagine how we are born again, there is really no physical process involved. It starts by us hearing the word of truth, then we believe it and voila! We are born spiritually! We are born again by that word we hear. That word of God germinates in our hearts and instantly becomes the new creation. Like Jesus, we too are spoken into being by the power of the Holy Spirit. That is why we are as righteous, perfect, just and as holy as the word which begat us. It is a spiritual operation or mystery that is really hard to explain in human terms but it is real. In fact, the invisible and spiritual new creation is more real than the flesh which came through physical birth.

    After the death and disposal of the old spirit nature of sin in the cross and grave of Christ, as Christ Himself rose again, upon believing Him; we are born again by the operation of the Holy Spirit, this time as new and perfect Spirits who are just like God. Actually, this new-born spirit is one with the Spirit of God. There is no difference between the two. You can't tell between them who is who. It is like when you mix juice and water. Afterwards, you can't tell what is juice and what is water because it is all juice-1 Corinthians 6:17. So, to be born again is to get rid of the old spirit of sin and to acquire a new spirit who is as righteous, holy and as perfect as Jesus Christ Himself. There is a scriptural backing to further buttress that overwhelming truth.

Ephesians 4: 24 *And that ye put on the new man, which after God is created in righteousness and true holiness.* (KJV)

This new man is the one referred to as the new creation in 2 Corinthians 5:17. In that same context, Paul cautions against viewing the new creation through natural eyes because if you do so, you will miss him. He says there was a time they saw Christ as a natural man because they only looked at His flesh but they have since repented.

Our natural birth was after Adam and in that former state, just like Adam, we were merely living souls-1 Corinthians 15:45a, 48a. That old man was born of the flesh, of the will of man and of the seed of man. The new creation takes after Jesus Christ-1 Corinthians 15:45b, 48b. Just as Jesus, this new creation is a life giving spirit. Anyone who is in Christ is not just a living mount of flesh and blood; he is a spirit, and a life-giver at that. That is why like Christ, we can heal the sick, raise the dead and lead men to salvation.

Long gone are the days when we considered and judged our fellow brethren based on their natural attributes. The people of Jesus' day did look at Him as an ordinary man-2 Corinthians 5:16. Some called Him the carpenter's son whose mother, brothers and sisters they knew all too well. While the first natural birth that brought us to the world was occasioned by the will of man and it happened through the seed of man, the new creation is a spiritual birth- John 1:13; 1 Peter 1:23. <u>Spiritual rebirth is an immediate replacement of the old spirit of sin with a brand new divine spirit.</u> That is why we say the new creation is a partaker of divine nature and has no past.

2 Peter 1: 4 *Whereby are given unto us exceeding great and precious promises: that by these ye might be partakers of the divine nature, having escaped the corruption that is in the world through lust.* (KJV)

That explains why there is a huge difference between the person who was before the second birth and the "you" after. That first person was a wicked spirit while the born again "you" is a righteous spirit. The old person sinned at will because he was of his father the devil and carried his nature. The new you does not rejoice in sin but in righteousness because he is of his Father God. The new creation has no past. You see, the old person died and was buried once you accepted Christ. The new you took the place of that departed old person. Once this truth sinks in, religious talk like the following will depart from your lips, "when I was a sinner, I used to do this and that …when I was…when I was…" You see, that person is long gone and you cannot still be referring to yourself in association with that dead person. The new you has no past at all. 1 Corinthians 6:11; 2 Corinthians 5:17.

1 Corinthians 6:11 *And such were some of you: but ye are washed, but ye are sanctified, but ye are justified in the name of the Lord Jesus, and by the Spirit of our God.* (KJV)

As far as God is concerned, the believer never existed before. The believer's past is dead and buried in the grave from which Jesus Christ arose victorious. The new you is not a modified or improved person, He's a totally new person who has never been before. The resurrected Jesus was the first born in this order of new spiritual species.

Revelation 1: 5 *And from Jesus Christ, who is the faithful witness, and the first begotten of the dead, and the prince of the kings of the earth. Unto him that loved us, and washed us from our sins in his own blood,* (KJV)

Colossians 1: 18 *And he is the head of the body, the church: who is the beginning, the firstborn from the dead; that in all things he might have the preeminence.* (KJV)

Thanks to God, we who are new creation take after the resurrected Jesus, not after the first Adam. <u>God's idea for this new spiritual species is to carry on the demonstration of God's glory and virtue, and to showcase the culture, power and majesty of heaven on earth, which began with the Lord Jesus.</u>

Ephesians 2: 10 *For we are his workmanship, created in Christ Jesus unto good works, which God hath before ordained that we should walk in them.* (KJV)

The new creation is by far the greatest gift handed to the human race by God. The church, which is the body of Christ on earth has more going for her than Adam had in a perfect environment at Eden. We are what creation had been waiting for all along-Romans 8:19-22.

The new creation is not like a young baby who has just

been born and needs time to grow. He is born complete in Christ. Complete means lacking nothing and perfect. The new creation is not a gradual improvement or modification or improvement of the old sinner. <u>The new creation is not getting better by the day. He cannot be improved upon in time or in eternity. He is not born to grow over time. He is born complete, and as Jesus is, so is this new creation now and here.</u> That is the case even if he was born just a few minutes ago. He cannot be made better by anything one does. First of all, his birth is not even remotely related to any form of human contribution, human activity or human merit. He is a perfect gift of and from God. He originates directly from God. His source is God and is one with God. <u>He's a chip straight from the eternal block that is God.</u> Just like God, the new creation cannot sin.

1 John 3: 9 *Whosoever is born of God doth not commit sin; for his seed remaineth in him: and he cannot sin, because he is born of God.* (KJV)

This verse has baffled a lot of Christians, confused others and even put others under fear and doubts. Like all other gospel scriptures, it is a blessing and not a curse. It is simply saying that as a new creation, you are incapable of sinning in and with your new spirit, although your soul and body are still capable of sinning especially if they are not sufficiently renewed and trained. This verse is dealing with the spirit because its context is very clear it is dealing with the part that is born of God. Your soul and body are not yet glorified and therefore you can't say they are born of God. They are still products of your parents. Anybody who thinks this verse is talking about not being able to sin (and I know there are people who think they are perfect and sinless even in the flesh) even at your soul and body level is deluded. We all fail but none of those failures are occasioned by the spirit. Those sins are in the flesh, never in and from the born again spirit.

Romans 7: 16 *If then I do that which I would not, I consent unto the law that it is good. 17 Now then it is no more I that do it, but sin that dwelleth in me. 18 For I know that in me (that is, in my flesh,) dwelleth no good thing: for to will is present with me; but how to perform that which is good I find not. 19 For the good that I would I do not: but the evil which I would not, that I do. 20 Now if I do that I would not, it is no more I that do it, but sin that dwelleth in me. 21 I find then a law, that, when I would do good, evil is present with me.* (KJV)

The new creation is not the old person modified. He is not the old person trying to perform better than how he did before the spiritual rebirth. The new creation is exactly as the name suggests – a new species, a new person and a brand new start.

Now, let us carefully dissect 2 Corinthians 5:17. What is the implication of this mind-blowing verse? It says *old things are past and all things have become new*. The revelation of that verse will transform you beyond your wildest imagination.

When God replaces your evil spirit with His own righteous and holy spirit, you are renewed only at your spiritual level at that point. Why then does the Bible tell us "old things are past and all things are become new?" At least we don't see our soul and body becoming new! When we are born again, those two remain unaffected in the immediate. For example, if you were eighty years old, you won't revert to thirty three like Jesus. If you weighed 200 pounds, your weight remains the same. At the soul level, if you were not very smart intellectually, there will be no noticeable change thereafter. If you had a quick temper before you got born again, things are likely to remain the same. Now, salvation can and should alter all these things. For example, by faith in God, you can renew your youth like an eagle even at 80. Ask Sarah of Abraham. Faith in God can renew your strength so that you mount up with wings as eagles, run and not be weary, walk, and not faint. Again, if you think you have excessive weight, you can solicit the Lord's help and He'll no doubt walk and work with you to scale it down to where you desire it to be. At the soul or intellectual level, if you don't think you are sufficiently smart, you can engage the mind of Christ in you and you can be as smart as you want to be. As for the short fuse, you can work with the Holy Spirit in you to bring out His fruit of patience. Even decades after one has been born again, they still don't attain perfection at the soul and flesh levels. Working on these two is a life time commitment.

So, why does scripture declare that all things become new when one is in Christ? I submit to you that it is at the spirit where everything is new. That goes to prove that man is not the body or the soul. Man is a spirit; he has a soul and resides in a body. In 2 Corinthians 5:17, the Bible does not even recognize the soul and the body. Where man is concerned, it recognizes only the spirit because man is a spirit. The implication is that our current body and soul are not of eternal value, only the new spirit. That is why God addresses the spirit only in this verse. That means that if you don't have it all together in the soul and body (no one has, or ever will), take courage because you have a new spirit from God. Count it all joy because God sees all things new in you. That is why He says <u>you are complete (perfect and lacking nothing) in Christ although He knows you still struggle in certain areas of your life. God is spirit and He sees you in spirit.</u> So, if you are in Christ, He sees everything new in you and that is all what matters in life and before God. Having said that, let me hasten to correct an impression that may form in the minds of many a readers. I don't mean to say that our bodies and soul don't matter to God. They do. God wants you sanctified wholly. He wants your whole spirit, soul and body preserved blameless unto His coming-1 Thessalonians 5:23. It still behooves us to renew our minds so that we can rule over our bodies. That is our responsibility and the Lord is eager for us to do it. However, Verse 24 says it is not you to sanctify your whole being for God. It is the Lord Himself to preserve you for Him. As for the Spirit, the work of the newly created spirit is totally and exclusively God's. Our only participation is to believe in the Lord Jesus. But, the part of renewing our minds and crucifying our flesh is ours although we do it with the help of the Lord.

By stating that all things have become new and all things are of God, the Holy Spirit is saying that the old wicked spirit is completely gone, discarded and done away with. It will never make a comeback. Jesus banished it totally and gave you a new spirit that is one with His own Spirit. This is the great mystery of the new creation that not even many Christians understand. Failure to understand is evident in how a lot of believers talk. They say things like: "only the Lord is holy and righteous; I am a poor wretched sinner saved by grace; no one is perfect; I am not a saint or an angel; I am a stronger and better Christian now than when I first began; I am trying very hard to hold on to Jesus so that when He returns He will find me still standing and not having backslidden; no one can be sure they will stand to the end, we need to pray hard so that we hold on to the very end; I am saved, I am being saved and I will be saved."

These and many other attitudes are common place in much of Christendom and they are all totally wrong and unfortunate. Let us examine some of them and determine how erroneous they are: Although the Lord is holy and righteous, so is every believer! We are partakers of His divine nature. That means we are also divine as He is. It is not because we worked hard for it but because He has qualified us in Christ to partake of His divine nature. As He is, so are we in this world! We are not poor wretched sinners saved by grace. We were sinners before we got born again. After we are born again, we are the righteousness of God in Christ and we cannot sin. I repeat again, a Christian cannot sin at his spiritual level-1 John 3:9. The real you, who is the spirit you, is the new creation and cannot sin. He's created by, and born of God and like God- in righteousness and true holiness. There is no sin in Him and He cannot sin. He delights in the perfect law of God. Sin can only be found in your soon-to-be-done-away with flesh and a partially renewed soul. When it comes to sainthood, every born again person is a saint right now! This nonsensical religious business of people being made "saints" decades or centuries after death and only after elaborate religious ceremonies is from hell. There is nothing godly or biblical about any of them. I never seem to understand why the masses shy away from clear and straight forward biblical teachings which only liberate, to embrace enslaving traditions and rules of wicked, rebellious and ignorant religious men. All the groups of people Paul and the rest of the disciples addressed were saints as they referred to them and none of them was dead. They were all very much alive. A believer who was born again just a second ago is a perfect saint for eternity! Don't follow the teachings of these lost and pagan religions that have nothing to do with God and Jesus. As a matter of fact, <u>you cannot be made a saint once you die if you were not one before you died.</u> You either sleep in Christ or die out of Him. If you sleep in Him, you sleep a saint. If you die out of Christ, you go to hell to await eternal damnation in the lake of fire. There is nothing anybody can do to help you after you've passed on. They can take your money and pretend to pray for you but only a living person can determine where they will spend their eternity and that window to make that determination is closed as soon as they take their last breath on earth.

Back now to our earlier discussion of how God relates to us based on who we are at the spirit level. God is not looking at the soul or flesh to deal with men, but only at the spirit.

2 Corinthians 5: 16 *Wherefore henceforth know we no man after the flesh: yea, though we have known Christ after the flesh, yet now henceforth know we him no more.* (KJV)

So, we say things like; "I am trying to get this word into my spirit." You can't get the word of God into your spirit. The whole Bible is in there already! Your spirit knows all things because he has the mind of Christ. Your spirit is not growing. He already has and is the full stature of Christ because he is one with Him. You cannot educate your spirit or sensitize him. He is the one who educates your soul. Your spirit is one with the Holy Spirit of God who wrote the Bible and who knows and searches all things.

(iii) WHAT ABOUT SPIRITUAL GROWTH?

When we talk about spiritual growth, I have heard some people liken new believers to toddlers who must be fed with food to continue growing and strengthening. They then apply that parallel to the spirit. They say that the new believer's spirit is to be nourished with the word of God to grow and be strong. That's a tragic fallacy. It is not our spirit who grows to maturity. It's the soul that grows and matures in the things of God through mind renewal. What we call spiritual growth is actually soul growth. It is the soul being fed with the word of God both through the senses (if we are talking about reading or hearing the word) and internally from the spirit. We call any Christian who has sufficiently renewed his soul, 'mature and spiritual.' The born again spirit cannot grow. He is complete in Christ, pure, perfect and he knows all things. Only the mind can grow in the things of God.

Remember, the soul of man is also spiritual in nature, in that you cannot touch it. You can't touch your emotions, intellect, imagination or will. You just see the effects of the soul but can't contact it physically. It is the spirit that trains, feeds, sensitizes and grows your soul, not vice versa. <u>The born again spirit cannot benefit from anything that comes from outside it through the senses or the soul.</u> Therefore, you read God's word to benefit your soul, not your spirit. Nowhere does the Bible ask us to renew our spirit. We are only told to renew our minds so that we will know what is that good, acceptable and perfect will of God. Your spirit is born new, perfect and totally godly. There is nothing to renew there. Once your soul has thus benefited, it can then be in the same page as the new creation. That can only result in a believer being as effective as Jesus Christ Himself. I re-iterate again here that you do not have any handicap at your spirit level; any shortcomings you may have lie in the soul. I have also heard it said that because the spirit is born of, or hails from the word and everything must be sustained by its source, then the spirit must continually feed on the word. I agree with the bit that the spirit is born of, and hails from the word of God. However, he cannot feed on the word because not only is he born of the word; he is also one with the word. He is full of the word because he is one spirit with the Lord-1 Corinthians 6:17. The word doesn't come from outside the spirit but is resident in there. That means we cannot talk of the spirit feeding on the word. What must feed on the word in order to survive and thrive is the soul. It is when we feed the soul with junk food from the world: the news generated by men, fears, worldly talk, movies, worldly novels, psychology and other kinds of worldly garbage that it develops constipation, withers and dies. Death doesn't have to be cessation of breathing: it can be depression, boredom, oppression, hopelessness and negativity. Hence, we can only talk of the spirit feeding the soul. That is what we call living from the spirit. It means being guided from the spirit as opposed to from nature and our surroundings. The spirit of man is the candle the Lord uses to lead us and to expose all the innermost motives so that they can be dealt with. Our spirits are directly inspired of the Lord and it is up to us to train our souls to stay tuned to broadcast from the spirit.

Proverbs 20:27 *The spirit of man is the candle of the LORD, searching all the inward parts of the belly.* (KJV)

Job 32:8 But *there is* a spirit in man: and the inspiration of the Almighty giveth them understanding. (KJV)

About perfection, I have already established that we are not yet perfect in the soul and body, but we are complete and perfect in the spirit. I will add that nobody has ever been, is and will ever be perfect in the soul and body until Jesus Christ returns with our glorified bodies and souls. If we were able to attain perfection in the soul and the body, then there would be no need for a glorified body upon Christ's coming.

1 Corinthians 15: 50 *Now this I say, brethren, that flesh and blood cannot inherit the kingdom of God; neither doth corruption inherit incorruption. 51 Behold, I shew you a mystery; We shall not all sleep, but we shall all be changed, 52 In a moment, in the twinkling of an eye, at the last trump: for the trumpet shall sound, and the dead shall be raised incorruptible, and we shall be changed. 53 For this corruptible must put on incorruption, and this mortal must put on immortality.* (KJV)

1 Corinthians 13: 9 *For we know in part, and we prophesy in part. 10 But when that which is perfect is come, then that which is in part shall be done away... 12 For now we see through a glass, darkly; but then face to face: now I know in part; but then shall I know even as also I am known.* (KJV)

And when we say "I am a stronger and better Christian now than before," that is only true if you are talking about your soul. Yes, you can have a better, more spiritual and more efficient soul courtesy of mind renewal. The more you renew your soul, the more mature you become stronger and more effective in the things of God. You can exercise yourself unto godliness. You can train your body to always be responding positively to the things of God.

1 Timothy 4: 7 *But refuse profane and old wives' fables, and exercise thyself rather unto godliness.* (KJV)

1 Corinthians 9: 27 *But I keep under my body, and bring it into subjection: lest that by any means, when I have preached to others, I myself should be a castaway.* (KJV)

However, you can't improve on, strengthen or even better

your new man. Your new man is complete in Christ, who is the head of all principality and power. On the same note, some people are shaken and even destabilized when someone who has been born again for decades is tripped by rather a not very 'strong temptation.' They cannot understand it. It is because they expect too much from the soul and from the body. Such people trust too heavily in their sections which are yet to be glorified. The reason why sin doesn't dominate us is not because we have been born again for long. It is not because we are stronger and better now in the soul and body. It is not because we have been in church for longer, have been praying, fasting, reading the word and doing other religious things for a protracted period of time. We dominate sin because we lean on God's grace solely and not in our flesh. The arm of the flesh shall surely fail you. No matter how old you are in spiritual matters, you are never too advanced to fall if you depend on your will power to defeat the evil forces that are against you. On the other hand, a newly born again believer can withstand any sin if all he depends on is the Lord's grace.

    Then there's this thing of holding on to Jesus so that we do not backslide. I know there are many songs written on holding onto Jesus but they are all wrong. The first reason why this notion is wrong is because if you are the one to hold onto Jesus, then that speaks of works righteousness. It means your safety and security lies in what you do to remain in Jesus. Works can never sustain you because salvation is by grace. If you are depending on your ability to stay in Jesus, then you will never rest and you are already at risk because your survival will depend on whether or not you will hold on without getting tired and releasing the grip. No matter how strong and formidable what you are holding onto is, if it is flying for example, you will soon suffer fatigue. If you release your grip as you surely will because of the force of gravity of the things of this world, then your fate will be sealed. On the contrary, if you let that formidable object hold you, you will be very safe. I will give the example of an airplane. When it is taking off, you can decide to take off with it in two ways: you can hold onto the landing gear externally, or you can just board it and take your seat comfortably. If you choose the first option, we will be arranging your funeral in a few minutes after the take-off and that is only if there will be any remaining parts of you to collect after the plunge.

It is the same in the spirit. We do not hold onto Jesus, we are in Him already! That is where we move, live and have our being. He is our environment. It is our position of grace in Him that assures us a secure ride and victorious life. People who talk of holding on to Jesus are mainly legalistic people who through works of the law try to "remain" in God's good books. That is religion. They soon burn out. True Christianity is Jesus living His own life in and through you, not you trying to live for Him.

About backsliding, those who talk of it, do they really know what exactly they mean? For some reason, I hate that concept because I associate it with religion. Is the new creation a pen so that he can be lost? Is salvation so temporary and flimsy that it can be misplaced? Are the names of those who are born again written on quick sand on the seashore so that they can be easily erased? Those who talk of backsliding, I doubt they understand what the new birth entails. Once somebody is born again, can he be 'unborn' again? Can he return to the "womb of God" or cease to exist again? You see why it is all confusing and senseless?

John 10: 27 *My sheep hear my voice, and I know them, and they follow me: 28 And I give unto them eternal life; and they shall never perish, neither shall any man pluck them out of my hand. 29 My Father, which gave them me, is greater than all; and no man is able to pluck them out of my Father's hand.* (KJV)

John 6: 37 *All that the Father giveth me shall come to me; and him that cometh to me I will in no wise cast out… 40 And this is the will of him that sent me, that everyone which seeth the Son, and believeth on him, may have everlasting life: and I will raise him up at the last day.* (KJV)

Romans 8: 35 W*ho shall separate us from the love of Christ?...... 38 For I am persuaded, that neither death, nor life, nor angels, nor principalities, nor powers, nor things present, nor things to come, 39…shall be able to separate us from the love of God, which is in Christ Jesus our Lord.* (KJV)

Some pastors say to their flock, "no one can tell whether or not they will make it to the end. Only God knows whether or not we are saved. No one can tell if they are out of the woods yet until the last trumpet." That is unfortunate. If the pastor doesn't know whether he has eternal life, then his members are to be pitied. God wants us to deal only with certainties. Christianity is not guess work. It is not charity sweepstake. If you believe in the Lord Jesus, you are in already. You have eternal life and no one and nothing can snatch it from you. Also, you are seated in Christ in heavenly places. For you to "backslide," God would have to expel you from heaven-John 3:16.

1 John 5: 11 *And this is the record, that God hath given to us eternal life, and this life is in his Son. 12 He that hath the Son hath life; and he that hath not the Son of God hath not life. 13 These things have I written unto you that believe on the name of the Son of God;* **that ye may know that ye have eternal life,** *and that ye may believe on the name of the Son of God.* (KJV) Emphasis added.

John 20: 31 *But these are written, that ye might believe that Jesus is the Christ, the Son of God; and that believing ye might have life through his name.* (KJV)

Anyone who believes that Jesus is the anointed son of God, the messiah and savior of mankind is born again. That person has eternal life and he can never lose it. He is saved for eternity. That is the gospel! Lastly, have you ever heard some people say, "I am saved, I am being saved, and I will be saved?" What exactly do they mean? Well, if they mean they already have eternal life in their new spirits, and they are in the process of renewing their minds and are banking on the hope of the redemption of their glorified bodies, then I agree with them fully. But, if what they mean is that they are not complete and perfect yet but have only a promise of future salvation which depends on how they conduct themselves, if they are in the mean time working for their salvation; then that is totally wrong!

2. THE NEW CREATION ARE VITAL SONS OF GOD

As I have already pointed out, one of the most misunderstood and least appreciated concepts in all Christianity is that of the new creation. Very few pastors even try to carefully pry into the nature and ability of this awesome super-being. A lot of people think the new creation is an improved sinner. They say things like "I am just a human." To most Christians, the new creation is just an ordinary, struggling religious person who hopes one day to make it to heaven. The born again person or the new creation is even more than just a follower or disciple of Jesus Christ. That is where most Christians are stuck and wonder why they are not excited about the Christian life and why they seem so powerless and defeated. The New creation is one Spirit with God. God did more than just transform us at salvation. He united us with Himself in a vital, inseparable, eternal union. That is what we mean when we say we are in fellowship with Him. It is that oneness, that unassailable union that even goes beyond spiritual to physical union. I am talking about divine membership in Christ's body. By that I mean that we are members of Christ's flesh and of His bones.

Ephesians 5:30 *For we are members of his body, of his flesh, and of his bones.* KJV.

Ephesians 4: 4 *There is one body, and one Spirit, even as ye are called in one hope of your calling; 5One Lord, one faith, one baptism,* KJV.

The new creation is not some distant servant of God. Tragically, religion likes to paint us as struggling servants of God trying to please Him by much effort. To explain what kind of a relationship God wants between Him and His sons, Jesus gave the parable of what we call the prodigal son in Luke chapter 15.

I will not deal here with the son who asked for his part of his father's estate and squandered it, but the one who was left at home and who I believe was even worse in terms of a terrible religious mentality. Many Christians have the attitude of that self-righteous fellow. He told his father that he had served him all those years yet he had never given him a calf to celebrate with his friends. That is how religious people are. They think they are doing the Lord a favor by being His 'servants' and 'working' for Him. They expect Him to duly reciprocate by raining down goodies. As a result, they get very frustrated and worked up when they see other believers who they perceive as either their juniors in the faith or not as holy and hard working as they are getting better results in life. They begin to imagine God as being a stingy and hard, unappreciative person who they have to work hard for and still no one is sure whether the pay will come. They believe they have to be good and work hard to get anything from God. They don't know that all things are ours. They don't know we are heirs of God, joint-heirs with Christ of all things. We have unlimited access to everything that God is and has. We don't need to be jealous of anybody; we don't need to covet anything and we don't need to be infuriated with God whenever we think He is not treating us as we would wish. God has never been our problem and He will never be. He can never withhold anything good from us although a lot of factors on earth can keep us from receiving what God has already given us. Some of those things can include trying to work for what we've been given on account of Christ's work or thinking we must be good first before God can bless us. All this is self-righteousness and it is the most tragic sin of all. We are joined as one entity with God. When we enjoy, God enjoys too because He is in us and we are in Him. He is our life. That being the case, how can God deny Himself every good thing? We are a vital part of God, an inseparable constituent of Jesus Christ. You see, we are not just a removed bunch of people who aspire to please God, imitate Christ and reach Him. We are born of Him. He is our Father. We carry His divine DNA. That is a settled fact. We carry His genes and we can't hide it. We are one with Him and that can't be taken back. You know, my daughter Keilah happens to resemble me almost 100%. The skin pigmentation, the hair, even the mannerisms are all akin to mine. Her resemblance of me is staggering. I can't take that back. I can't help it. There is nothing I can possibly do to reverse or erase that fact. Everything in me is genetically replicated in her. I can never deny her. She is my seed forever. So it is with us and Jesus. God gave birth to us. The same way a woman goes through labor pains and gives birth, Christ travailed in labor and gave birth to all of us who believe. We are His children. Our spirits are direct offshoots of His Spirit. That is why we are one spirit with Him according to 1 Corinthians 6:17. That is why the Bible doesn't call us co-heirs with Christ, but joint-heirs with Christ in Romans 8:17. Co-heirs would denote some distance between the heirs, but joint-heirs is indicative of inseparable oneness. It means everything is owned jointly together. It means we must enjoy it together. That is part of what it means to be partakers of God's nature in 2 Peter 1:4

God's nature, character and personality are all over imprinted on our spirits. That is why a lot of scriptures in the Old Testament do not apply to the new creation. I still hear Christians applying scriptures like Isaiah 55:8-9 to themselves.

For my thoughts are not your thoughts, neither are your ways my ways, saith the LORD. For as the heavens are higher than the earth, so are my ways higher than your ways, and my thoughts than your thoughts. (KJV)

One could be wondering, "What is wrong with that scripture? Why is it not applicable now? Isn't it in the Bible?" First, if you are still reading and applying that verse at the present, then you ought to get born again. Unlike in the Old Testament where men were lowly sinful creatures, God has now elevated us to His own class, the God-class. We are now partakers of divine nature. We share in the life of God and are participants in divinity. I am not saying we are God; just that after God, it is us.

Hebrews 2: 7 *Thou madest him a little lower than the angels; thou crownedst him with glory and honour, and didst set him over the works of thy hands:* (KJV)

The more correct rendering of the first part of that verse may be, "thou reddest him a little short of God." The angels are God's messengers to minister for those of us who are heirs of salvation. We are the most privileged creation in the universe. Jesus is our senior brother. We are sons of the Most High God together with Him. After God the Father, we share the next most privileged spot with Jesus who is God eternal in His own right. You see how highly exalted and glorified in Christ we are by God?

John 20: 17 *Jesus saith unto her, Touch me not; for I am not yet ascended to my Father: but go to my brethren, and say unto them,* ***I ascend unto my Father, and your Father; and to my God, and your God.*** (KJV) Emphasis added.

By His grace, God has elevated us to the highest position in the universe to where we are seated in His son by His right hand, a position of power and authority far above any operations of anything created and named not only in this age but also in the one to come.

I will put it here for the umpteenth time that not every scripture in the Bible is applicable to the new creation. If every scripture was to be applied without discrimination, then we would have to go back to the old covenant of law. We would have to start slaughtering animals for sacrifice, observing all the ceremonial law, all the festivals, holy days and Sabbaths of the Old Testament. But we don't do that because Jesus came and made everything new, including us. That is why we are called new creation. There are a lot of things that were true of old creation men that do not apply to us now. That is why we must rightly divide the word of truth if we are to be liberated from the shackles of the Old Testament. It is not enough to read the Bible; it is critical to glean the present truth encapsulated in that part of scripture you are reading.

2 Peter 1:12 *Wherefore I will not be negligent to put you always in remembrance of these things, though ye know them, and be established in the present truth.* (KJV).

By present truth, it doesn't mean God changes with time. God is the same throughout all time and eternity but He has had different terms of dealing with men depending on which dispensation those men are living. Back to Isaiah now and I am saying that God's ways are no longer mysterious to us. His ways have become our ways; His thoughts have become our thoughts; His power is ours and His abilities our abilities. His mind has become our mind and we have become one spirit with Him. God's wisdom, righteousness, holiness, knowledge, will and power are now readily available in our Spirits awaiting utilization.

1 Corinthians 1:30 *But of him are ye in Christ Jesus, who of God is made unto us wisdom, and righteousness, and sanctification, and redemption:* (KJV)

1 Corinthians 2:16 *For who hath known the mind of the Lord, that he may instruct him? but we have the mind of Christ.* (KJV)

God has made provisions for us to be synchronized with Him in thoughts and actions. Remember the words of Jesus in John 5:19-20. *Then answered Jesus and said unto them, Verily, verily, I say unto you, The Son can do nothing of himself, but what he seeth the Father do: for what things soever he doeth, these also doeth the Son likewise. For the Father loveth the Son, and sheweth him all things that himself doeth: and he will shew him greater works than these, that ye may marvel.* (KJV)

This scripture is not true for Jesus only, but for us as well because we are joint-heirs with Him. Remember Christ said that if we believe in Him, we would do the works He did, and even greater works. Our Father God yearns for us to have a rich, prolific and glorious daily fellowship with Him. He wants us to operate in complete sync with Him. He wants us to be in such oneness of the spirit with Him that we will know and carry out what He is thinking in real time. That is exactly what Jesus did and it explains why He was so effective. Jesus didn't even say this glorious life was His preserve only but that He actually shared it with us.

John 15:15 *Henceforth I call you not servants; for the servant knoweth not what his lord doeth: but I have called you friends; for all things that I have heard of my Father I have made known unto you.* (KJV)

This is the fellowship of the top, most powerful and reigning spirits in the universe. That is how serious God is. He has elevated us to a divine partnership of reigning with Him in the universe as associates of His class, and partakers of the divine nature. Not even the angels (including Michael and Gabriel) have that privilege. As a matter of fact, the people of the old creation and angels alike marveled at the sweeping and exceeding privileges, prerogatives and glory accorded to us by God through His grace.

1 Peter 1:10-12 *Of which salvation the prophets have enquired and searched diligently, who prophesied of the grace that should come unto you: 11 Searching what, or what manner of time the Spirit of Christ which was in them did signify, when it testified beforehand the sufferings of Christ, and the glory that should follow. 12 Unto whom it was revealed, that not unto themselves, but unto us they did minister the things, which are now reported unto you by them that have preached the gospel unto you with the Holy Ghost sent down from heaven; which things the angels desire to look into.* (KJV)

I kindly implore you to read those things with an open mind. Don't let what the Sunday school teacher (no offense: many have revelation and do a splendid job), or a particular pastor, or some person said to derail you from benefiting from what the Holy Spirit is ministering to you through this work. It is the antiquated beliefs, Bible misinterpretation, lack of understanding, ignorance and the traditions of men that render God's word of none effect in the lives of His people.

Mark 7:13 *Making the word of God of none effect through your tradition, which ye have delivered: and many such like things do ye.* (KJV)

3. THE NEW CREATION ARE ONE ENTITY WITH GOD

The new creation is one entity with God. He has become one joint person with God. God's Spirit has merged with his spirit and together they have become one. Being given birth to by God means at that very point of that second birth, God translated us from the realm of natural life to a far higher realm of the supernatural and even the divine. In that realm, we don't walk by sight (facts and information gathered by the senses) but by faith (what the word of God says no matter what the facts show). That simply means we don't live guided by the five senses but guided by God's word. Ordinary men are guided by what they can smell, hear, touch, feel and taste. On the basis of that they make their decisions. That is why they live such limited lives. You see, if your life is governed by the senses only, there is only so much you can do because you can't transcend what governs your life. When Jesus came, every human being on the planet was ruled by the senses. It all resulted from Adam's fall from a glorious being to a carnal creature. Jesus then demonstrated the practicability of living in the supernatural realm, in the natural. He walked on water defying gravity. Instead of sweating like a mule, He simply spoke to a tree and it died forthwith. He gave thanks and a few loaves of bread and fish became a feast for thousands of people. That supernatural, glorious life is now no longer a preserve of Jesus now that He died and resurrected to never die again. As many as have believed Him, He has given the power to be partakers of His very divinity. So, we can not only do the things He did but greater things. Although still living in the earth, the new creation lives concurrently also in the higher supernatural realm of faith which is the realm of God Himself. The new creation perceives things that ordinary men living by physical senses can't pick. But, for the new creation to be able to pick up things in the spirit that bypass ordinary men, he must train his soul by renewing it to hear from God through the spirit. God is forever speaking through the spirit of man but those who are carnal or those who are tuned to the things of the earth can never hear Him. You can't think like the old creation after Adam and expect to get the results of a new creation. Jesus invaded space and time so that He could set us free from the limitations of it and fling us to timelessness and eternity. That is why the new creation doesn't die. He just lays aside his body for a while when he needs to, because he will pick it again at the advent of Jesus. It seems that these biblical truths on the new creation are so staggering they destabilize the mind of the religious man. The religious man says, "God is holy and righteous. God is not a man. He cannot associate with dirty and sinful men. God cannot fill a dirty vessel and therefore you must be perfect in the spirit, body and soul for Him to fill you with the Holy Spirit. Man cannot know the mysteries of God. God's ways are very far from man's ways"

A lot of those statements may have been true in the Old Testament, but we have more revelation of God now. It is true God is holy, righteous and His ways are far from natural. But, He rend the Heavens. He came down and became a man. He has further become one with the men who believe in His son. He has made them equally righteous and truly holy. He no longer enjoys that state of absolute perfection and purity alone but has incorporated us in His league also. Although we are conscious of His righteousness and holiness, we are more conscious of His unsearchable love for us. Whenever He appeared, Old Testament sin-conscious people said, "Depart from me for I am a sinful man!" We can't say that now. He doesn't even appear to us anymore. He has made a permanent abode in us. Today, we enjoy His fellowship on a continual basis. We can't tell Him to depart from us because He is holy and we are undone. Instead, we thank Him perpetually that by His sacrifice and not by our conduct, He has made us as holy and as righteous as Himself. On that basis, we can commune with Him boldly and without hindrance. In the beginning was the Word, and the Word was with God, and the Word was God. The same was in the beginning with God. This is John chapter 1:1-2, yet we can add to it; "and the word gave birth to the new creation (born again of the incorruptible seed of the word of God), and became one with the new creation." That is not blasphemy. That is not adding to the scriptures. It is paraphrasing a Bible-stated-truth.

A lot of what we arrogate to ourselves in the new covenant would have been blasphemous in the old.

1 Corinthians 6:17 *But he that is joined unto the Lord is one spirit.* (KJV)

Not only is the born again person one spirit with Him, he is also one flesh with Him! That truth is staggering. We have always known we are joined unto the Lord spiritually and are therefore one spirit with Him. But that is not where the Bible stops. We are being informed that our bodies are members of Christ!

1 Corinthians 6: 15 *Know ye not that your bodies are the members of Christ? shall I then take the members of Christ, and make them the members of an harlot? God forbid.* (KJV)

He who is joined unto a harlot is one body with the harlot. They have become one joint thing. It then applies the same analogy with the new creation. The new creation is the one joined unto the Lord and both he and the Lord have become one Spirit. That is why we say that "as Jesus is, so are we in this world." In other words, if you are a new creation, then your spirit is one entity with the Spirit of Christ. That makes your body the house of Christ. Not only so, your physical body also becomes a member of Christ's overall body, with other believers constituting other parts or members. This is one of the most mind-blowing scriptures in all of the Bible and I can hardly get over it. Can you imagine it is saying that not only is your spirit joined unto the Lord, even your very physical body that is not yet glorified is a member or part or an organ of Christ! That means your entire physical body is inundated with the life of Christ. That means sickness can't attack you successfully because the Holy Spirit who is one with your born again spirit, and who raised Jesus from the dead now quickens or gives life to your mortal body.

Yes, that is the great news. Our physical bodies are members or parts of Christ. That means your hand is the hand of Christ. Your hand is not the hand of and ordinary human being but of Christ. That is why Jesus said if the new creation lays his hand on sick people, they shall recover. The hand of an ordinary human cannot do that. That has to be the hand of Christ. That is why the apostles gave people materials from their bodies and the sick who came into contact with them recovered. When Peter walked, ill people would be laid on both sides of His path. When his shadow fell on them, they would instantly be healed. Other than the new creation and an Old Testament prophet called Elisha who had a double portion anointing, it is unheard of that since the creation of the world, an ordinary human healed any disease. They did have traditional medicine men, witch doctors and other native healers but all they did was guess work. Their concoctions were no more than products of trial and error.

John 9: 32 *Since the world began was it not heard that any man opened the eyes of one that was born blind. 33If this man were not of God, he could do nothing.* (KJV)

Besides healing diseases that baffle even the best of trained medics, only super men in Christ can cast out devils. The natural man cannot know what to do with demons and devils. It does not help even if he has accumulated millions of learning accolades. He would still be beaten by devils hands down. But a new creation can cast out even the chiefest of devils with a slight wave of his tiniest finger in the name of Jesus. Only the new creation can literally take up serpents and not be hurt by them.

Acts 28: 3 *And when Paul had gathered a bundle of sticks, and laid them on the fire, there came a viper out of the heat, and fastened on his hand. 4 And when the barbarians saw the venomous beast hang on his hand, they said among themselves, No doubt this man is a murderer, whom, though he hath escaped the sea, yet vengeance suffereth not to live. 5And he shook off the beast into the fire, and felt no harm.* (KJV)

Only the new creation can gulp any deadly thing and not be harmed by it. The new creation is truly the real and original superman.

Hebrews 11: 33 *Who through faith subdued kingdoms,*

THE MARVEL OF THE NEW CREATION SUPERMAN

wrought righteousness, obtained promises, stopped the mouths of lions. 34 Quenched the violence of fire, escaped the edge of the sword, out of weakness were made strong, waxed valiant in fight, turned to flight the armies of the aliens. 35 Women received their dead raised to life again: and others were tortured, not accepting deliverance; that they might obtain a better resurrection:

I like to say that I am divinity clothed in humanity. I am God-possessed. I am full of the power of God. The divine life of God is a renewing life; it is continually at work in me renewing every cell of my blood, every organ, fiber, muscle, sinew, bone, gland and nerve of my body. Age cannot not limit or thwart eternal life which is the life of God in me. This renewing process is going on in me regardless of age. As I continue to believe that God's life is present in every cell of my body; as I hang on to the truth that strength, wholeness, and vitality are God's will and desire for me; my body is continually renewed and revitalized. I give up all belief in age or illness; I no longer give the power of my thought to disease. I declare that God is renewing every cell and atom of my being. I thank the Lord for body-building divine energy throughout my body temple and for a resurgence of new strength. Blessed be God. Amen.

Your limbs are God's tentacles for touching the world. It is instructive to note that Christ does not call the new creation "My people." He calls the new creation "me." When Saul was persecuting the early believers, Jesus didn't strike him down and blind and say; "Saul, Saul, why are you persecuting the Christians?" Instead, He asked, "why are you persecuting me." In Christ's mind, He is one with His people. There is no difference. Christ came, He lived among men, He then became one entity with those who believed, and continue to believe in Him.

That is exactly what we mean when we say our fellowship is with God and with Jesus Christ.

1 John 1:3 *That which we have seen and heard declare we unto you, that ye also may have fellowship with us: and truly our fellowship is with the Father, and with his Son Jesus Christ.* (KJV)

1 Corinthians 1: 9 *God is faithful, by whom ye were called unto the fellowship of his Son Jesus Christ our Lord.* (KJV)

<u>The highest purpose of Christ coming to die and be raised</u>

<u>back to life was to restore the fellowship we enjoyed with God at the garden of Eden. Every other purpose flows from that supreme one.</u> Forgiving our sins, sanctifying us and making us righteous were all means to the end of restoring the broken fellowship between God and man. That was the goal of God in the plan of redemption. Man could not associate with God because of sin. Sin had to be taken out of the way, and courtesy of Jesus's sacrifice, it was. This is why religion is such a tragedy. Religion dwells in the means to the end and never gets to that end. It is stuck perpetually in sin consciousness, fear of the terror of God, condemnation, guilt and penance.

Religious, legalistic and judgmental people need to know they make a very poor Holy Spirit. It's not our duty to judge and condemn people over how they wear, where they go, how they appear and even what they do. If we don't think they wear decently, or, if we think they should not wear tattoos, or, if they are confused about their sexual orientation, or, if we think they apply too much make-up or they club too much; it's not our job to condemn them over those things and try to get them out of those habits by human effort. Such human efforts usually include judging and condemning them, making them feel unworthy before God and threatening them with hellfire. To be sure, all the things named above are destructive. Indecent dressing has its problems. First, it is unethical and even immoral. It adversely affects not just those who dress indecently but other people as well. It is not consistent with the law of love. Tattoos were expressly forbidden in the Old Testament and children of God should steer clear away from them. The Bible is also clear on God's position regarding all forms homosexuality. They are an abomination before the Lord. When it comes to make-up, I really don't know what the hullaballoo is all about. I believe that if your face needs some improvement and you have the means to do it, go right ahead. The only thing is, there is no need to overdo it because our beauty and glory is not based on our physical appearance but on our inner man who after God is renewed in righteousness and true holiness. That inner glory is what radiates all the way to the outside until we become radiant and very attractive. That is the message the apostle Peter was passing across as captured in 1 Peter 3:2-4. Having said that, God has not tasked us with the responsibility of being moral policemen; whereby we try to get people off those destructive lifestyles by our own means. We must know that God does not expect us to change people. Our role is just to share the gospel with them and to reveal to them the truth. That includes pointing to them the errors they are involved in. After that, it is very important to help them understand that God loves them at whatever point of spiritual growth they are and that He wants them freed from any bondage to things that are against His will. They should also know that He is not condemning them but has goodwill and grace toward them, and grace is God's power to them to say no to all ungodliness and worldly lusts. Mostly, in the Old Testament, God recorded and kept the wrongs of people. He also punished them for their sins. That is why David looked ahead and envied the man upon whom the Lord would not impute sins. We are those men! When reading the stories of men in the Old Testament, you notice there is a difference in the recording, even where the same man appears in both covenants. For example, in the Old covenant, God recorded the mistakes of people in many places. But, in the new covenant, God only records the strengths of those same people. Down here we see God recording the weakness of Moses.

Exodus 2:14……. *And Moses **feared**, and said, surely this thing is known. 15 Now when Pharaoh heard this thing, he sought to slay Moses. But Moses fled from the face of Pharaoh, and dwelt in the land of Midian: and he sat down by a well.* (KJV) Emphasis added.

We see here Moses' criminal behavior of murder and subsequent fear exposed. Now, check how God puts forward Moses' strong points only in the New Testament;

Hebrews 11: 24 *By faith Moses, when he was come to years, refused to be called the son of Pharaoh's daughter; 25 Choosing rather to suffer affliction with the people of God, than to enjoy the pleasures of sin for a season; 26 Esteeming the reproach of Christ greater riches than the treasures in Egypt: for he had respect unto the recompence of the reward. 27 By faith he forsook Egypt, not fearing the wrath of the king: for he endured, as seeing him who is invisible. 28 Through faith he kept the passover, and the sprinkling of blood, lest he that destroyed the firstborn should touch them.* (KJV)

Don't you see there is a vast difference between how God regards people in the new and Old Testaments?

When the Lord appeared to Abraham and Sarah and promised them a child, Sarah who was eavesdropping as she prepared a meal laughed as an expression of doubt. The Lord even commented on it back then.

Genesis 18: 12 *Therefore Sarah laughed within herself, saying, After I am waxed old shall I have pleasure, my lord being old also? 13 And the LORD said unto Abraham, Wherefore did Sarah laugh, saying, Shall I of a surety bear a child, which am old?* (KJV)

The Lord recorded the same incident again in the New Testament but this time, He disregarded the doubting part and only majored on the believing part of Sarah.

Hebrews 11: 11 *Through faith also Sara herself received strength to conceive seed, and was delivered of a child when she was past age, because she judged him faithful who had promised.* (KJV)

Abraham himself made a lot of blunders in his time. He lied, doubted, was selfish and also reckless in protecting his wife, being willing to let wicked men take advantage of her. However, God called him friend and laid the foundation of God's family in the earth on this faulty man. When He recorded about him in the New Covenant, He was all praises for the man who was actually supposed to be in jail.

Romans 4: 16 *Therefore it is of faith, that it might be by grace; to the end the promise might be sure to all the seed; not to that only which is of the law, but to that also which is of the faith of Abraham; who is the father of us all, 17 (As it is written, I have made thee a father of many nations,) before him whom he believed, even God, who quickeneth the dead, and calleth those things which be not as though they were. 18* **Who against hope believed in hope, that he might become the father of many nations,** *according to that which was spoken, So shall thy seed be. 19* **And being not weak in faith, he considered not his own body now dead, when he was about an hundred years old, neither yet the deadness of Sarah's womb: 20 He staggered not at the promise of God through unbelief; but was** *strong in faith, giving glory to God; 21 And being fully persuaded that, what he had promised, he was able also to perform.* 22 And therefore it was imputed to him for righteousness. (KJV) Emphasis added.

Wow! How that encourages us to know that God has only goodwill for us and only records our strong points. He is urging us on to believe Him more and do more for the kingdom we love. He is not seeking to condemn but to affirm, strengthen and bless. Am I in any way trying to excuse sin and sloppiness? That is not the case at all. I am just saying that God is not focused on our failures but on our acts of faith. He is not imputing our sins unto us because He judged them very harshly in Christ so that now He imputes the righteousness of Jesus to us. He sees us as righteous as Jesus. That is why we are not afraid of the Day of Judgment because as Jesus is, so are we in this world. Likewise, don't be sin conscious. Be righteousness conscious like God because that is what He has made you-His own righteousness in Christ. Being sin-conscious is not a mark of piety and humility. In fact, it smacks of rudeness, unbelief and foolishness. Religious peoples' lives are centered on sin while people of grace have their focus on Christ. As a new creation, your conscience should be as pure and as perfect as the perfect sacrifice of Jesus for you, not as your conduct is. Why focus on the gloom, doom, sin and the ugly when you can actually dwell on grace, glory, power, victory and every other thing in the altogether lovely Jesus? Why be fixated on darkness when you can just deal with light alone? I would never waste my time thinking about and fighting satan and demons who hate me when I can be obsessed with the all-powerful Jesus who defeated them all and who loves me 'insanely'. Dwelling in sin-consciousness is telling Jesus that He did not do a thorough job of taking away your sins and you still need to do some little payment of your own through sorrow, fear, penance and other religious rituals. It reeks of unbelief because you don't believe that God will not impute sins unto you. Some people go throughout the day trying to imagine what wrong they may have done so that they do what they call confession and repentance. Our sins are not forgiven through confession and repentance but by faith in Jesus Christ. Once we believe in Jesus Christ, all our sins for all time are erased by the eternal blood of Jesus offered once over 2000 years ago and from then on, we begin a new life as new creation without a past. Think of it; to be saved, we are not told to confess sins but to just believe in Jesus Christ.

John 3: 15 *That whosoever believeth in him should not perish, but have eternal life. 16 For God so loved the world that he gave his only begotten Son, that* **whosoever believeth in him should not perish, but have everlasting life. 18 He that believeth on him is not condemned:** *but he that believeth not is condemned already, because he hath not believed in the name of the only begotten Son of God.* (KJV) Emphasis added.

John 5:24 V*erily, verily, I say unto you, He that heareth my word, and believeth on him that sent me, hath everlasting life, and shall not come into condemnation; but is passed from death unto life.* (KJV)

Acts 10: 30 *And brought them out, and said, Sirs, what must I do to be saved? 31 And they said,* **Believe on the Lord Jesus Christ, and thou shalt be saved,** *and thy house.* (KJV) Emphasis added.

Romans 10: 9 *That if thou shalt confess with thy mouth the Lord Jesus, and shalt believe in thine heart that God hath raised him from the dead, thou shalt be saved.* (KJV)

There are many more scriptures that repeat this same thing of believing in Jesus as the only requirement for one to obtain eternal life. What does it mean to believe in or on Jesus? Romans 10:9 above has the details. It is to give up all attempts of self-righteousness or works of the law and to put your total faith for forgiveness of sins and your hope of righteousness and holiness in the completed work of Jesus at the cross.

There is nowhere in the grace dispensation where we are required to confess our sins so that we can obtain eternal life. The requirement is always to believe in Christ and failure to so believe is the only sin the Holy Spirit convicts people of and it is also the only one which will send people to hell. Once one believes in Jesus Christ and trusts in His name, all of his sins are eternally remitted. The Lord shall never remember his sins and lawless deeds anymore and He is no longer imputing sins to that believer.

Acts 10: 43 *To him give all the prophets witness, that through his name whosoever believeth in him shall receive remission of sins.* (KJV)

That scripture makes it very clear that we are not forgiven because of our confession but based on our faith in Christ Jesus. Religious traditions of men that have no roots in the Bible have confused very many in the church. For example, when many people give an alter call or during communion time, they ask people to confess all their sins as they remember them. They tell people to confess all their sins for God to forgive them, and the people start remembering all their sins and try to confess everything they know and don't even know. What the devil does is, after you have confessed all the sins you can remember, as you leave the church, he reminds you of the sins you did not recall to confess. He then tells you that you were insincere and that salvation or blessings are not really for you. Hear this! God didn't say to confess all your sins for salvation or for communion. Those are not occasions for remembering how dirty you are. They are times for reminding you how gracious and loving God is. The requirement for salvation is to confess with your mouth "JESUS IS LORD," and believe in your heart that God raised Him from the dead for the forgiveness of your sins.

As for communion time, what we remember is the costly sacrifice of love of Jesus, not our sins. We are required to remember the sacrifice that took away our sins, not those sins. The religion of sin-consciousness has really muddied the waters of genuine faith and one has to sift through mountains of religious garbage to get to the real gospel. That is the essence of this publication. Blessed be God!

Having said that, I will still repeat it here again that there is nothing wrong with acknowledging before God where we are struggling in life and leaning on His grace to banish those weaknesses from our lives. That we must do. But there is everything terribly wrong with being obsessed with sin-consciousness and ever trying to bring before the Lord our failings. When we try to constantly remember where, how, when and in how many things we may have wronged God so that we can inform Him and seek His forgiveness; that demeans the costly sacrifice of Christ and lowers it to where it is no different from the blood of animals which couldn't permanently perfect the consciences of worshippers. In fact, it is largely for that purpose that Christ came so that by His one sacrifice for sins forever, He would end all sacrifices for sin because we being once purged should have no more consciousness of sins. Do the people who constantly oppose those of us who preach radical grace ever read their Bibles? How much more could the Bible be clear?

Hebrews 10: *For the law having a shadow of good things to come, and not the very image of the things, can never with those sacrifices which they offered year by year continually make the comers thereunto perfect. 2 For then would they not have ceased to be offered? Because that the worshippers once purged should have had no more conscience of sins. 3 But in those sacrifices there is a remembrance again made of sins every year. 4 For it is not possible that the blood of bulls and of goats should take away sins.* (KJV)

The new creation has no sins because he has no past. His past is God and there is no sin in God. Here is the thing: as new creation, we have sin in us, that is, in our flesh. But, we don't have sin on us, meaning in our spirit nature. We have effects of sin in our flesh but our spirits are as pure as God Himself. In other words, our bodies are dead because of sin but our new spirits are life because they are as righteous as Christ is now-Romans 8:10.

Romans 7: 20 *Now if I do that I would not, it is no more I that do it, but sin that dwelleth in me. 21 I find then a law, that, when I would do good, evil is present with me. 22 For I delight in the law of God after the inward man: 23 But I see another law in my members, warring against the law of my mind, and bringing me into captivity to the law of sin which is in my members.* (KJV)

Believing in Jesus is tantamount to subjecting the old person or the Adamic nature to death with his sins and being born a new without sin.

Amazingly, people who are ever sin-conscious never take to account the very many godly things they do in a day. Many of them are reasonable and responsible people who daily wake up early, they pray, groom themselves, provide for their families, go to work, study the word of God, assist others and do many other commendable things that God is very proud about. Yet, all they are mostly conscious of are the few things they fail in. It ought not to be so. <u>Sin-conscious is deadly sin in itself.</u>

We have not been given the ministry of condemnation which is the ministry of death. We have the life-giving, gracious and strengthening ministry of reconciliation, of grace, goodwill and of peace where we don't impute peoples' sins unto them. For those who are still struggling with ungodly practices, we should then pray for them, love them and help them receive more and multiplied grace through the knowledge of God and of Jesus. We can further serve to them as a living love letter and an example of righteousness. That's just as far as our job goes. We should not arrogate to ourselves roles that are the Holy Spirit's. The Lord is more than willing and able to help them deal with whatever needs to be dealt with in their lives. If we try condemning them, we should know it works counterproductively because it drives people further away from God while love, grace and mercy draw them to Him. We cannot sow the seed of grace in their lives and pretend to help it germinate and grow. Our part is to sow and water it with the word and then the Holy Spirit nurtures it and delivers the increase-1 Corinthians 3:6-7. Always remember it is the goodness of the Lord, not His hot temper and judgment that draws us to God and leads to repentance. Did you know there are very many people who used to call themselves Christians but they drifted away from God and in fact are ardent God-haters? They now rebel against God because the religion of law, works and condemnation made them regard God as one exacting and hard task master who demands perfection and is strict and judgmental.

Religious people keep thinking there is an unrepented sin and that the Lord is angry and about to strike. God has called us to fellowship not to religion. Religion is man's way of trying to get to God. It's all about trying to defeat sin and satan, it's about penance, lighting candles, going to church trying to please (and bribe) God, it's about rituals, recitals and empty activities. On the other hand, fellowship is oneness. It includes association, communion, intimacy communication, co-working, contribution, partnership, sharing power, participation, joint-heirship, Joint ownership and many others. We don't teach a religion of rituals and practices. What we have is a grace relationship in the family of God. There is no religion in a family. My daughter Keilah Maia does not relate to me religiously through rituals, works of the law, confessions and the many other religious things people do in the name of trying to contact God. What she has with me is a loving family relationship. There is nothing she tries to do in order to qualify to be my daughter or to qualify for my blessings. She was just born to me out of my own will and there is nothing I can ever do to reverse that-John 1:13;

James 1:18 *He chose to give us birth through the word of truth, that we might be a kind of firstfruits of all he created.* (KJV)

Religious people think they were born again of their own will. We are born again by the will of God. In other words, being born again is not our idea but God's. So, if He chose to give birth to us, how can we again be afraid that He will disown us just because we mess up as if our second birth was our project? No! We are God's project for ever and He will continue working on this project until He comes back for it.

My daughter is mine forever. Not only so, she qualifies for everything I am and have by virtue of being born to me. In a family, the members just love each other and respect the senior members in that unit. We don't do religious things like singing, giving, praying, fasting and confessions in order to fit in the family. We become part of the family of God by faith and then in honor of the seniors who are the God-head, we can then praise, worship, give and do other things that responsible sons do; but they must not be religious. Religion is a creation of blind and carnal men and it is the very reason many people are staying away from the things of God in their droves-Matthew 23:13. The gospel we propagate is about life in the family of God. It is not about works or performance but about a loving, gracious relationship between God and His beloved and blood-bought sons. <u>The gospel is not about us working for God. It is the great news about how completed all the work is for us and all we do is receive by faith and propagate the kingdom of our Father which is also our inheritance.</u> In our kingdom, we don't work. All we do to make what Jesus did become ours is just put faith in Him. After we receive, we can then share out of love with those who are still in darkness. <u>The highest point of Christianity is the realization of our inextricable oneness with the Lord.</u>

John 17:20 *Neither pray I for these alone, but for them also which shall believe on me through their word; 21 That they all may be one; as thou, Father, art in me, and I in thee, that they also may be one in us: that the world may believe that thou hast sent me.* (KJV)

We are in Christ and God, and they are in us. Our lives are hidden with Christ in God. We are one with divinity.

John 14:23 *Jesus answered and said unto him, If a man love me, he will keep my words: and my Father will love him, and we will come unto him, and make our abode with him.* (KJV)

You now understand why Paul screamed, "We are more than conquerors in Christ Jesus" How can you lose with a divine team like that? <u>We are the highest of the highest of all of God's creation and we reign with Him in the universe.</u> That ought to put a shout in a dead tree!

4. THE NEW CREATION ARE A SPECIES OF gods

1 Peter 2: 9 *But ye are a chosen generation, a royal priesthood, an holy nation, a peculiar people; that ye should shew forth the praises of him who hath called you out of darkness into his marvellous light;* (KJV)

I like the way the Holy Spirit did not mince words in this scripture. He says the believers may still share the earth with the Jews and Gentiles but they are a separated race of people. They are new creation. Outwardly, they may appear natural, with a body just like any other person but let not that fool you. These are priests and kings. They are a separate nation of people; a strange group that defies human explanation. The only similarity between the new creation and non-believers is the outward body. This body does not matter very much because it will soon be changed anyway. In the twinkling of an eye, it will be shed and its place taken by a perfect body that is as glorious and as capable as Jesus'. You see, in the universe, there are different levels of existence. First, there is the heavenly level. That is the realm where God Himself is in charge. That is also the realm of holy angels and other heavenly beings. Then, there is the realm of satan and his other fallen sidekicks called heavenly places. Soon, this realm will be emptied of its inhabitants because they will all be cast into the lake of fire for eternity. Then there is the earthly level where we live. You could say there are also the nether regions beneath the earth's crust where currently hell is situated and where the souls of those who die without Christ are temporarily contained to await eternal damnation as well. That too will be emptied and hell itself with its inhabitants will as well be cast into the lake of fire-Revelation 20:14.

You will notice I mentioned the most common actors in each of those realms. It goes without saying that God fills all of those realms with Himself. David said that even in hell, God is still there. In fact, we should not look at the whole wide universe-seen and unseen-and think God is contained in there. God is not a resident of the universe because even the highest heaven cannot contain Him. On the contrary, it is the universe that is contained in God. The whole universe is inside God. He is self-existing and self-sufficient, needing nothing. He lives by His own power of an endless life.

2 Chronicles 2:6 *But who is able to build a temple for Him, since even heaven and the highest heaven cannot contain Him? Who am I then that I should build a temple for Him except as a place to burn incense before Him?* (KJV)

Jeremiah 23:24 *"Can a man hide himself in hiding places So I do not see him?" declares the LORD. "Do I not fill the heavens and the earth?" declares the LORD.* (KJV)

Psalm 139: 7 *Whither shall I go from thy spirit? or whither shall I flee from thy presence? 8 If I ascend up into heaven, thou art there: if I make my bed in hell, behold, thou art there. 9 If I take the wings of the morning, and dwell in the uttermost parts of the sea; 10 Even there shall thy hand lead me,* (KJV)

When we narrow down to the earth, we find that there are three kinds of life: there is plant life, animal life and human life. Then, there is another kind of life that came to effect after Jesus was raised from the dead. Tragically, few people know it or what it entails. You see, the quality of life determines either the creature or being. Plants have plant life. Animals have animal life. Human beings have human life. Then, gods have divine life. When applied to the new creation, that life is specifically called eternal life. It is not the life of plants, animals or human beings. The non-believer has human life. That life is not very far from animal life unless it is replaced by divine life. In fact, God does not even count it as life. From where God stands, the non-Christian is dead already.

John 3:36 *Whoever believes in the Son has eternal life, but whoever rejects the Son will not see life, for God's wrath remains on them.* (KJV)

<u>Divine life or eternal life is the God kind of life, the indestructible, indomitable, invincible, shatterproof life</u>. History tells us that of all the apostles of Jesus; John was the last to sleep. Wicked men tried all they could to kill him but they couldn't. One time they tried to fry him in oil like a fish but he came out unscathed. Now that is called divine life. No wonder he is called St John the divine. You see, our Father has not kept His life all to Himself. He has shared it with His sons, who we are. He has given us His very life. That is why Jesus said not only would we do the things He did but greater things even. It is because His life is at work in us. We have become one with Him. His life is our life. His righteousness and holiness are ours, His wisdom is our wisdom and His mind is ours.

1 John 5:13 *These things have I written unto you that believe on the name of the Son of God; that ye may know that ye have eternal life, and that ye may believe on the name of the Son of God.* (KJV)

John 6:56 *Whoever eats My flesh and drinks My blood remains in Me, and I in him. 57Just as the living Father sent Me and I live because of the Father, so also the one who feeds on Me will live because of Me. 58This is the bread that came down from heaven. Unlike your fathers, who ate the manna and died, the one who eats this bread will live forever."...* (KJV)

1 Corinthians 15:45 *So it is written: "The first man Adam became a living being;" the last Adam a life-giving spirit...48 As is the earthy, such are they also that are earthy: and as is the heavenly, such are they also that are heavenly.* (KJV)

That last scripture from 1st Corinthians is so radical most people just pass it over and refuse to imagine that it can real. God is saying that there are two models of men. One model is Adam who was a living soul. He was just alive. Nothing more is recorded of him. He came from the dust of the earth and therefore he was earthy. He was not divine. He did not belong to the God-class. Then the Bible says natural and unbelieving men take after him. They are just alive and soon they wither and die like animals to never count again. But then there is the second model-the last Adam, Jesus. He was not from the soil. He was not earthy but heavenly. His seed came not from men but from God. Jesus was not just a living soul; He was a life-giving Spirit. Then the Bible adds a most staggering revelation. It says that as Jesus is, so are they who are in Him. <u>As is Jesus the heavenly- a life-giving spirit, so are they who are heavenly-the new creation. That means they are life-giving spirits as well. That is why we point to cancer and it dissolves.</u> We rebuke HIV/AIDS and it disappears to oblivion. We call back the spirits of the dead and they oblige. No challenge is too big for us. We can do all things in Christ who is our life. We know no impossibilities. We are the only people on the planet who clearly know their future and their destiny. We know exactly what will be happening a billion years from now and where we will be and what we will be doing. The rest of the population is simply groping in the darkness, lost in one vast ocean of ignorance. *<u>On this same earth, there are men and then there are spirits. Those of us who are born again are spirits in motion.</u>* Ordinary men cannot understand us. We are a mystery. They see us eating fries and chicken just like them and they think we are the same. How mistaken they are! They think we hail from Adam like they do. What they don't realize is that we may have been born through the Adamic lineage but we switched to a divine lineage through a second birth. We applied to be born again from heaven and it happened in a flash. The heavenly birth then cancelled the first earthly birth. We are now not born in the similitude of Adam but of Jesus. That is why all generational curses and all disadvantages brought about by the law are totally annulled in our lives. We have no past. The fellow who was born in the likeness of Adam died and his place can be found no more. Now, only the new birth counts.

Galatians 3: 26 *For ye are all the children of God by faith in Christ Jesus. 27 For as many of you as have been baptized into Christ have put on Christ. 28 There is neither Jew nor Greek, there is neither bond nor free, there is neither male nor female: for ye are all one in Christ Jesus.* (KJV)

Natural men can never comprehend the mystery of this original superman called the new creation. They have no capacity to explain who we are. We are even ourselves still coming to terms with who we really are. We are a mystery even to ourselves. In fact, the finite minds we still have can never fully grasp the awesome reality of what and who the Lord has made us. We are a sign and a wonder. Great things are spoken of us. We are not limited to earth only. We straddle both Heaven and earth. We are seated in Christ in Heaven but our operations are on earth in the meantime. We are reborn with a completely divine genetic makeup. We own all things. Together with Christ our head, we inherit God Himself. We are awesome creation in Christ

John 3: 8 *The wind blows wherever it pleases. You hear its sound, but you cannot tell where it comes from or where it is going. So it is with everyone born of the Spirit." (*NIV)

I will go deeper. Did you know genes determine the physical, social and intellectual characteristics and even capabilities of a thing? It is good news that we no longer contain the genes of fallen Adam but the genes of Christ.

2 Corinthians 5: 16 *Wherefore henceforth know we no man after the flesh: yea, though we have known Christ after the flesh, yet now henceforth know we him no more. 17 Therefore if any man be in Christ, he is a new creature: old things are passed away; behold, all things are become new. 18 And all things are of God,* (KJV)

Galatians 2: *19 For I through the law died to the law that I might live to God. 20 I have been crucified with Christ; it is no longer I who live, but Christ lives in me; and the life which I now live in the flesh I live by faith in the Son of God, who loved me and gave Himself for me.* (KJV)

Ephesians 4: 24 *And that ye put on the new man, which after God is created in righteousness and true holiness.* (KJV)

If we still possessed the genes of the lineage of Adam, we would still be subject to all the diseases, curses and limitations of ordinary men. For example, while ordinary men have average and slow minds because they are descended from Adam, the new creation has the mental capability of Christ.

1 Corinthians 2:16 *For who hath known the mind of the Lord, that he may instruct him? But we have the mind of Christ.* (KJV)

We have the mind of Christ in our spirits and we must renew our souls with that mind for it to be manifested. That means if I was involved in any form of altercation with someone, I must never tell them "I will give you a piece of my mind" The reason is, my mind is the mind of Christ. I have no other human mind from where the old man who died was born. Yet I still find supposed Christians who are still proud of where they were born after the natural man and what they are boastful of are shameful traits of anger, stealing, covetousness, superstition, stubbornness and other satanic characteristics that should never be mentioned among God's people. The bloodline of Adam comes loaded with the burden of all manner of setbacks resulting from sin. When we ditch that bloodline, we escape them all. We are no longer subject to inherited illnesses and conditions, and other consequences of the fall. We are even disengaged from all the stereotypes that men attach to different race groups, blood groups and other physiological considerations. For example, I hear men talking about how people of this or that race are predisposed to behave and fair in life. You can't fit the new creation into those strait jackets. You can't tell me I am predisposed to be squeezed into one or a few of four temperaments only- so called choleric, sanguine, melancholy and phlegmatic.

Ephesians 4: 22That ye put off concerning the former conversation the old man, which is corrupt according to the deceitful lusts; 23 And be renewed in the spirit of your mind; (KJV)

Romans 12:2 *Do not conform to the pattern of this world, but be transformed by the renewing of your mind. Then you will be able to test and approve what God's will is--his good, pleasing and perfect will.* (KJV)

My temperament is that of Christ and if I catch myself manifesting any other, then I should immediately call a meeting with me and repent by renewing the attitude of my mind. Sadly, people have brought these weird man-made teachings to the church as if we have no sound doctrine from the Bible to teach. Can you imagine a pastor who paid school fees to be trained who then comes on Sunday to teach sons of God how all of them can be fitted into only four temperaments that are found in fallen men! What a waste! He doesn't even tell them that the new creation cancels all of those human traits and they have only the traits of Jesus who is their life!

The only explanation I can give is because they don't spend time in the word and so they don't know what it says. So, they have to fill up time with such junk or they will be forced to close shop.

Titus 1:14 *Not giving heed to Jewish fables, and commandments of men, that turn from the truth.* (KJV)

Matthew 15: *But in vain they do worship me, teaching for doctrines the commandments of men.* (KJV)

A lot of people who claim to be called to ministry spend too much time trying to 'prepare a sermon.' They sleep late scratching their heads trying to concoct some motivational or even legalistic and no doubt humanistic presentation from books authored by fallen men. That is not what the will of God is. God wants you to share the life He has deposited in you with His people. He wants you to pick up the Bible and take your people through it line upon line, distilling the pure revelation of grace that is able to build them up and deliver them divine inheritance among those who are called. One of the best ways to minister is to just be able to take the Bible even if they woke you up at midnight and turn to one book or epistle or psalm and bring out the present truth from scripture. That way, people can understand the gospel of grace in a more consistent way.

I have no apologies to make for asserting that the new creation people are a race of gods. People who say we are not gods are carnal fellows who want to confine us to the carnal realm. Even the things that Jesus called us to do cannot be done human beings. They can only happen through people who are God-possessed and we call them new creation. Mere men can't cast out satan. He is their master. They can't raise the dead; they are scared stiff at its very mention. Ordinary men can't cleanse lepers or supernaturally heal diseases; they are victims of those same illnesses. Everyday men can't speak in the new tongues. They can only speak in a language they have been taught for years. Those of us who have a little more revelation of the gospel have been accused of blasphemy but I am here to set the record straight:

John 10:34-35 *Jesus answered them, is it not written in your law, I said, Ye are gods? 35 If he called them gods, unto whom the word of God came, and the scripture cannot be broken...* (KJV)

Those were the words of Jesus Himself. He affirmed the very words from Psalms 82:6; *I have said, ye are gods; and all of you are children of the Most High.* (KJV)

Let me clarify that I am not saying we are God, as in Jehovah. There is only one of those. He is the Father of our Lord Jesus Christ, our own Father and the creator of everything that is. He has no competition and no rivals. He created us but then exalted us to where we are below Him in order of hierarchy and then the rest of creation. We are subordinate to Him. That is why we worship Him. But I am saying we are His offspring. That is, we are gods. God gave birth to us. We carry his image, his likeness, his genes, his nature, his character, his power, his authority and his ability.

1 John 3:9 *Whosoever is born of God doth not commit sin; for his seed remaineth in him: and he cannot sin, because he is born of God.* (KJV)

1 John 3:2 *Beloved,* **now are we the sons of God,** *and it doth not yet appear what we shall be: but we know that, when he shall appear, we shall be like him; for we shall see him as he is.* (KJV) Emphasis added.

God is not offended, blasphemed or threatened when we call ourselves gods or when we say we are one with Him. He is very elated because His sons are finally coming of age to assume their place. Come to think of it, if we who are born of God will inherit God jointly with Jesus Christ, how then is it abnormal to aver that we are associates of the God-class? Aren't we partakers of divinity?

The 82nd Psalm we read above proceeds to state in verse 7 that the subjects Asaph was writing about would die like mere men; that they would fall like every other ruler. That has significance for us in the New Testament. The truth being passed here is that if we reject the settled fact of our divinity in Christ; if we resist and push away that privilege in the pretext of humility; then, all we would get are average human results. Our lot would be no better than of any pagan. We would waste our entire lifetime living naturally rather than supernaturally.

2 Peter 1:4 *Whereby are given unto us exceeding great and precious promises: that by these ye might be partakers of the divine nature, having escaped the corruption that is in the world through lust.* (KJV)

For a prince or princess to reject that he or she is royalty is not humility but ignorance, immaturity and even an affront to the reigning monarch or whoever the parent may be.

The way a prince or princess makes the progenitor happy is not by rejecting or downplaying the fact of his or her royalty; it is by embracing and affirming it. Then, the progenitor will be assured of safety and continuation of the kingdom. A lot of woes that face Christians and Christianity result from the fact that Christians are either ignorant of, deny and downplay who they are, what they have and what they are capable of doing in Christ.

One of the most prolific generals of God in the past era was John G. Lake. He was one of the foremost faith healers of the New Testament church so far. His healing and other miraculous exploits were mind blowing. It is reported he could touch active pathogens being viewed under a microscope and they would all instantly freeze. There is a reason he was so successful. He knew clearly that he was one with God and went ahead to act accordingly. John would wake up and dress up ready to go and conquer the world-and conquer the world he did. As he was dressing, he is reputed to have had the habit of saying these words; "God dwells in this suit of clothing and wherever this suit goes, God goes"

Christ wants His children to be bold and assert; "I am a direct offspring of Christ and I can do all things through Him. I am one with Him and I have all authority to exercise God's power on earth. I can do all the supernatural works Christ did and greater works can I do." You know, when the new creation speaks the word of God in faith, heaven hears and agrees; hell also hears and obeys. The devil and his lot cannot resist us. We are too much for them. They must do our bidding if we command them to do anything in the name that is above all names.

The truth of the Bible is that those of us who are new creation are not ordinary human beings. We are spirit beings. We perceive all things, yet no man can perceive us. We have the mind of

Christ. We are one with Christ. We know all things. As Christ is, so are we in this world. We have the health, safety, wealth, peace and victory of Christ. That list can proceed on and on. Scriptures tell us to look unto the rock from which we were hewn.

Isaiah 51:1 Hearken to me, ye that follow after righteousness, ye that seek the LORD: look unto the rock whence ye are hewn, and to the hole of the pit whence ye are digged. (KJV)

The Old Testament believers looked unto Abraham the father of faith. For us in the new covenant, we still look unto Abraham because we are his seed but we see beyond. We see Jesus who is before Abraham and through whom our Father God has spoken to us lastly. We are Christ's. We are members of his body, of his flesh and of his bones. Where he is we are. What is true of Him is true of us. His destiny is ours and his divinity we are partakers of.

Only gods can terminate age-old diseases. Only gods can walk on water like Peter did. Only gods can raise the dead like Paul and Peter did. Only gods can effect a supernatural prison-break like Peter, Paul and Silas did. . Only gods can casually shake off a deadly viper and characteristically walk away unharmed like Paul did. Only gods can be boiled in super-hot oil and come out unscathed like extra-biblical accounts tell us John the divine did. "But brother, all those examples you've cited happened in Bible times with the apostles and they no longer happen!" if I were to narrate to you the kind of things that are happening in the body of Christ, you would be blown away. I am not even sure many people would believe it unless they saw it with their eyes. Sons of Jesus are performing miracles that baffle even themselves. It is, of course, the Lord Himself working in and through them. We are witnessing terminal and chronic illnesses dismissed with ease. It is common place to see supernatural restoration of missing organs and limbs. We have seen lengthening of uneven limbs and renewal of affected skin. We have seen total healings of allergies, asthmatic conditions and all manner of other complications that doctors had given up on. More people have been raised from the dead in the last few decades than probably the rest of all that other period going back to the time of Christ.

Are we claiming to be gods in and of ourselves? Not by a long shot. Everything we are, have and can do is a function of our position in Christ.

Colossians 1:27 *To whom God would make known what is the riches of the glory of this mystery among the Gentiles; which is Christ in you, the hope of glory:* (KJV)

The great news is that we can never be outside Christ because he can never deny his own and neither can he leave us nor forsake us. That is the reason we can make these bold assertions, while ordinary human beings and carnal Christians wait for death and anticipate growing old and decrepit before that terminal reality calls; we look forward to live long, healthy and productive lives productive even in old age-Psalm 92:14. While other people's strength diminishes with age, the converse applies for us.

SHARERS OF DIVINITY: MEMBERS OF THE GOD-CLASS

2 Peter 1: 4 *Whereby are given unto us exceeding great and precious promises: that by these ye might be partakers of the divine nature, having escaped the corruption that is in the world through lust.* (KJV)

This is one of the most inspiring scriptures in the entire Bible. If this is not one of your favourite verses, then there is a lot you are missing out on. By this verse, Peter is telling us that we areparticipants or shareholders of divinity. That means we play in God's own league. We are members of the God class. Come on, don't read the Bible like a religious person. Take it at what it says and don't dilute it. This scripture is saying that the believer is involved in the God-life or the divine experience. That means one thing: we share the life of God with Him. That is why we have His Spirit as one spirit with our spirit. We know what God knows and have what He has. As He is, so are we in this world. God is no longer living that special life all by Himself. He has made us associates of Him. I am now a certified conveyor or carrier of God-life. This means I am set with Christ far above normal human and earthly life, far above defeat and far above any demonic activity. I see believers climbing up mountains, skyscrapers or even flying on airplanes to draw near satan's turf and fight him there. I think that is very foolish. We are not earthbound. We are not just earthlings. We come from heaven and that is where we are seated in Christ. So, we don't resist satan from beneath here; we operate from far above where his dirty nose can't even catch the slightest wind of what is happening. We dominate the devil and his sidekicks from above where our seat of authority is, not from below. We don't "rise up to counter the devil," he licks the dust of our feet. I heard a brother saying that if you ever want to pass a message to the devil, scribble on the sole of your shoe because that is where Jesus put that crook. I like that. He has been defeated badly by Jesus and put beneath us as our footstool. We command him and put him where he belongs by the authority we have in Christ. The only thing about us that is earthly is our souls and bodies. Otherwise, we are spirits born from heaven by God Himself. We don't have plant, animal or any other kind of earthly life; we have eternal life, the supernatural, divine, God-life. We are super human and that is not subject to debate. This always troubles non-believers and carnal Christians. It is very disturbing to tell a man who only operates with the senses that you hail from heaven. They look at you and think you've lost your mind. But think about it, Jesus made the same claim. He told His listeners that He was from above but they were from below. The onlookers looked at Him and asked; "is this not the carpenter's son? His parents and sibling don't we know?" Ordinary people trust their senses too much and that is their undoing. <u>Senses destroy faith. To be carnally minded (sense ruled) is death while to operate by faith is life and peace.</u> The truth is, Jesus' body may have come through Mary, but Jesus was not His body. He was the eternal Spirit who came straight from His Father in Heaven. That is what He was referring to when He said He came from Heaven. Also, even Jesus' flesh was not the result of the will of man. There was no human seed involved in His conception and birth. God supernaturally planted the seed of Jesus' body in the womb of Mary. Mary is not the "Mother of God" as one cultic pagan religion which styles itself as Christianity likes referring to her. I know they get the term from Luke 1:43 but God cannot have a mother as He is the source of everything that is. He has no beginning and no end. He created everything and gave all life and is Himself not created or born. These preposterous claims by cultic religions are what make some of the other sister earthly pagan religions mock Christianity as well. For example, Islam says that Jesus cannot be God because God neither begets nor is begotten. It is true God can never be begotten but He begot Jesus. Father simply means source and sustainer and God is the Father of Jesus. Let us examine what Jesus says about us.

1 John 4: 4 *Ye are of God, little children, and have overcome them: because greater is he that is in you, than he that is in the world.* (KJV)

A lot of people misunderstand this verse to mean that we belong to God because we are called by His name and are associated with Him. This is more than association. It means we come from Him. He is our source because He has begotten us. We are His direct offspring. So, don't let these physical bodies we possess and our local connections and relations fool you like those people of Jesus' time were confused.

2 Corinthians 5: 16 *Wherefore henceforth know we no man after the flesh: yea, though we have known Christ after the flesh, yet now henceforth know we him no more. 17 Therefore if any man be in Christ, he is a new creature: old things are passed away; behold, all things are become new.* (KJV)

The only thing about us that is from here is the body and to a certain extent, the soul. Otherwise, our spirits are born from above.

Satan is no longer a viable factor in the life of the new creation, at least not the one who is aware of his true identity. We have power to tread over serpents and scorpions and over all the ability of the enemy and nothing can by any means hurt us. If that is not divine life, then what is? That means we are inoculated and insulated from every attack, every fiery dart, and every onslaught of the dark powers. We are immune to their ability to affect us adversely. No wonder Jesus said, 'fear not.' Fear not Satan's attacks because they are all futile manipulations.

Psalms 46:1 *God is our refuge and strength, a very present help in trouble. 2 Therefore will not we fear, though the earth be removed, and though the mountains be carried into the midst of the sea; 3 Though the waters thereof roar and be troubled, though the mountains shake with the swelling thereof. Selah.* (KJV)

The only thing I know from scriptures that we are not delivered and exempted from is persecution. But when it comes to accidents, terrorists attacks, climatic upheavals, crime and other such like dangers; the Bible is very clear they cannot touch us.

When some villagers in the island of Melita saw a venomous snake latch on to Paul's hand, they expected him to drop down dead in minutes, if not seconds. But he just shook it off. Paul didn't pray; "o God protect me, be with me and let the venom not affect me." He was just conscious of the God-life in him. The villagers thus called him a god. They were right. Paul knew he had eternal life: disease killing life, venom-destroying life, the impregnable and uninfectable life of God. With the new creation, the old things of the law and normal, ordinary, human life have passed away. All things have become new and these new things are divine because they are of God. That means we have been transmuted by the life of God into the nature (substance) of Christ. We have been transfigured in the spirit into the image and likeness of the son of God. <u>The human life with which I was born by my parents has been supplanted by the supernatural life of God. That is why I am not subject to generational curses, hereditary diseases and other such humanly transmitted disadvantages of life.</u> The last vestiges of that old life are to be found in my physical body and my soul but they are on their way out and will exit completely the moment Jesus appears in the clouds with awesome power and great glory.

But even the new creation's body is a divine instrument of imparting blessings. If we are believing believers rather than unbelieving ones, whatever comes out of our bodies can be so blessed that it causes blessings and miracles to those who come into contact with it. Even a simple handshake or a word from us can impart power and solve someone's problem.

Deuteronomy 28: *3 Blessed shalt thou be in the city, and blessed shalt thou be in the field. 4 Blessed shall be the fruit of thy body, and the fruit of thy ground, and the fruit of thy cattle, the increase of thy kine, and the flocks of thy sheep.* (KJV)

We know this to be true because Jesus' spit healed a blind

man, Peter's shadow healed the sick, and handkerchiefs and aprons from Paul's body drove out evil spirits and healed diseases. That means at the very least, you can't be sick and stay for long with that sickness because even health flows from your body.

Colossians 3:17 *And whatsoever ye do in word or deed, do all in the name of the Lord Jesus, giving thanks to God and the Father by him.* (KJV)

Anything that proceeds from your body: children, ideas, work, business and words are all blessed. Your children are mighty in the land. That simply means their words and actions run the world. One could be asking, 'if that is true, why don't we see most Christians' children excelling in their fields of endeavour?' You see, the word of God does not come to pass automatically. It works only for those who believe it and apply it. If you have not been speaking those promises over your children, don't expect any results. A lot of Christians don't speak and apply the word to their lives. They just sit there and expect everything to fall in place. That simply doesn't happen because if it did, all Christians would have similar results because the word of God has the same power and effect towards all of us. Repeat these words please:

"I am an associate of God. I function from the standpoint of advantage, victory, dominion and power because I am born of God and conscious of His life in me. What is born of human is natural but what is born of God is divine. I'm guided and propelled by His divine wisdom to do His will and fulfil my destiny in Christ, in Jesus' name. Amen."

5. THE NEW CREATION IS GOD'S ULTIMATE DELIGHT

Because God is the one who has perfected you forever in Christ by His grace (not by your good works), He is exceedingly pleased with you. He cannot stop thinking about you. He even breaks into a song at the mere thought of you. He has engraved you in the palm of His massive hand so that you are ever in His sight. As He forever beholds Christ on His right hand, He sees you too because you are in Christ and constitute His very body. That is radically different from what religion has been telling people that God is recording their sins, is angry with them and wants to strike them in punishment for their wrong doings. God can never be angry at His own children who are junior brothers of Jesus. He loves and esteems them in the same way He does Jesus.

I heard one preacher say that people who write and say things like these are guilty of two things: They demote Jesus and God to the level of man and elevate man to the level of God. That is the opinion of a religious fellow who doesn't God and doesn't know himself too. I want that preacher to know that through faith in Christ, God elevated us from pathetic lowly humans to divine creatures of His own class. <u>God wanted us for associates of His kind, not religious slaves.</u> That is why we are heirs of Him, joint heirs with Christ. All things belong to us. In eternity, we will be reigning in the universe with Him. We are members of the God class. Yes, I repeat that God has elevated man into His own class of being! We're supermen from Zion. We are superior to Satan and have dominion over the forces of darkness. We operate in Christ from far above any principality and power and any name that is named not only in this world but in the one to come! Hallelujah! I am not saying we are God but that we have been recreated after Christ who is our senior brother, the firstborn among the new creation. He is the divine template of the original supermen. Unless you want to say that Christ is a man only, then you can't argue against my assertion. Fasten your seatbelt because next come statements that can destabilise the religious mind. Because I am in Christ, I am so precious to my Daddy God that He cannot even stop thinking about me. He has a portrait of me in His palm which He is ever delightfully beholding. He loves me so much that He rejoices over me with joy. He rests and rejoices in His love for me. Jesus is a physical bundle or package of love from God. He's God's love letter to humanity. Jesus is God's practical statement of love. Just by looking at Jesus, we are able to physically see God's love in action. When we pry into the scriptures and see Jesus having compassion on the sinners, the sick, the oppressed, the lost, the confused, the suffering, the hungry and all manner of disadvantaged people, we see a compelling evidence of God's love. Jesus Himself told us that he who had seen Him had seen God. Today, don't ask where God is.

Turn to your Bible and see Jesus in action. That is God!

Additionally, God has songs He sings as He rejoices over us. The Lord cannot have enough of us just like I can never have enough of my young lovely daughter Keilah!

Psalm 139: 17 *How precious also are thy thoughts unto me, O God! how great is the sum of them! 18 If I should count them, they are more in number than the sand: when I awake, I am still with thee.* (KJV)

Zephaniah 3:17 *The LORD your God is with you, the Mighty Warrior who saves. He will take great delight in you; in his love he will no longer rebuke you, but will rejoice over you with singing."* (NIV)

Malachi 3:12 *And all nations shall call you blessed: for ye shall be a delightsome land, saith the LORD of hosts.* (KJV)

Psalm 149: 4 *For the LORD taketh pleasure in his people: he will beautify the meek with salvation.* (KJV)

When we put it like this, some people think; "but all these things are only true when I do right and never sin. I can only be righteous, holy, pleasant and delightsome to the Lord if I have done everything right and kept all the commandments." Who is talking about doing right here? Who is even talking about working for righteousness? Righteousness is not doing right; it is the very nature of God imputed unto you freely without consideration of your conduct but only because of your faith in the righteous Christ. What do I mean when I say you are the righteousness of God in Christ Jesus? That is a good question. I mean you are just like God in nature. You are complete in Christ, lacking nothing. You are as perfect, excellent, pure and as divine as Jesus is right now; your conduct notwithstanding.

Hebrews 10: 14 *For by one offering he hath perfected forever them that are sanctified.* (KJV)

Colossians 2: 10 *And ye are complete in him, which is the head of all principality and power:* (KJV)

1 John 4: 17 *Herein is our love made perfect, that we may have boldness in the Day of Judgment: because as he is, so are we in this world.* (KJV)

The Christian journey starts with perfection and

completeness in Christ and then proceeds to demonstrate or manifest that perfection in real life. That is contrary to what most Christians think. They think that after we are born again, we begin a journey of gradual perfection and completeness over lifetime. That is not true. We are made perfect and complete in the spirit at the point of the second birth and then we walk in that completeness, not work for it. <u>Christianity is not about doing to become. It is about what Jesus did so that we become sons of God and His brothers without working for it.</u> Think of it like this, you didn't do anything to become your parents' son or daughter. You were just born in the family and were a complete and bona fide child of it before you could do anything good or bad. It is the same with the new creation. You were born into the massive family which is named after God in heaven and earth and instantly became a son there and a junior brother of Jesus. Whatever is in Jesus is in you and whatever is His (which is everything that is) is yours as well.

So, what does all this mean and what is the implication of being perfect before God and being absolutely pleasing in His sight? It means you never have to feel condemned, you never have to fear, you never have to perform to please God or to be accepted by Him and you never have to feel inferior or inadequate. It means sin never has to have dominion over you because you are under grace and not under law. It also means you can do the very things Jesus did while He was here and greater things can you do too.

6. THE NEW CREATION IS NOT LIMITED TO LIFE IN THE THREE DIMENSIONAL NATURAL WORLD

Philippians 4:13 *I can do all things through him who strengthens me.* (ESV)

One of the major problems of being trapped in a carnal mindset is that even if you are a Christian, you unconsciously place limits on God. You harbor a limited view of who He is, and what He's capable of doing. Instead of seeing God for who He is, you bring Him down to the level of natural men. So, if something is impossible to you, you also imagine it is impossible to God. Notice below here how Jesus described God's illimitable nature:

Luke 1:37 *Nothing is impossible for God!* (CEV)

Jeremiah 32:27 *Behold, I am the Lord, the God of all flesh: is there anything too hard for me?* (KJV)

Matthew 19:26 *But Jesus beheld them, and said unto them, with men this is impossible; but with God all things are possible.* (KJV)

The human mind can't grasp the overwhelming enormity of God. Therefore, being so limited in their ability to accurately fathom who God really is, automatically, men think of God as a man and His capacity as that of man. No wonder the Bible lets us know that the natural man receives not the things of the Spirit of God for they are foolishness unto him; neither can he know them for they are spiritually discerned are spiritually discerned-1 Corinthians 2:14.

For example, there're those who cast aspersions on the virgin birth of Jesus. Thinking like the natural men they are, they ask small questions like, "How can God, who is neither a woman nor a man, have a son?" Even Islam asks that same question. In an attempt to make the whole thing sound humanly palatable, some even try to come up with stupid concocted hypotheses of how the Jesus project was possible. I had a close brother in Christ who was very level headed until he went to a Bible college (I have utterly nothing against grace based and genuine New-Testament-teaching Bible schools). When we met later and we tried to share about Christ, we drifted and found ourselves discussing about the virgin birth. That brother told me, "Oh, that one, I have since learnt from a particular professor that actually, God must have found a way to get Joseph's seed into Mary without intercourse" I was baffled for a moment and couldn't find my tongue initially. I knew that ignorant, religious and unbelieving instructors with big titles had destroyed his mind. I later tried to make him understand how it was of utmost importance for Jesus to be born free from any human blood for Him to qualify to be savior. I told him that if Jesus had even one drop of blood from Joseph, then His blood would be tainted and unuseful in the work of redemption. That is why Jesus couldn't undergo blood transfusion. His blood was purely from God. That is why He kept telling His hearers that they were from below but He was from above.

Such questions or musings are unfortunate. They relegate God to the realms of ordinary human beings to where He is also subject to the same biological processes as men. As a Christian, never make the costly blunder of sinking to the lows of trying to drag God down to the league of men. What will happen is that God Himself will not lose His altitude to come down. He will remain God and will still be up there.

Psalm 90:2 *Before the mountains were brought forth, or ever thou hadst formed the earth and the world, even from everlasting to everlasting, thou art God.*

However, that will severely hamper your ability to receive anything from God. You need to know He's God and not a man! You need to know He is a willing giver and nothing is impossible to and with Him. You also need to know you are a receiver and God is more that delighted to give to you and bless you. When you know and believe that, then you will receive from Him.

Matthew 8:3 *Jesus reached out his hand and touched the man. "I am willing," he said. "Be clean!" Immediately he was cleansed of his leprosy.* (KJV)

Numbers 23:19 *God is not a man, that he should lie; neither the son of man, that he should repent: hath he said, and shall he not do it? or hath he spoken, and shall he not make it good?* (KJV)

Ordinary men live in the three-dimensional natural world, and all they know is limited to that realm. But, God exists in a far much higher dimension which is unfathomable to natural men. In the Old Testament, He did pull the curtain a bit to invite a few selected men to view things from His perched dimension.

2 Kings 6: 12 *None of us, my lord the king," said one of his officers, "but Elisha, the prophet who is in Israel, tells the king of Israel the very words you speak in your bedroom...16"Don't be afraid," the prophet answered. "Those who are with us are more than those who are with them." 17And Elisha prayed, "Open his eyes, Lord, so that he may see." Then the Lord opened the servant's eyes, and he looked and saw the hills full of horses and chariots of fire all around Elisha.* (NIV)

Modern earthly security people talk of intelligence gathering but nothing comes anywhere close to what the king of Israel enjoyed during the time of Prophet Elisha. Even the very thoughts the opposing king entertained in his bedroom, Elisha relayed them to his king. Then the poor natural fellow thought of capturing Elisha. How can you plot to capture a guy who you've just been informed by your officers that he can hear your thoughts and eavesdrop into your most private conversations? Natural men are desperately slow. So, when his miserable forces thought they had surrounded the man who is an Old Testament shadow of our Lord Jesus Christ, it was Elisha's equally natural servant who was baffled. That morning, Elisha knew some soldiers were posturing outside but he didn't even think it was an emergency worth waking up to attend to. So, he took his time and continued to enjoy his well-deserved rest. He however asked God to lift his poor servant from the three dimensional realm of men to His own unlimited and exalted dimension. When that happened, the servant could see clearly and what he beheld was glorious. When Elisha eventually woke up, he had heaven strike the hapless men blind before leading them like small puppies to the king of Israel. He had them given some food and sent back to their natural master. They never dared attack Israel again. Is that awesome or what!

That is what I mean when I say that although we are in this natural world, we need not be limited to and by it like natural men. We can be in this world but have the experiences of heaven. In fact, that is the will of God for us. We should not be as confused, fearful, helpless, sick and as negative as the unbelievers. We should learn to see things from God's perspective because we are seated in heaven in Him. What baffles natural men should be an easy piece of cake for us. You don't find anywhere in the Bible where Jesus was wringing His hands because things were hastily heading south. In all things, He was composed and had solutions ready. There never was any situation that arose which He could not control. He had ready answers for everything, everywhere and at any time. Somebody may be saying, but He was God! That must never be an excuse. We have the same anointing of Jesus, His mind and we know all things-John 14:12; 1 John 2:27; 1 Corinthians 2:16. There is no reason why any Christian should be stuck in life. Our lives should be so glorious, so stable and so unshakeable that unbelievers keep searching for the secrets of our unassailable success and prosperity. When natural men talk of incurable diseases, we ought to show them that any illness is as easy to cure as a simple cold. When they talk of economic downturns, we should be singing, enlarging the place of our tents, lengthening the cords and strengthening our stakes. We should be expanding when others are talking fear because we are supplied from heaven. We live according to God's glorious riches in Christ, not according to the economies of men. When others say there is a casting down, we should show them we are always lifted up. Trouble does sure come to everybody who lives on earth but for the new creation, the life of God in him should put him over even where ordinary men are sinking. You see, the same sun that melts the wax hardens the clay. It just depends on what material you are made of. The new creation is made of divine material and should be able to weather any kind of trouble by the Spirit of God. There ought to be a huge difference between the results of a person whose source is God and people who depend on earthly systems for sustenance. When others are afraid of the future, we should astonish them with the unparalleled peace we enjoy in all circumstances and the bright future we look forward to. When they are panicky, we should be enjoying absolute rest and bliss because no evil can come near our dwelling. When they are talking fear and dread, we should be spreading faith, optimism and hope.

Just like the natural people of Jesus' time couldn't fathom Him out, those who are in the flesh do not understand us.

John 3: 8 *The wind bloweth where it listeth, and thou hearest the sound thereof, but canst not tell whence it cometh, and whither it goeth: so is every one that is born of the Spirit.* (KJV)

1 Corinthians 2:15 *But he that is spiritual judgeth all things, yet he himself is judged of no man.* (KJV)

Although we are physically in the three dimensional world with them, we at the same live in another spiritual dimension which is what makes all the difference. The spiritual dimension is the game changer for the Christian. It is not limited to length, height and width. It is not governed by biological, physical and chemical processes. Once you realize that, you will then know how come God could send His Word through an angel to the Virgin Mary and it produced a child without the participation of man. You will even understand that Jesus is the word of God and that the word can take the form of flesh and remain just as powerful and anointed. You will also find out that the new creation that is you is made of the word also, not of flesh. As such, you cannot get the results of a fleshly man but of a spirit man. You should get the word results because everything produces after its kind. Natural men are born of flesh only, and they hail from the soil. We are born first of the flesh but then we are born again a second time of the word by the Spirit of God from heaven.

John 3: 6 *That which is born of the flesh is flesh; and that which is born of the Spirit is spirit.* (KJV)

John 17:16 *They are not of the world, even as I am not of the world.* (KJV)

Being born of the word of God just like Jesus, you should assume the nature and character of that word and get the results of that word because it fails not-1 Peter 1:23. That explains why we triumph always in Christ and without exception so-2 Corinthians 2:14. Being born again of the word, we have the same power and effect the word has. That is why we heal, introduce light where there is darkness, raise the dead, cast out demons, save, provide solutions, avert disasters and do everything Jesus did. Refuse to live your life according to standards, speculations and theories of natural men. There's a higher knowledge and realm of life. Follow the Word. Just like our Father God, we are not to be restricted by man's limitations. Never allow what man's version of reality which is derived from carnal observation determine how your life goes. You are a spirit and are unlimited. You live above science, technology and every other intellectual pursuit of natural men. You beat them all. Glory to God! Amen.

7. CITIZEN OF HEAVEN, NOT EARTH.

The new creation's citizenship is in Heaven, not on earth.

Philippians 3:20 *But our citizenship is in heaven. And we eagerly await a Savior from there, the Lord Jesus Christ,* (KJV)

The Bible says we are sojourners on this sordid earth. We don't belong to this corrupt planet. Thank God after He concludes time, a new earth and a new heaven will be unveiled and we shall be back to where God always wanted us-heaven on earth.

John 17: 16 *They are not of the world, even as I am not of the world.* (KJV)

On this current earth, we are ambassadors, not citizens. Ambassadors never become citizens of the country they are sent to. They go there strictly to represent the interests of their country in the foreign territory.

2 Corinthians 5: 20 *Now then we are ambassadors for Christ, as though God did beseech you by us: we pray you in Christ's stead, be ye reconciled to God.* (KJV)

This passing earth has no claim on us. We are not even subject to the vagaries here because we live under the system and economy of heaven though we are still here. We are God's family on earth and are called by His name.

Ephesians 3: 14 F*or this cause I bow my knees unto the Father of our Lord Jesus Christ, 15 Of whom the whole family in heaven and earth is named,* (KJV)

An ambassador doesn't live by the standards of the country he is posted to but of the country of his origin. Even if the country he is posted to is poor, he carries the environment of his source country with him. He does not become subject to the circumstances of the foreign country. Also, the place where the embassy of his country is situated is property of his country, not the host country. That means the home of the Christian is the embassy of heaven. Begin looking at your home in that light. Your office is a piece of heaven on earth and you are the ambassador. What a privilege!

Now, the thing that makes the new creation special is because unlike ordinary men who are dead spiritually, he possesses a new and perfect spirit which is from Zion, not below. His spirit is as perfect as God Himself who is spirit as well. He is in Zion, at the same time as he is on earth. We are strange creatures!

Hebrew 12: 22 *But ye are come unto mount Sion, and unto the city of the living God, the heavenly Jerusalem, and to an innumerable company of angels, 23 To the general assembly and church of the firstborn, which are written in heaven, and to God the Judge of all, and to the spirits of just men made perfect,* KJV.

Besides stating that the new creation has a perfect spirit, this verse is also saying that we have come to God's City of Zion already. Religion is still telling Christians they are marching to Zion and they may or may not make it to there depending on their conduct in between. <u>The new creation is a special species of aliens from a radically superior realm.</u>

1 Peter 2:11 *Beloved, I exhort you as aliens and sojourners, to abstain from fleshly desires, which war against the soul,* (Berean Literal Bible)

The new creation is not a regular or ordinary human being. His citizenship is registered not in earth but Heaven. <u>The new creation is not an African, an American, an Asian, a European or an Australian. He is not even a Jew. He is a citizen of heaven on a brief loan to earth.</u>

Ephesians 2: 19 *Consequently, you are no longer foreigners and strangers, but fellow citizens with God's people and also members of his household* (NIV)

Hebrews 13: 14 *For here we do not have an enduring city, but we are looking for the city that is to come.* (NIV)

1 Peter 2:11 *Dearly beloved, I beseech you as strangers and pilgrims, abstain from fleshly lusts, which war against the soul;* (KJV)

The new creation is currently in Heaven, and at the same time on earth.

Ephesians 2:6 *And hath raised us up together, and made us sit together in heavenly places in Christ Jesus:* (KJV)

Whenever I hear people singing the song "Let us go to Zion the city of the Lord" I always wonder whether they ever read their Bibles. We are in Zion already!

Hebrews 12: 22 *But ye are come unto mount Sion, and unto the city of the living God, the heavenly Jerusalem, and to an innumerable company of angels,* (KJV).

The only reason why we don't believe we are in Zion already is because most of us still walk by sensory perceptions, not by faith. So, we expect to see ourselves seated in Heaven with our physical bodies. It doesn't work like that. We don't walk by sensory perceptions but by faith without which we can forget about pleasing

God. You have to believe that what the word of God says is final regardless of how the circumstances appear in the physical realm. So if the word of God says we are seated in Heaven in Christ; that settles the matter. It is upon you to now take that word and educate your mind that your spirit is one with Jesus' in heaven and your body is a member of Christ and wherever Christ is seated, His members are there as well. It is called mind renewal. A non-renewed mind is a burden to its bearer. This is because it cannot receive the things of God because they are spiritually appropriated yet such a mind is totally in the flesh. A non-renewed mind is death because it rejects and disregards spiritual things which constitute the life of God.

    The only thing that the new creation is waiting for is a new body and a supernatural soul. Otherwise, his spirit is as perfect as it will ever be in eternity. It will not require some more modification, cleansing or perfecting. The new creation is not a changed man; He is an exchanged or transformed man. But sir, what about spiritual growth? Isn't it growth of the spirit? No! Spiritual growth is nothing more than renewal of the soul by the spirit. After the new birth, the only thing that remains for the believer to do for life is to renew the mind so that it conforms to the new spirit. The problem for the believer is always a non-renewed soul because it is the interface between the spirit world on the one side, and the body and the physical world on the other. If the soul is renewed, there is a high chance the will in there will propel the body to do what is in line with the spirit. Every time the soul is in agreement with the spirit, the believer has hopes of winning but whenever the soul rejects or is ignorant of the will of God which is in the spirit, the believer stands a high chance of losing in that particular situation. Once the soul is renewed with the word of God, it will automatically cooperate with the spirit and the two have a better chance of crucifying the body so that it doesn't succumb to the desires therein. The body ought to be a slave and servant of the soul but it has its own desires and it can militate against its master. The will, emotions and intellect reside in the soul and they determine which direction the soul goes. That is why you can be nursing depression and disturbance in your soul but then suddenly your spirit reminds you that the Lord is your life, your hope, strength, strong tower and that His joy is your strength. You will then discover that the turmoil that is going on in your soul that has affected even your body is superficial and carnal. In that case, there is a possibility that when the countenance in the soul shifts from sadness and heaviness to joy and happiness in light of that new revelation, the body also benefits. When the heaviness lifts, the body will be healthier, stronger, relaxed and more productive.

Psalm 43: 5 *Why art thou cast down, O my soul? and why art thou disquieted within me? hope in God: for I shall yet praise him, who is the health of my countenance, and my God.* (KJV)

This was David's spirit talking to his sullen soul. We have something David could only dream of, a new spirit. That means we should be talking to our souls and educating them from the spirit with the word of God. We shouldn't let our souls have the upper hand in our lives so that we are ruled by emotions, senses, human intellect and the motions of a non-renewed mind. Talk to your soul and inform it of the marvelous things that been done by Christ so that you are prosperous and are in health, even as your soul prospers. When the soul prospers by way of being inundated with the word of God, the body is put in a likely position to prosper as well. Studies have uncovered an undeniable link between a troubled soul and many somatic health complications. It is just that they only discovered an old wisdom in the Bible.

Proverbs 17: 22 *A merry heart doeth good like a medicine: but a broken spirit drieth the bones.* (KJV)

Isaiah 26: 3 *Thou wilt keep him in perfect peace, whose mind is stayed on thee: because he trusteth in thee.* (KJV)

Also, the more you renew your mind, the more you mature as a son of God. But, you are not becoming more of a son of God. That would mean your spirit is still growing. When my daughter was a few minutes old, she was as much my child as she is now that she is older. She is not becoming more of my daughter. The only thing that is happening is that she is discovering more of who she is and behaving more like that. The new creation is born complete in Christ. Nothing needs to be added to or subtracted from him. Immediately at salvation, you become a fully-fledged son of God but you start off on a journey of self-discovery until you come to where you know who you are and are living that fully.

Ephesians 4: 13 *Till we all come in the unity of the faith, and of the knowledge of the Son of God, unto a perfect man, unto the measure of the stature of the fullness of Christ: 14 That we henceforth be no more children, tossed to and fro, and carried about with every wind of doctrine, by the sleight of men, and cunning craftiness, whereby they lie in wait to deceive;* (KJV)

It is at the time when we sufficiently mature as sons of God that we place ourselves in a position to receive what the Lord has kept safely in store for us. It is not the Lord who determines when we mature and when we receive the things He has for us as religion teaches. Religion says that the reason you have not received a particular thing from the Lord is because as far as the Lord is concerned, you are still a baby Christian. It is true the reason you have not received is because you are still a toddler but it is not the Lord who is keeping it from you. You are keeping it from yourself by refusing to grow up. In fact, you can be a decades old Christian and still be a spiritual baby and never receive any meaningful substance from the Lord though it was ready throughout the time. The Lord has set up the spiritual system to automatically give you your inheritance immediately you attain maturity. You see now it is in your best interests to take the word and renew your soul to where you know who you are in Christ, what you have in Him and what you are capable of doing. When you get there, you will not even need to ask for anything from the Lord. You will know what you have in Him and personally command it and appropriate it. That is very good news. It is just the same way a child grows up naturally to find out what has been bequeathed to them by their parents and as they do, they just take it and benefit from it! I have seen teenagers who are responsible and are enjoying the fruits of their inheritance. Sadly, I have also seen other people who are past thirty and forty but have refused to grow up and their inheritance is still in the hands of custodians and trustees.

Galatians 4:1 *Now I say, That the heir, as long as he is a child, differeth nothing from a servant, though he be lord of all... 4 But when the fulness of the time was come, God sent forth his Son, made of a woman, made under the law, 5 To redeem them that were under the law, that we might receive the adoption of sons.* (KJV)

2 Corinthians 2: 12 *Now we have received, not the spirit of the world, but the spirit which is of God; that we might know the things that are freely given to us of God... 15 But he that is spiritual judgeth all things, yet he himself is judged of no man.* (KJV)

No one can ever fully renew their minds and no one can ever mature totally in this life but we can do it to the extent that we think more like Christ and are beyond the place where we cease to be victims of life and of cunning treachery of the devil and crafty men. The soul and the body will still have to be transformed to conform fully to the new spirit at the first appearance of Christ in His glorious return.

Philippians 3:21 *who, by the power that enables him to bring everything under his control, will transform our lowly bodies so that they will be like his glorious body.* (KJV)

1 Corinthians 13: 9 *For we know in part, and we prophesy in part. 10 But when that which is perfect is come, then that which is in part shall be done away. 12 For now we see through a glass, darkly; but then face to face: now I know in part; but then shall I know even as also I am known.* (KJV)

Hebrews 10: 39 B*ut we are not of them who draw back unto perdition; but of them that believe to the saving of the soul.* (KJV)

YOUR NEW SPIRIT TRAINS, DEVELOPS, TEACHES AND RENEWS YOUR SOUL, NOT VICE CERSA

Some people ask, if we are already perfect in the spirit, then why do we still fail? Why do we still have all manner of problems? Why are some people still poor, sick, dominated by sin and suffering? We must understand that the spirit is the real us. We are neither the body nor the soul. Before we were reborn, we had a wicked spirit that we inherited from Adam. The spirit is the driver of man. The spirit is supposed to be man's sure guide in life. The spirit of man became corrupted when Adam fell. It ceased to be a sure guide. It became defiled and undependable. It guided people towards its father the devil. At salvation, the Holy Spirit incised away that foul spirit and installed a new, perfect and godly one.

Titus 3: 3 *For we ourselves also were sometimes foolish, disobedient, deceived, serving divers lusts and pleasures, living in malice and envy, hateful, and hating one another. 4 But after that the kindness and love of God our Savior toward man appeared, 5 Not by works of righteousness which we have done, but according to his mercy he saved us, by the washing of regeneration, and renewing of the Holy Ghost;* (KJV)

To answer the question at hand, that old spirit that we call old sin nature left behind some of that foolishness, disobedience, deception and the rest of that list. It is the same way computers work. Computers are run by software. Computer applications or *apps* fall under this category. Basically, software is simply a program that determines what a computer does or that enables a computer perform its tasks. In our case, the spirit would be our software while the body is the hardware. The soul which is very close to the spirit would be the user interface. It is the nexus between the spirit and the body. When a software becomes either outdated or needless, it is usually either updated or uninstalled from the computer and a new and updated one installed in its place. Usually after uninstallation, not everything about that software goes with the application. Some residues are left in the computer. As a result, an additional program called registry cleaner is required to hunt down and completely eradicate all those residues. Fortunately for computers, those residues do not harm the machine although some people think they slow down the system. That has been proven to be untrue time and again and it's even safer to leave those residues alone. In the case of man, salvation was not simply an upgrading or updating of the old software (read spirit). It was a complete uninstallation. It left behind in the soul residues that adversely affect our Christian lives big time and they must be totally uninstalled. That registry cleaner is the word of God. We must employ it to uproot all those diabolical programs from the old sinful man and install the knowledge, wisdom and will of God. After that, we can begin thinking and operating like God again.

Ephesians 4: 23 *and be renewed in the spirit of your mind, 24 and that you put on the new man which was created according to God, in true righteousness and holiness.* (KJV)

1 Peter 1: 14 *As obedient children, not fashioning yourselves*

according to the former lusts in your ignorance: (KJV)

The special cleaning software of the word of God comes in to sanitize the soul so it can be updated according to the new spirit. We call it mind renewal. The word of God is spirit as well. It's the spiritual software that we use to update the mind so that it can catch up with or be in sync with the perfected spirit.

John 6: 63 *It is the spirit that quickeneth; the flesh profiteth nothing: the words that I speak unto you, they are spirit, and they are life.* (KJV)

Contrary to what most people say, we don't read the word to educate, strengthen, train, inform, build or develop the spirit or to get the word into the spirit: the entire Bible is in the new spirit already, including the entire counsel of God. We have no trouble with the spirit. The spirit is one entity with God and he knows all things. He has the mind of Christ.

Colossians 3: 10 *And have put on the new man, which is renewed in knowledge after the image of him that created him:* (KJV)

You can't teach your spirit anything. He is the one who teaches your mind to renew it. There is nowhere in the Bible where we are told to educate, inform or improve the spirit in any way. In him resides all the resources of wisdom and knowledge because he is joined as one with Christ.

In the spirit is where the perfection spoken of in so many places in the New Testament is. The spirit is the perfect man born in righteousness and true holiness. What we have trouble with is the non-renewed mind. The Bible doesn't tell us to renew the spirit. You can't show me one verse which instructs us to renew, strengthen, build, inform, train or teach the spirit. But, I can show you many places where we are told to renew the mind with the word of God. <u>Until you renew your mind with the word of God, you will continue to think like a pagan, though you are born again. You will also continue to get the results of a pagan though you should be getting the results of Jesus.</u> As you think, those are the results you will get. The reason why Jesus was different and got different results from everybody else is because He thought differently. He knew things nobody else knew because nobody else had the original information from heaven as He did. If you want to be different and to get different results, you must think differently from ordinary men. You must think like Jesus and His thoughts are contained in the Bible. If you want to get the same results Jesus got, you must be a friend of the Bible. It doesn't come any other way. The anointing comes through knowledge, not through prayer, fasting, laying on of hands or any of these other shortcuts religious people have devised. If you are ignorant, even if a million apostles lay their hands on you until you lose all your hair, the Lord will still reject you. By rejection I don't mean He will condemn you to hell. Rejection here means "to not use." God does not use ignorant people who have rejected knowledge or are too lazy to seek it. If they purport to work for Him and they are ignorant, they will embarrass and even disadvantage His majestic kingdom. That is tough but it is right.

Hosea 4: 6 *My people are destroyed for lack of knowledge:* ***because thou hast rejected knowledge, I will also reject thee,*** *that thou shalt be no priest to me: seeing thou hast forgotten the law of thy God, I will also forget thy children.* (KJV) Emphasis added.

Proverbs 18: 15 *The heart of the prudent getteth knowledge; and the ear of the wise seeketh knowledge.* (KJV)

Proverbs 20: 15 *There is gold, and a multitude of rubies: but the lips of knowledge are a precious jewel.* (KJV)

Proverbs 4:7 *Wisdom is the principal thing; therefore get wisdom: and with all thy getting get understanding.* (KJV)

<u>Information and instruction from the word of God brings about transformation of the soul.</u> This knowledge is required in the mind to renew it so that it can stop resisting the spirit in carrying out what is godly in the life of the person. When a mind is renewed, it always agrees with the spirit and the will of man subjects itself to the will of God which is in the spirit of the new creation. A lot of people say the eyes or even the mind is the doorway to the spirit. I beg to differ. At least that's' not true for the new creation. There is nothing in the environment that the spirit doesn't know of so that it now requires to be educated or informed through the senses by the soul. Furthermore, the re-born spirit doesn't even require that information from the environment because he has the original information (which is the definition of truth) from God, being one spirit with the

Lord. Here is the thing though; the soul is the spirit's avenue to the body and to the outside environment. <u>God wants a lot of work done in the earth. He lives in the new, pure and sanctified spirit of man. He wants to touch the world through the body of that man.</u> So, He influences the soul in a bid to have the will of that man agree with the will of God. Let's say God wants to heal a sick person. He will speak to the soul of a nearby born again person and He will make it known in the spirit of that man. That man may say, "I want to help that sick man." That is how God speaks to us. He speaks in the first person so that we think it is just our desires but actually it is Him influencing us through our new spirits to do His will. He works in us to will to do His will. If we delight ourselves in Him, He gives us the desires of our hearts. In other words, if we fellowship with Him, He makes us desire the same things He desires. If the mind of that particular Christian is sufficiently renewed, it means he is responsive to the will of God. It means his will is surrendered to the will of God. Hence, he will not resist but agree with the will of God in his spirit. A righteous man has two wills in one person. He has the will of God in his new spirit, and a will of his own in his mind or soul. The person who has properly renewed his mind has sacrificed his will and merged it with the will of God. The two wills are synchronized. That is part of what we call offering one's body as a living sacrifice, holy (dedicated unto the Lord) and acceptable to the Lord. Almost nobody has ever submitted themselves to the Lord so completely that they had only one will, the will of God in them. Not even Paul the apostle. We all are at various stages of submitting ourselves to the Lord. So, that believer who has his will in sync with the will of God will then have his will push his hand and lay it on the sick man and the will of God (healing) will happen on earth as it is done in heaven. If it is preaching to a lost person, the same process is repeated. Today, I was standing somewhere and a man came and sat nearby with the intention of selling to me something. I didn't need the thing and I politely declined his overtures to turn me into his client. He borrowed something from me and I gave him. For a short time, there was silence between us. In those few moments, the Lord was speaking in my spirit. He wanted that man preached to. I was not willing at first. But, the Lord through my spirit prevailed on my will and I gave in. Then, my will moved my lips and I began to share the liberating and powerful gospel of God's grace (which is His power to salvation) with that man for several minutes. He ended up opening up to me that he was a drug addict and was actually undergoing rehabilitation. Ultimately and after planting the seed of the incorruptible word of God in his heart, I gave him my contact for follow up and we parted ways. That is how it works. <u>It is not about trying to get anything to the spirit; it is about God in the spirit trying to transform the soul so that through it He can get His work done on earth. God's desire to carry out His work on earth either succeeds or is aborted in the soul of the person involved.</u> If the soul is not renewed and stirred up, God's mission suffers. The converse is also true. Other than the spirit trying to get something done in the earth; for the rest of the time, the spirit tries to renew the soul with the word. This is how it happens: there is a constant desire generated in the spirit to feast on the word. The spirit influences the soul to get into the word. If the will of man is thus conquered, then it gets the body to find a Bible and have it read. As the person reads with the brain in the mind, the spirit from within brings out the revelation in that word so that the soul benefits from it. In other words, the spirit takes that opportunity of Bible reading to educate the mind and transform it. When that happens, the soul prospers and hence the whole person benefits as well.

The spirit operates at the same pace with the Lord Jesus. He operates at the speed of the Holy Ghost. The soul is the slow man here who requires needs daily doses of the quickening word of God. Some other people say speaking with tongues edifies or builds up the spirit. That is the result of men reading into the Bible. Speaking in tongues cannot be for building the spirit because it is that same spirit that is prays in those tongues. He is praying the hidden wisdom of God. He is speaking the mysteries of God who resides in him. The official Bible position is that he who speaks in an unknown tongue edifies himself, just like he who prophesies edifies the church. It doesn't say he who speaks in an unknown tongue edifies the spirit. Paul here is simply stating that he who speaks in an unknown tongue is building up his own life all around. He is building his life like an edifice to where above all things he can prosper and be in health, even as his soul prospers. You cannot purport to build up the spirit; it is the one that builds you up. Saying you can build up the spirit is like trying to edify God. The spirit is where the divine life of God resides. Some people say that reading or meditating on God's word is feeding the spirit. They say the word is food for the spirit. That is untrue according to the word. There is nowhere in the New Testament where we are told to do anything to improve the new spirit. We are only expressly instructed to renew our souls. The new spirit of the born again man is born of, and made of the word. It is actually the word of God sheathed in human flesh. On the other hand, the word of God is food for the unregenerate soul. If you don't feed the soul with the word, it will be hungry and depraved, and the manifestations will be depression, boredom, fear, anxiety, worry, confusion and all manner of other ills. As all these unfortunate things happen, you will be still be born again and your spirit will be full of the word and all the answers that you will ever need, yet you will not be utilizing them. However, a soul that is properly fed is satisfied and its fruit is perfect peace, faith, hope, joy, boldness confidence and productivity. Just like Christ, we too are life giving spirits because as is the heavenly Christ, so are we that are heavenly. <u>By far, the most important thing in all of life is to get born again and acquire a new spirit. The next most important thing is to renew the mind.</u> Renewing the mind is replacing the human or worldly thinking with word-of-God-based thinking. Now, salvation or the new birth is a one-time event, while renewing of the mind is a life-long process. The moment we stop renewing our minds with the word of God, we stunt our spiritual growth and begin deteriorating rapidly towards carnality. <u>If you are not growing spiritually, you are growing in the flesh.</u> In fact, the Christian who fails to renew his mind is no different from a pagan. He may eventually make it to Heaven but such a person will be useless to the kingdom of God on earth. The result of a non-renewed mind is a powerless, ineffective, almost useless Christian.

Ultimately, it means you have everything you need for life and godliness. You are not trying to get anything more from God into your spirit. In the spirit resides all your inheritance from God. You have all the grace, righteousness, holiness, wisdom, knowledge, material things, love, joy, peace and faith you will ever need in life. It is all there in your perfected spirit. Even the whole Bible is in you because you are one spirit with Jesus; you have His mind; you know all things and need not be taught anything; and, you have all treasures of wisdom and knowledge-1 Corinthians 1:30; 1 Corinthians 2:16; Romans 12:3; 1 John 2:20-21, 27; Colossians 2:3. All these things are in your born again spirit, not in your soul or body but they need to be delivered there through renewing of the mind. There is nothing your perfect spirit lacks. There is nothing you are trying to deposit there. Instead, your new spirit has everything you require. You don't even need to deposit into the spirit more righteousness and holiness. You just need to get them from the new spirit and manifest them through a righteous and holy life. You don't need to get more faith. Every believer has the very faith of Jesus in their spirit-Galatians 2:20. It's not faith they lack but knowledge and appreciation of it. You get born again fully loaded and totally equipped for life. That means you don't receive more of anything. Religion is still keeping its victims busy singing terribly inaccurate songs like; "more, more, more of you Jesus. I want more of you. Touch me once more." You can't have more of Jesus and you can't have more power, more peace or more of anything else. You have the Holy Spirit without measure just like Jesus had. That is why you should be busy doing the same things He did and greater ones even, not singing silly songs and asking for what you already have. You don't need anybody's touch either. Jesus didn't just touch you; He filled you. You need to acknowledge that you have everything you need for life and godliness and begin putting it to work. All you can do now is only to grow up into what you have in Christ, which is superabundance of everything. Babies in the faith are trying to get more of all manner of things from the Lord but the mature sons know they have everything and all they do is figure out ways to get it out from the spirit:

Galatians 4:1 *Now I say, That the heir, as long as he is a child, differeth nothing from a servant, though he be lord of all; 2 But is under tutors and governors until the time appointed of the father.* (KJV)

Philemon 1:6 *That the communication of thy faith may become effectual by the acknowledging of every good thing which is in you in Christ Jesus.* (KJV)

8. THE NEW CREATION HAS ALL PAST, PRESENT AND FUTURE SINS FORGIVEN.

The spiritual word of God says that God in Christ has made us new creation. All things are now new and old things are passed away. All things are now of God, who hath reconciled us to Himself, not imputing our sins unto us. After reading such a word, a non-renewed mind will look at the physical and see no change. It will see "nothing" new. It will not even believe that God has forgiven all the sins and doesn't even remember our trespasses anymore. It wants to see forgiven sins physically. Just because the mind doesn't feel forgiven, the person will go by feelings and not by the explicit word of God. Consequently, such a mind will say, "The Bible is full of metaphors, myths and fantasies. One can't quite take anything literally in the Bible." So, the carnal mind will think the Bible is engaging in a play of words and not meaning what it says. It will therefore conclude that at salvation, nothing changed. Furthermore, that mind will not believe that God imputes no more sins unto us because He imputed all of them to Christ. In that regard, the carnal mind will fail to receive the peace that comes with knowing that God is not out to get us but to bless us. It will continue to wallow in sin consciousness. That will lead to condemnation which leads to fear, which in turn leads to stress and then all manner of illnesses and then death.

A lot of people don't know that part of the reason why Job was befallen by the tragedies satan brought his way is because he was sin-conscious. He had this constant fear that his children might sin and curse God in their hearts and so he offered burnt offerings for each one of them continually.

Job 1: 5 *And it was so, when the days of their feasting were gone about, that Job sent and sanctified them, and rose up early in the morning, and offered burnt offerings according to the number of them all: for Job said, It may be that my sons have sinned, and cursed God in their hearts. Thus did Job continually.* (KJV)

The word continually in this verse means that Job never

rested. He was constantly worried about what his children were up to and he suspected they could sin any time and therefore he was constantly appeasing God. Job is like modern day Christians who are ever doing what they call "confession" and "repentance." They never rest because they are ever examining themselves and checking what wrong they may have done so that they can confess it and repent of it. They keep muttering confessions under their breath until they look weird to the public. Do you think a sinner observing your life can ever want to have what you have? Who wants to live under that oppressive religion of 'confessing' and 'repenting' of every sin? What if you forget some sins of which you are guaranteed to do? What about the unknown sins which are probably more than the known ones? What if you sinned and either died quickly or Jesus returned before you had chance to confess it? Life is hard and complicated enough even without religion. What people are looking for is for a way to make it a little bit bearable. They are not looking for more complications and burdens of religions. Strangely, Jesus answered their longing but religious people keep them from accessing what Jesus brought. Jesus heard the cry of the people and told them He had not come to make things even more unbearable. He said He came to simplify life and roll away the burdens. He invited all who were heavy laden, oppressed, crushed, isolated by religion and who labored; to come unto Him because He brought rest for their weary souls. We have been called to a life of rest, not of condemnation, fear, anxiety and restlessness. Let us not entangle ourselves again with this religion of constant groveling in sin-consciousness by keeping in mind that God said He is merciful to our unrighteousness; and our sins and iniquities He remembers no more. I have never met a genuine Christian who doesn't believe that our sins all the way toAdam; or at least since we were born are forgiven at the point of salvation. Where we have problems is believing that our future sins are taken away as well. That is easy to explain. First, God says in Hebrews 8:12 that our sins and iniquities He will remember no more. If God doesn't remember our sins, then who are we to remember them unless we want to pretend to have a better memory than Him or even to know better than He does? Secondly, God is not imputing sins unto us-2 Corinthians 5:19. Thirdly and very convincingly, when Jesus died, all our sins were future and He dies no more for sins. He died only that one death on the cross and it was enough to purge all sins of all men for all time. Did you know that fire can't burn again where it has burnt already? Firefighters actually employ that tactic to contain fires. When they see bush fire approaching, they go ahead of it and deliberately burn a section of the vegetation which lies along the path of the fire. When the fire gets to the burnt section, it stops immediately and contains itself. The fire of God's wrath for our sins came upon Jesus and He took it all and sheathed it in His body. God's justice was satisfied by Jesus at the cross, not by our performance. What I mean is that God was justified to rain down fire and brimstone as judgment for our sin. He was justified in serving death to us all as our reward for disobedience. Instead of that judgment falling on us, Jesus came in between and took it for us. He became our substitute. God cannot now judge the sins of the person who is in Christ. That would have to be what they refer to in justice lingo as double jeopardy where a crime is punished twice. God is just and He can never do that. He was completely satisfied by the sacrifice of Jesus and He doesn't even want any more human sacrifices. Any human sacrifice now of penance and works of the law is an affront to Jesus, is sacrilegious and an abomination. I can prove to the experts in this 'confession' business that they don't even confess and repent of the real sins which are unbelief, fear, self-righteousness and other sins of omission like not doing good yet they know to. They also don't confess for doing things that are not of faith. They only confess of what they consider 'big' sins like adultery, fornication, lying, murder and others. I have come to learn that only religious people classify some sins as big and others as small. Actually, the real definition of <u>sin is anything or anybody which or who falls short of the standard of God which is Jesus. The Ten Commandments are not the standard of God.</u> So, now that we know that no man has ever or can ever attain the standard of Jesus in the flesh, anybody who wants to be accepted with God has to believe in the one who is the accurate standard of God. That is the only way out. The way out is not trying harder to measure up to Jesus so that you can be blessed or acceptable to God. It is faith in Jesus that does the trick. Have I said it is wrong to be sorry for sins and to acknowledge them before God? Never! It is crucial to do so. It is just like when we wrong another member in the family and we say sorry to the wronged party and determine to do everything in our ability never to repeat it. Likewise, we also have an eternal family and God is the head there. He is our loving Father. We ought to say sorry to Him when we blow it. We ought to acknowledge our shortcomings before Him. However, here, we don't confess our sins in order to be forgiven. We do it because we are forgiven already and God is not counting our sins against us because He is merciful to our unrighteousness and our sins and lawless deeds He will remember no more. Acknowledging our failures before God doesn't really affect our standing before Him, but it affects our relationship with the devil who is ever waiting to accuse and condemn us in our hearts once we fail. Acknowledging sins before God silences the devil and seals all the loopholes he uses to destroy us through guilt and sin-consciousness. However, our relationship with God is always secured in Christ because we are eternally saved by what Jesus did, not by our performance. Also, unlike in a natural family situation, we don't swear to God to never repeat mistakes again because for one, God takes no pleasure in human oaths and secondly, we are bound to once in a while repeat the same things and because we swore to God, we will be susceptible to feel condemned, unworthy before Him and try to keep away from Him. God doesn't condone that because our fellowship with Him is not based on how well we promise to never sin again or how effectively we 'confess' sins, how holy we live or on any other thing we do or don't do other than a simple faith in Christ Jesus. Any other condition or consideration on which we try base our fellowship with God amounts to law and human works and they don't cut it with God. Once we acknowledge our failings before God, we just ought to tell Him also we are not leaning on willpower and swearing never to repeat it again. Swearing to God to never repeat a particular thing is not only totally uncalled for and unnecessary, but it is also foolish. God doesn't require our promises because He knows we still have a flesh to contend with. He loves us the way we are, not after we fulfill some righteous requirement of the law or after we defeat all sin and become perfect. The correct thing to do is to thank Him for forgiving us in Christ over 2000 years ago and not imputing our sins unto us. We should thank Him because where sin increases, grace much more superabounds. It is also important to thank Him because His power is available to help us so that we don't become slaves to sin, poor habits and human weaknesses going forward. People who think that by human will and self-righteousness they can promise God to never repeat their mistakes and keep that promise usually fall back into the same pit usually before the day is over and they become victims of guilt, shame, condemnation, fear, low self-esteem and broken fellowship with God. Some of these are the religious types who fail so many times after their vows to keep clean that they give up, feel like hypocrites and failures, and some even do what in religion they call "backsliding." I still don't know what they mean by that term but hey! I am not expected to know because that is the domain of religion which I shunned long time ago. I have never heard of a son who for any reason backslid from being his parents' child. What I know is that once a son, always a son. Even the son who planned on backsliding to the lower rank of a servant in Jesus' parable of the prodigal son was not allowed by the father to do such a thing. He was received warmly and his position of son-ship maintained without question. His position was always there all the time he was gone. His confessions were not even given time and he found himself talking alone. There was so much excitement in that man's home that nobody ever listened to his sorry stories of how he had sinned against man and God. That loving father in that story represents God and His attitude towards those who feel like they are beyond repair. Those like me who don't swear anything to God but just appeal to Him to cause us to lean more on His present help in us to dominate sin never set themselves up for failure, condemnation and fear. All I can say regarding this issue of Christians who are ever confessing sins is that <u>there is a practice or imagination that seems right to a religious person but the end thereof is death.</u> What about James 5:16? It says; *"Confess your faults one to another, and pray one for another, that ye may be healed. The effectual fervent prayer of a righteous man availeth much."* A lot of people have taken this verse to mean that we should tell others what sins we have committed as if we are telling it to God. That is not what this verse is about. Whole religious doctrines and rituals have been developed out of this one verse. In some religions, people go into cubicles to empty the dirty contents of their lives before a priest who then purports to forgive them. That is impudence on the part of that fellow who thinks men seated in some ungodly conference somewhere can confer upon him the power to pardon sin. These are the same fellows who think John 20:23 is giving some "super-Christians" power to forgive sins or withhold forgiveness. Who did these pretenders die for so that people can confess sins to them and for them to then pardon? Since when did God grant a mere man authority to determine the eternal destiny of another? The weighty matter of forgiveness of sins can never be left at the whims of man. Anyway, we can't confess sins to men for several reasons: One, they are not God and there is nothing they can do even if we told them. Two, they have sins of their own they are dealing with and they are really no better. Three, God knows as soon as you tell them about your sins, they will be broadcast to others and you will be walking in public as one who is naked. Four, people really are not interested in hearing about all the rotten things you are struggling with because it will depress them. So, what does this verse mean? This verse is saying to share with others where we have some challenges (not necessarily direct sins) and weaknesses in life. I believe we should disclose this information only to mature, confidential and godly people who are preferably our mentors in Christ. They should be confidential people who can then walk with us the journey of overcoming those challenges. That journey may include praying with and for us, holding us accountable as they take stock of our progress, and, helping us apply scriptures in our lives. This is what works to banish weaknesses and overcome challenges which lead us to fail. It is always very easy to overcome when we know we have a trustworthy confidant who is walking and working with us for our very best. Confidants like these are few and far between and we must be very careful and even prayerful when finding one. We should depend on God to help us locate one although such a person will definitely be someone we have developed a cordial and godly relationship with over time and we know them well.

  By Jesus' death once for sins forever, He removed all the

sins of all those who had died before Christ but believed in God; of all those who were alive at the time of Jesus and believed on Him; and, the sins of all those who would ever come and believe on Jesus. Jesus is seated in Heaven; He is not up in the altar offering sacrifices for sins daily like what the Old Testament priests used to do daily. This one supreme point seems to evade the vast majority of Christians for whom preoccupation with thoughts of whether or not they have sinned is a constant diet every day.

Hebrews 10: 10 *By the which will we are sanctified through the offering of the body of Jesus Christ once for all. 11 And every priest standeth daily ministering and offering oftentimes the same sacrifices, which can never take away sins: 12 But this man,* **after he had offered one sacrifice for sins forever, sat down on the right hand of God;** ... *14 For by one offering he hath* **perfected** *forever them that are sanctified.* (KJV) Emphasis added.

The Bible says without the shedding of blood, there is no forgiveness of sins.

Hebrews 9: 22 *And almost all things are by the law purged with blood; and without shedding of blood is no remission.* (KJV)

If you couple these scriptures in Hebrews chapters 9 and 10, you find that it is the eternal blood of Jesus that cleansed us once and for all from sin, not what religion erroneously calls confessions or repentance. Blood as the only remover of sin is a truth that cuts across both the new and old covenants. When the old covenant people brought animals to be sacrificed because they had sinned, it was not time for confessing or apologizing for sin. There was not even room for such apologies. God didn't require them. It was time for atoning for sin. The only acceptable response to sin was atonement, not making apologies, confessions, repentance or promises to never repeat it again. It is only when the animal was offered in the place of the sinner that they could make a trip back home satisfied that they were in God's good books. Even if there was one religious fanatic who came to the temple compound and apologized to God the whole day, repenting, confessing all known and unknown sins and, cut himself until he bled trying to appease God; they would still go back home with their sins and the wrath of God would still be upon them.

The question for us really is whether we have sinned and fallen short of God's glory. The answer is yes. That means our sin must be removed. The next question is whether there is such blood in place that can take away our sins. John the Baptist answered that question for us when He saw the Lamb of God who takes away the sin of the world. The apostle John confirms again in the book of Revelation that Jesus did indeed cleanse us from our unrighteousness.

Revelation 1: 5 *And from Jesus Christ, who is the faithful witness, and the first begotten of the dead, and the prince of the kings of the earth. Unto him that loved us, and washed us from our sins in his own blood,* (KJV) Emphasis added.

Hebrews 1:3 *Who being the brightness of his glory, and the express image of his person, and upholding all things by the word of his power, when he had by himself **purged** our sins, **sat down** on the right hand of the Majesty on high:* (KJV) Emphasis added.

1 Corinthians 6:11 *Such were some of you; but you were **washed,** but you were **sanctified,** but you were **justified** in the name of the Lord Jesus Christ and in the Spirit of our God.* Emphasis added.

I would like you to take keen notice of all the tenses used in all these scriptures. They all denote a finished work of washing, cleansing, purging, justification and perfection. None of those things is being done continuously. They were done, completed and Jesus sat down. The way Jesus dealt with sin is radically different from the way the Old Testament priests with their animal sacrifices did. Jesus didn't cover sins like it was done throughout the Old Testament; He took the sins away for them to never again count against those who believe.

Three things stand out clearly in the scriptures above: one, the tenses employed are all past. It means the work of taking away our sin is an accomplished mission, not an ongoing duty. It is done and concluded. Secondly and very importantly, we were not the ones who washed ourselves from our sins. It is Jesus Himself and we know He does a thorough and perfect job. After that, we are assured in the last scripture up here that because of Jesus' finished work for us, we are made holy and justified or made righteous. Thirdly, it says that after Jesus had finished purging (taking away) our sins, He sat down on the right hand of God. That is a picture of rest. It indicates a completely finished work. Jesus is no longer busy in heaven dealing with our sins. He completely finished that business by the sacrifice of Himself once. All who like to take advantage of His finished work of purging our sins simply put their trust in Him and they receive their eternal pardon from His eternal work. It is not the religious confessions and repentance which take away sins; it is faith in the blood of Jesus. The Old Testament priests who were mere shadows of Jesus could not rest because their work was never finished. They could never permanently purge the sins of the worshippers. So, they never rested but were ever busy with daily sacrifices which would never take away sins. In fact, it is reported that there were no seats in the temple. The reason is because there was no time to rest because covering sins was a constant occupation.

Hebrews 9: 25 *Nor yet that he should offer himself often, as the high priest entereth into the holy place every year with blood of others; 26 For then must he often have suffered since the foundation of the world: but now once in the end of the world hath he appeared to put away sin by the sacrifice of himself... 28 So Christ was once offered to bear the sins of many; and unto them that look for him shall he appear the second time without sin unto salvation.* (KJV)

So, if the work of taking away our sins is accomplished, what is our part? Our part is to believe God's report. That is the way we receive what the Bible records was done for us. But, just how many sins did the blood of Jesus take care of? The blood of Jesus cleansed every human being from all their sins for all time if they believe in Christ. Some people have a problem with that position but I have a water-tight case to defend it. Some ask, how can Christ cleanse future sins I have not committed? Well, you have no option but to believe He did because when He died, all our sins were future because none of us was born yet. Not only did He forgive sins in advance, He also forgave sins of those who had long died. Our sins were forgiven ahead of time, and those who were dead had their forgiveness backtracked if they died believing in God. Jesus' sacrifice for our sins was not like that of goats and other animals. It was a one-time perfect job for all people and for all time.

Hebrews 9: 12 *Neither by the blood of goats and calves,*

*but by his own blood he entered in once into the holy place, having obtained **eternal redemption** for us.* (KJV) Emphasis added.

Hebrews 10: 10 *By the which will we are sanctified through the offering of the body of Jesus Christ **once for all**.* (KJV) Emphasis added.

The word redemption in Hebrews 9 above is translated forgiveness of sins twice in Colossians 1:14 and Ephesians 1:7. That means Jesus' blood afforded us eternal forgiveness of sins, not just forgiveness until one sins again which is where religion is mostly stuck.

Colossians 2: 13 *And you, being dead in your sins and the uncircumcision of your flesh, hath he quickened together with him, **having forgiven you all trespasses;*** (KJV) Emphasis added.

This verse is not saying God is going to forgive all our sins or is continuing to forgive them; it clearly states He has already done it and is through with it. It is a done deal! The verse doesn't define which sins have been forgiven but it says all. That means all past, present and future sins of all people. All we do is believe and receive that completed work. We also know the forgiveness is eternal because Hebrews 9:12 confirms it. When believers begin to question whether they are truly forgiven for good, it leads to all kinds of insecurities, fears, destructive bondages and condemnation. The Bible defines redemption as the forgiveness of our sins in Ephesians 1:7 and Colossians 1:14. It doesn't say we will have forgiveness of sins but that we have it in our possession now! Jesus resurrected and ascended to heaven with His precious blood and applied it in the mercy seat at the eternal and original heavenly temple there for us. That was an eternal transaction which will never be repeated again. By that one application, He wiped out completely all the sins of all those who had died believing in God, and all the sins of all those who would ever believe in Him. Jesus is an eternal being, not a mortal character like the Old Testament priests. That can only mean He did an eternal job of taking away our sins for good, not just covering them temporarily like those Old Testament priests. I don't know why this always eludes religious people. How can God whose mercies endure forever save us temporarily only up to when next we sin?

9. THE NEW CREATION OWNS ALL THINGS

The new creation owns all things.

1 Corinthians 3: 21*Therefore let no man glory in men. For all things are yours; 22Whether Paul, or Apollos, or Cephas, or the world, or life, or death, or things present, or things to come; all are yours;* (KJV)

Again, the fellow who has not renewed his mind may say "All things can't be mine because Look, I can't even properly afford food, clothing or pay my rent. Paul could not have been serious!" That is the burden of a carnal mind. It walks not by faith (God's word) but by sensory perception (what it can see, feel, touch, hear, smell or prove in a laboratory). I particularly find such carnal folks intolerable to live with. I like to be around people of faith. I like the company of People who read the word, dream the word, breathe the word, 'eat' the word, and live the word. I do not even know how the faithless and doubting lot survives. They must have a very rough life here on earth. You see, things work in our lives only when we acknowledge every good thing that is in us in Christ Jesus.

Philemon 1:6 *that the fellowship of your faith may become effective, in the knowledge of every good thing which is in us in Christ.* (New Heart English Bible)

Things only work in our lives when we first know what is in us in Christ, and mix God's word with Faith, not with unbelief. Only then shall we be able to rest. To rest is to bask in the green pastures of Jesus' finished work by taking full advantage of them.

Hebrew 4:2 *For unto us was the gospel preached, as well as unto them: but the word preached did not profit them, not being mixed with faith in them that heard it.* (KJV)

The other tragic mistake most Christians make is to try to interpret God's word by our circumstances. In that case, if what the carnal Christian is experiencing is not what the Bible promises, then he dismisses the Bible as not true and realistic. If the Bible promises healing and divine health but what you have is sickness, then don't disadvantage yourself by claiming that the Bible doesn't work. The truth is that it works always but you may not always know how to work it. The correct procedure should be to inform our circumstances of what the word of God says, not try to fit the word of God into our circumstances. It is our circumstances that should be forced to fit in the word of God. For instance, if you find yourself sick or poor, do not say "that is the way it goes on earth." Don't say, "poverty and sicknesses are inevitable; it is a fallen world." You are supposed to subject your experiences to the obedience of the word of Christ.

Here is the thing: God has already spoken to us through His son, not prophets as He did with the people of the old. He has appointed that son heir of all things.

Hebrews 1:1 *God, who at sundry times and in divers manners spake in time past unto the fathers by the prophets, 2Hath in these last days spoken unto us by his Son, whom he hath appointed heir of all things, by whom also he made the worlds;* (KJV)

We are heirs of God, joint heirs with Christ. Do you know the magnitude of that statement? Christ is saying that you are not an ordinary person but a joint heir with the supreme Monarch of the universe. We are members of His body, of His flesh, and of His bones. That means we can't go anywhere or do anything without Him. He's in us and with us always to guarantee our success in life. This is what Christianity is all about! Christianity is not about us struggling to live for Jesus; but finding out who we are in Him and being exactly that; Jesus-men on earth. Even our speech is supposed to be so seasoned with the word of God that if someone was listening to us but couldn't see us, they would be forgiven for thinking that they were listening to Christ Himself. What is Christ's is ours and what is ours is Christ's. Christ is no longer a far removed and aloof God. He has come down to our level. He did not leave us at that low level however. He elevated us to His own class where we share everything with Him.

Romans 8:17 *And if children, then heirs; heirs of God, and joint-heirs with Christ; if so be that we suffer with him, that we may be also glorified together.* (KJV)

Luke 15:31 *And he said unto him, Son, thou art ever with me, and all that I have is thine.* (KJV)

What a staggering truth! Even in the face of those glaring realities. Some religious folks still say, "but all things will be ours when we get to Heaven. In the earth, we will struggle and suffer. Even Jesus said the poor will always be around"

Religious people have a knack for getting around scriptures to push everything that is good to the sweet by and by. I realize it's a cope out. It's a convenient way of managing failure. They push health, wealth, success, peace and victory to when they get to Heaven. They have no idea that we are really not even going to heaven; it is heaven that is coming to a new earth and God who is coming to make His abode with men. I don't even know where this discussion of going to heaven came from. Some people still think Jesus went on a construction spree and is still making mansions in heaven till now and that it is the reason He hasn't returned yet. Two things quickly: We don't need houses in heaven because we are spirits and spirits don't need housing. Secondly, Jesus is resting, not in a construction mode. Jesus may not have been talking about literal houses but opportunities and chances in the kingdom of God for His people. I personally believe He was talking about preparing our new earth. Earth can never go away. It abides forever and God's eternal plan is for man to reign on earth forever.

Revelation 5:10 *You have made them to be a kingdom and priests to serve our God, and they will reign on the earth."* (KJV)

God did not create the earth to put man there for a moment and then take him to heaven. We don't see that anywhere in the scriptures. What will happen is that this old and corrupted earth will be destroyed with everything in it and in its place installed a brand new one which is the home of the righteous and the location of the New Jerusalem; the eternal capital of God and His saints. This is where groups like the Jehovah's Witnesses get it wrong. They think we will inherit this same old, dirty, tired, punitive, beaten and corrupted earth. Never! Everything which reminds us of sin, satan and the terrible experiences of this pathetic life will be stamped out together with the perverted planet itself.

Revelation 21: 4 *And God shall wipe away all tears from their eyes; and there shall be no more death, neither sorrow, nor crying, neither shall there be any more pain: for the former things are passed away. 5 And he that sat upon the throne said, Behold, I make all things new. And he said unto me, Write: for these words are true and faithful.* (KJV)

Please do not get me wrong. I know the Bible says absent from the body means present with the Lord. It is true that immediately we are out this body, we shift location to where the Lord is but that is only for a while. I am aware that all things are ours, and that includes even heaven but God has given this particular unique planet to man. You cannot show me a single scripture which says Christians will dwell in heaven for ever but I can show you many which put man permanently on earth. Actually, what the Bible promises is heaven and God coming to the earth. Yes it will still be heaven, but the location is earth, not where God is right now.

Revelation 21:1 *Then I saw "a new heaven and a **new earth," for the first heaven and the first earth had passed away**, and there was no longer any sea. 2 I saw the Holy City, the **new Jerusalem, coming down out of heaven from God**, prepared as a bride beautifully dressed for her husband. 3 And I heard a loud voice from the throne saying, **"Look! God's dwelling place is now among the people, and he will dwell with them.** They will be his people, and God himself will be with them and be their God.* (NIV) Emphasis added.

Jesus never promised heaven to anyone and neither did the subsequent apostles. What He spoke about was entering the kingdom of God, not entering heaven. People who promise heaven have no other scripture to quote but this one:

1 Thessalonians 4:17 *Then we which are alive and remain shall be caught up together with them in the clouds, to meet the Lord in the air: and so shall we ever be with the Lord.* (KJV)

This verse doesn't disclose where we will be with the Lord but in Revelation 5:10 and 21:1-3 above, John was not silent about it. Heaven was never our place and if we were to live in heaven for ever, then the devil would have succeeded in thwarting God's plan for humanity. Earth is our eternal home and the Lord is just preparing a new one. The New Jerusalem that will drop from heaven together with the new earth is our eternal capital. Okay, for those who say our eternal destination is heaven, for who then is the new earth and the New Jerusalem which will drop down out of heaven from God designed? Every Christian is going to Revelation 5:10 and chapter 21:1-3. That is the culmination of everything including even the millennial reign. You better start preparing for that eventuality so that you are not shocked. There was even no mention of us going to heaven throughout the Old Testament. Anyway, that is a discussion for some other time but in the meantime, you can refer to the following scriptures and many more like them: Revelation 21:1-3; Ecclesiastes 1:4; Psalm 115:16; Matthew 5:5; Isaiah 45:18; Isaiah 65:17-19.

Back to what we were discussing now and the Bible doesn't say all things will be ours when we get to heaven. That is a done deal here and now! It's a present hour reality. It's not a promise, it's done! We begin enjoying everything here until we get to the other side of eternity physically. How about these sweeping scriptures?

3 John 1:2 *Beloved, I wish above all things that thou mayest prosper and be in health, even as thy soul prospereth.* (KJV)

2 Corinthians 9:8 *And God is able to make all grace abound toward you; that ye, always having all sufficiency in all things, may abound to every good work:* (KJV)

Philippians 4:19 *But my God shall supply all your need according to his riches in glory by Christ Jesus.* (KJV)

Matthew 6: 32(*For after all these things do the Gentiles seek:) for your heavenly Father knoweth that ye have need of all these things. 33But seek ye first the kingdom of God, and his righteousness; and all these things shall be added unto you.* (KJV)

It is out of this realization that David screamed "The Lord is my shepherd, I shall not want." These scriptures are certainly not talking about Heaven. Even if the poor and the sick will always be around, you don't have to be numbered in their statistics. You can trust God to gladly elevate you from poverty and to give you cities you did not develop, houses you did not build, wells you did not dig and olive groves and vineyards you did not plant. In other words, God can give you estates and businesses you did not toil for. It's all part of the Sabbath rest for the children of God. <u>Those who trust God's word completely and without wavering find His word completely true.</u> One thing with God is He will never force you to be prosperous. If you are happy and content being poor, He's a gentleman. He will not disturb your "comfort." He will love you poor. But what a tragedy to forfeit the privilege of material prosperity which you could use to bless the kingdom of God and reap from the benefits for eternity!

You see, there are many people who say they don't want to be wealthy. Some say they are just content with getting by with enough to eat and survive and they think they are being humble. I will say here that <u>godliness with contentment is a great gain, but complacency is evil.</u> Such an attitude of complacency is not humility. It is actually ignorance and selfishness put together. The truth is, you can do effective Christian ministry much more with wealth than with poverty. It takes money to reach unreached groups of people around the world and to run ministries. Still, if you are saying that you don't want a lot of money because you have enough to get only you by, then you are a very selfish individual because you don't care about other needy people who covet your help. But I think such people are usually lying because I am yet to meet anyone who is not interested in more money. Plus, why would anyone wake up early everyday if they didn't want to make a little more? I opine that it's all hypocritical. A lot of our own patriarchs were fabulously wealthy. Talk about Job, Abraham, Isaac, Jacob, David, Solomon and others. You can be surpassingly wealthy and still love God exceedingly as long you don't trust your money. All said, if you don't fancy wealth, Let the Lord give to me all that was due to you and I will be all so happier.

So, when we say the new creation man owns all things, what is included? The universe! The universe means everything everywhere. That includes Heaven itself, the heavens, the earth and all the galaxies. It is everything that we know and don't. Jesus owns it all and we own it with Him. So, next time you see people fighting over petty earthly things like money and estates, don't be party to that. The Lord has already bequeathed everything everywhere to you.

10.   THE NEW CREATION IS INVINCIBLE

As new creation, we are not even aware that we can be successfully sick; we are not aware that danger can come near us, or that any form of evil (other than persecution) can adversely affect us.

Psalm 91: 5 *Thou shalt not be afraid for the terror by night; nor for the arrow that flieth by day; 6 Nor for the pestilence that walketh in darkness; nor for the destruction that wasteth at noonday... 10 There shall no evil befall thee, neither shall any plague come nigh thy dwelling.* (KJV)

A lot of Christians think that stating they weather all the things that affect mere mortals on earth is saying too much. So they shy away from it. They say things like: "the earth is a very cruel place; anybody can contract any disease at any time. Anybody can have an accident happen to them. Death is inevitable. No one can tell what the future holds. Tomorrow belongs to God." These and many more wrong things do religious Christians say thinking it is a mark of humility to reason like that. That is carnal mindedness and it is death. It is carnal because it is based on the philosophies of men and not the Bible. The Bible in the verses above says no accident or terrorist attack can happen to a new creation. Please note I am not saying that sicknesses, dangers, climatic and economic upheavals don't come to believers. They do but we don't face them with fear, powerlessness and hopelessness as the unbelievers. We have the power of the Holy Spirit and tons of guarantees to triumph over everything the devil throws at us. We are supposed to face the adversities of life with such calm, peace, wisdom, power, mastery and triumph that those who are outside God come to find out how we do it. When they respond by saying the same things ordinary, natural men are saying; Christians mean that they are no different from heathens and true to their confession; they get the same results as those who have no hope and no God. Some Christians think that what the non-believers are afraid of, it is okay for them to be scared of as well. They think it is in order to respond to adversities like the heathen. If that is so, then what is the difference between the two and what is the purpose of our faith? Is it for taking us to the other side of eternity only? Christians who believe the word come out of all these misfortunes just fine. The problem is, there are a lot of them who don't believe the Bible and those ones suffer big time.

Psalm 91: 7 *A thousand shall fall at thy side, and ten thousand at thy right hand; but it shall not come nigh thee. 8 Only with thine eyes shalt thou behold and see the reward of the wicked. 9 Because thou hast made the LORD, which is my refuge, even the most High, thy habitation;* (KJV)

This Psalm 91 can make a very bold Christian! See what it is saying here? That though thousands may be dying all around you, that danger shall not touch you. Only with your eyes shall you witness those who don't believe in God's word having it very hard. You may be in the same hard economy as other people; you may be in the same insecure place as other people; you may be in the same plane that crashes or the vehicle that is involved in an accident: you may be in the same terrible situation that everybody else is in, but you are different if you are in Christ. You can't suffer like the unbelievers. As the rest of unbelieving Israel was being ravaged by a severe drought, Elijah was enjoying himself at the brook Cherith, relishing fresh bread from heaven delivered by birds. If that happened in the Old Testament, what do you think God has prepared for us in the New Testament? Even with our Old Testament patriarchs, many of them defied the prevailing circumstances of their time and thrived against all odds. While a terrible famine mercilessly ravaged his homeland, Abraham prospered in the foreign land of Egypt.

Genesis 13: 2 *And Abram was very rich in cattle, in silver, and in gold.* (KJV)

Remember, this is the same Abraham who is the father of us all who believe and with whom we are blessed. We are not only spared from desperate times, we also thrive in spite of them. After Abraham came his natural son Isaac. Again, there was such a disastrous famine in the land that he thought of going to Egypt where his father had once visited in lean times in the past. Isaac moved to Gerar from where God told him not to venture further to Egypt. I know why God gave him that seemingly weird instruction. You see, many of us are like Isaac. We think the place we are in determines whether or not we prosper. So, many people flock into the so-called lands of opportunities. God dissuaded Isaac from going to Egypt where there was plenty because He wanted him to know that it was not about where he was but who he was with. It was far better to be with God in that foreign land where he lived as an alien and possessed nothing, than to be in productive Egypt without

Him. There is a great lesson there for us: that what counts is not where we are and how many opportunities exist in the locality. What matters is who is with us or in us. With God, we don't go looking for opportunities. Rather, we are the opportunity the creation has been waiting for. We are the creators of whatever opportunity is required at any given place and at any time. We are the light of the world and salt of the earth. Part of what that means is that we carry the solutions the world so desperately needs. We should not be moving from place to place like the pagans looking for opportunities. <u>The new creation is a mobile solution and opportunity station.</u> We should provide practical solutions to every pressing problem where we are because we have the anointing and we know all things. We should be able to do all things through Christ who infuses us with strength. So, Isaac stayed in the foreign land of Abimelech, sowed and reaped a hundredfold. He became so successful in that foreign land that king Abimelech asked him to depart from his country because he was mightier than the whole nation-Genesis 26:16. Is that a blessing or what? Later, a grandson of Isaac called Joseph would be sold to the same foreign land of Egypt. One would think it would be the end of life for a young boy who is sold as a slave (completely without rights and possessions) who faces the double tragedy of being thrown into jail. The Bible records that even in jail which is a place of complete desperation, the lad was successful because "the Lord was with him"- Genesis 39:2. Again, I repeat here that prosperity has nothing to do with your location and the prevailing circumstances there. It has everything to do with who is with you. Against all odds, Young Joseph rose through the rungs to become the number two most powerful individual on the planet back then. He also fed the whole world and saved the nation of Israel from complete annihilation in a time of a devastating famine.

      One politician in the U.S.A said, "It's the economy, stupid" Although that may be what is happening in the physical world, the economy need not be stupid where you are concerned. You are supplied from Heaven according to God's riches in glory. God has infinite ways of supplying for His own. Sometimes, the surrounding circumstances may actually affect the believer. His business may go down or he may be affected in any other way just because he is in the same fallen and misbehaving environment. However, God has a standing guarantee to see to it that the believer doesn't suffer. He can employ literally infinite ways to get the supplies to the believer. He can send birds, animals, wind, people and even angels. The problem is, so many Christians are so carnal that they have no capacity to expect any supernatural intervention of heaven on earth. They are so focused on their meager resources and unreliable means of livelihood that their hearts are shut to the Lord. They cannot imagine that the Lord is their source. All they see is their unstable jobs and businesses. The Christian need not be bothered about how things seem to be taking a turn for the worst. He is rooted firmly in the unshakable ground of Jesus where nothing goes wrong and even if it attempted to, then we have the means to force it to line up with God's word.

Isaiah 43:2 *When thou passest through the waters, I will be with thee; and through the rivers, they shall not overflow thee: when thou walkest through the fire, thou shalt not be burned; neither shall the flame kindle upon thee.* (KJV)

The Lord is repeatedly stating here and in other places that His elect people are different from the rest of the pack. They give in to no obstacles and to no dangers. They cut through mighty waters and raging infernos and come out victoriously because they dwell in the secret place of the Most High. The Israelites were the elect of God in the Old Testament. One time they needed to cut through the formidable obstacle that is the Red Sea. Moses simply directed the waters on what to do with his staff. The Egyptians tried to cross as well but they were all swept away together with their contraptions of war. The same seabed the Israelites had walked through dry a few minutes earlier proved to be a deadly trap minutes later for the unbelieving Egyptians. The same deluge that buoyed Noah and his family and hoisted him up out of danger is also the one that killed all the wicked people of his time. Noah survived because he was in the secret place of the Most High called the ark which was an Old Testament shadow of Christ, in who we are.

Shadrack, Meshack and Abednego were thrust into a furious inferno that had been superheated seven times more than ordinary. Their tormentors were surprised to see the men enjoying themselves in fellowship with Jesus. When they came out, they didn't even reek of smoke. The same fire that did not even singe them had earlier on licked up those who threw them in. Daniel was also thrown into a den of hungry lions and the beasts could not touch him. That is counterintuitive! When He came out the following day and the same favor was returned to his accusers and in that same den, only fragments of their bones reached the ground. Can't you tell there is a massive difference in outcomes between those who believe in God and those who don't? The Bible tells us all these Old Testament actors managed all these supernatural feats because of the force of faith in their lives. It was their faith in God that enabled them to stand out and get completely different results from what everybody in the same environment and under the same circumstances was getting. It boils down to whether you believe the word or you are just a superficial religious fellow and therefore a hypocrite.

Hebrews 11: 32 *And what shall I more say? for the time would fail me to tell of Gideon, and of Barak, and of Samson, and of Jephthae; of David also, and Samuel, and of the prophets: 33 Who through faith subdued kingdoms, wrought righteousness, obtained promises, stopped the mouths of lions. 34 Quenched the violence of fire, escaped the edge of the sword, out of weakness were made strong, waxed valiant in fight, turned to flight the armies of the aliens. 35 Women received their dead raised to life again: and others were tortured, not accepting deliverance; that they might obtain a better resurrection:* (KJV)

Do you really believe the word of God or are you like the religious types who don't think God really meant exactly what He says? I pray that you become a rabid believer of God's word. I pray that you become so fanatical and possessed by the word that it's all you will be meditating. I pray that you will become one with the word. I pray that you will only think the word, believe the word, talk the word, live the word and apply the word. I pray that you will become the word of God walking on two feet. I pray that you will be an embodiment of the word or the word personified. Say amen!

11. THE NEW CREATION HAS ACCESS TO ALL AUTHORITY ON EARTH.

This is one of my favorite chapters in this work. It is because the thing that really sets apart the new creation is the authority he has in the name of Jesus Christ. With this authority, he can do all things. The new creation has access to all authority on earth in Christ Jesus. We get this from Matthew 28:18-19:

Then Jesus came to them and said, "All authority in heaven and on earth has been given to me. 19 Therefore go and make disciples of all nations, baptizing them in the name of the Father and of the Son and of the Holy Spirit. (NIV)

As immediately as Jesus finished stating that all authority is already given to Him in Heaven and in earth, He gave us access to the same in the following verse.

That is the implication of the phrase "Go ye therefore" in the beginning of verse 19. You see, if all authority is given unto Jesus (as son of man not as son of God because as son of God, He did not need anybody to give Him any authority. He possessed it all already) and we are joint-heirs of God with Him, then it follows naturally that His authority is available to us as well. Some people say we, just like Jesus, have authority in heaven and earth. I don't know about us having authority in heaven and I think it is highly debatable. This is what I believe; we really don't need to exercise any authority in heaven because that place is perfectly governed. Earth is where the trouble is and where the exercise of our authority is required now. Let's reign on earth first before we can think of exercising authority elsewhere. There is no power vacuum in heaven but on earth. Heaven is well covered and perfectly ruled. Earth is where problems are and that is where we must occupy till our Lord Jesus comes. I also need to clarify another very important point: a lot of people say the authority is ours. There are many teachings on the "believers' authority." Technically, the believer has no own authority per se. It is Jesus' authority but the believer has an unlimited access to all of it. If the believer had authority, he would not need to use the name of Jesus. We use the name of Jesus to exercise his authority. That is why we don't go around saying; "demon come out by my authority." The authority is in the name of Jesus, not in our name. Demons only obey the name in which all authority is vested. That is why those sons of Sceva found themselves in trouble. They were trying to exercise an authority they did know where it lay. When you understand this concept of authority properly, your life will change before your very own eyes. You will cease to use the name of Jesus at the end of prayer as a religious appendage. You will begin to reign on earth in that name; commanding every circumstance you encounter to line up with God's word and nothing shall by any means resist you. By saying 'in Jesus' name,' we are saying that by the authority vested in the name of Jesus, we command the situation as if we were Jesus Himself. In other words, we are acting in the place or in the stead of Jesus. Jesus is no longer here bodily. We are His body; His hands, His feet and His mouth piece. When we speak, we are not representing ourselves; we are speaking on behalf of Jesus. That is why just like there is no devil that resisted Jesus; none can resist us as well. Jesus said that he send us just as the Father had send Him. How did the father send Him? Well, it is clear in the following passages.

John 5: 19 *Then answered Jesus and said unto them, Verily, verily, I say unto you, The Son can do nothing of himself, but what he seeth the Father do: for what things soever he doeth, these also doeth the Son likewise. 20 For the Father loveth the Son, and sheweth him all things that himself doeth: and he will shew him greater works than these, that ye may marvel.* (KJV)

John 8: 26 *"I have much to say in judgment of you. But he who sent me is trustworthy, and what I have heard from him I tell the world."... 28 So Jesus said, "When you have lifted up[a] the Son of Man, then you will know that I am he and that I do nothing on my own but speak just what the Father has taught me.* (NIV)

The Father sent Jesus by giving Him ability to do the same things He was doing and showing or revealing to Him what He (the Father) was doing. Likewise, Jesus has given us His own authority and explained to us openly what to do. He has also given us His Holy Spirit to lead us in all things and to order our steps. Jesus said He doesn't call us servants but friends because he has revealed to us all things. Now, it is very interesting the way we exercise Jesus' authority. I say this because most believers know there is some authority to be exercised but they don't quite know how to go about it. Many of those who try to exercise authority do it ignorantly. We need to be acquainted with a few critical guidelines on exercising Jesus' authority on earth. The first one is that to exercise authority is to enforce God's word or law on earth just like a policeman enforces the law of the land. In short, we are the enforcers of the will of God on earth. That is why Jesus trained His disciples to pray that the will of God happens on earth as it does in heaven. We can't pray like that now. We make it happen with the authority we have in the name of Jesus. We are God's policemen who ensure His laws are abided by throughout the face of the earth. Let me explain that with an example: all evil on earth comes from satan and his fallen sidekicks working through men who submit to them. Jesus was manifested to destroy the works of the devil. When He was here bodily, He healed all diseases, dealt with poverty, raised the dead, confronted darkness and prevailed over misbehaving weather. All those were actions of destroying the works of the devil. Jesus is no longer here in His physical person. According to the law of God, He cannot exercise power here without His physical body. His only physical body here is the body of believers also known as the body of Christ. That means the only way for Christ to continue destroying the operations of the enemy is for His body to exercise authority in His name to paralyze the devil. That is how we come into the picture. This power is not available to just a few 'super' believers who know a lot of theology or have been to seminary. It is available to every single believer including the one who was born again a few seconds ago. Jesus said in Mark 16:17-18 that demonstration of the power of God shall follow all who believe. The only qualification for one to exercise Jesus' authority is to believe in Him and apply God's power in His name. Many Christians think that those who demonstrate God's power most are those who live right, pray and fast more, those who have been born again for long, have read through the Bible many times, have been to seminary or even are special. Nothing could be further from the truth. As many as are in Christ and have revelation of and faith in their authority in the name of Jesus, they are ready to destroy every work of the devil they encounter. For example, sickness is not God's will ever. There is no sickness in heaven and God doesn't expect any sickness on earth. That is why Jesus destroyed every sickness He encountered in the people He ministered to. Sickness is one of the evil works He came to destroy. Now that we are the ones who function in the place of Christ, God now expects us to banish sickness completely from our spheres of influence. That way, we will have obeyed the call to make happen on earth God's will as it happens in heaven. Jesus didn't intent for that 'our Lord's prayer' to be chanted mindlessly as a religious ritual. He wants it actualized in the lives of His sons and in the earth where they live now. We cannot still be praying for God's kingdom to come and for His will to be done on earth as it is in heaven. We enforce that will here in the name of Jesus. When we do so, we then bring the kingdom of God to bear in such a situation as we impose God's power on. Jesus said:

Matthew 12:28 *But if I cast out devils by the Spirit of God, then the kingdom of God is come unto you.* (KJV)

Luke 10:9 *Heal the sick in that town and say to them, 'The kingdom of God has come upon you!'* (NET Bible)

For us, we can say that if we heal the sick and cast out demons by the name of Jesus and in the power of the Holy Spirit, then we have brought the kingdom of God unto His people. The so-called Lord's Prayer was not meant to be recited as a religious magic wand.

We are supposed to take our authority and actualize it. Religion has so badly muddied the waters of faith that most Christians have been reduced to powerless complainers instead of being a mighty and an overcoming force.

The next question to deal with would be how much of Jesus' authority we have. The answer is absolute or unlimited as long as we operate within the limits of the word of God. We cannot exercise authority without being governed by the word. We must operate within the confines of the word of God. For example, I have heard some people who called themselves men of God try to throw their weight around and try to curse people they didn't think treated them well. There is nowhere in the word we are given authority to curse people. Instead, we are instructed to bless only and never curse. <u>We have been liberated from the curse of the law, from being cursed, from the curse of Adam and from cursing others.</u> Whenever you overstep the boundaries of the word of God in exercising authority, you cancel your right and ability to exercise it. A police officer exercises authority only as stipulated by the law of that land. He cannot exercise extrajudicial authority because that again becomes a chargeable offense. You cannot just take it upon yourself to enforce your own religious dogmas that have no basis in the word. Your authority ends where the word ends. All this means one thing; you cannot exercise Jesus' authority if you don't know God's word or if you are Old Testament minded. A police officer cannot exercise authority if he doesn't know the law. How will he even know whether or not the law has been transgressed? Police officers are supposed to be informed people as far as the constitution is concerned. In fact, some prosecutors are drawn from police ranks. Then, you must have both faith and boldness to enforce God's will on earth. There is no place for timidity if we will be effective sons of God. Can you imagine a police officer who is unsure of his authority and is trying to stop speeding cars but because he is not established in knowledge of his authority, he does it anxiously because he thinks some cars may knock him down! Experienced police officers are so sure of their authority when they have their uniform on that sometimes they just stretch their hands to halt oncoming traffic without even looking at that direction. They know every qualified driver knows the whole country is behind that uniformed officer. Likewise, every 'qualified' devil in hell recognizes the uniform of Christ on us. Remember we are clothed with Christ. Christ lives in us and it is in His stead we operate. No demon can resist that. We were not even called to interview demons the way I see many people doing. Some people are spending dozens of minutes or even sometimes hours carrying out strange conversations with demons! That in itself is demonic. First, where do you even get that time? Secondly, since when did demons start telling the truth? If you ask a demon a question, you know you will be lied to because the devil has no capacity to tell the truth. Even if the devil was to make a blunder one day and tell the truth, it would have to be taken as a lie. Our duty is very easy. If you find a demon, just order him out with a simple command in the name of Jesus.

Also, now that Christ is ascended to heaven, the new creation is now the minister of reconciliation on earth. We have the authority to reconcile men unto God. We are 'saviors' together with Jesus.

Obadiah 1: 21 *And saviours shall come up on mount Zion to judge the mount of Esau; and the kingdom shall be the LORD's.* (KJV)

Don't get me wrong, I don't mean we are saviors in the sense of dying for sinners. There was only one of those-Jesus Christ. What we have been committed is the responsibility of reconciliation and whoever does not heed our word from Christ is condemned. When we as the body of Christ speak His word, it's just as authoritative as if Christ Himself said it.

Ephesians 1:22 *And hath put all things under his feet, and gave him to be the head over all things to the church,* (KJV)

John 3:35 *The Father loveth the Son, and hath given all things into his hand.* (KJV)

(i) GOD IS SOVEREIGN BUT NOT IN CONTROL IN THE EARTH; WE ARE.

God sent Jesus by giving Him as son of man, complete authority to make decisions based on what He saw His Father doing. He also did it by giving all things into His hand. That is the same way Jesus sends us. With that in mind, you can appreciate scriptures like these:

Mathew 16:19 *And I will give unto thee the keys of the kingdom of heaven: and whatsoever thou shalt bind on earth shall be bound in heaven: and whatsoever thou shalt loose on earth shall be loosed in heaven.* (KJV)

Notice Jesus doesn't say that what is passed in Heaven men must pass on earth. He is saying He has so much faith in the new creation that he trusts the decisions they make because genuine new creation people will always make decisions guided by the word of God and the Holy Spirit. That is why heaven sanctions them. Wow! Of course, these must be mature, Spirit –filled and Spirit-led men. God is not aware that they will make mistakes. So, you see, it is not enough to have faith in God; it pays as well to know that God has faith in you because His Spirit is at work in you. The only hope God has of carrying out His will on earth is through the body of His son, the church. God cannot now just come to sidestep the church and start doing things on His own. He works through His sons. His power works in them.

That shatters to oblivion this nasty and tragic doctrine of religious people that "God is sovereign." By "sovereign," they mean that God controls everything in the earth and that nothing happens that He doesn't either do directly or sanction. That misguided thinking is manifested in a lot of the statements that people make. They say things like: "God is in control; nothing can happen if God does not allow it; satan is like a dog on God's leash; satan is God's errand boy. If it has happened, it must be God's will. God has allowed it to happen because it serves some divine purpose that only He knows." Even if most people don't use those exact words, what they say amounts to the same message these statements are conveying. The message is that God controls everything that happens on earth. That He either causes everything directly or allows satan to do it-both the good and the bad. That is just about the most terrible and inaccurate statement in the history of Christianity. Ignorantly, what they mean is that God either directly causes or sanctions all the diseases, all the violent and deadly weather, all the wicked things people do, all the wars, all the wicked governments in the world, all the prejudices, all the greed and its manifestations, and, all the sorrows that happen on earth. That is the implication of saying that God is totally in control.

God is sovereign but sovereignty doesn't mean to control and manipulate like one would do a marionette. Whether they like it or not, that is most peoples' description of the 'sovereignty of God' and it is a page straight from the religious man's concordance of vain imaginations. Sovereign means supreme ruler or monarch. It means possessing supreme or ultimate power. That is the dictionary definition of the adjective sovereign. Notice it doesn't say sovereign means supreme controller or ultimate manipulator. God is the supreme ruler of the universe. He wields absolute power. He's comfortably perched on the top of the food chain. He eternally dominates the pecking order. He has no rivals, no threats to His position and no competition. That is sovereign. The thing I object to is when people say God determines every single thing that happens everywhere – good or bad. That is a fallacy. The religious definition and idea of the sovereignty of God is that nothing happens on earth without God doing it Himself, originating it or allowing satan to do it. That position is wrong on so many levels. Many of our nations are sovereign in the sense that they are self-governing and no one from outside comes to tell them what to do. However, their sovereignty doesn't mean they control their people or everything that happens in those countries. What they have are laws to govern life and outline the aspirations and will of the government. After that, it is up to the citizens to decide whether or not to follow those rules. The people have freedom to make personal choices as long as they are above eighteen years of age. Those choices may have consequences but they are free to make them anyway. It would be very wrong to say that everything that happens inside those sovereign countries is initiated, committed directly or sanctioned by the state. People in there break the laws every day and that is why jails exist.

It is the same thing with God. He is sovereign. No one tells Him what to do. He doesn't even take counsel from anyone because He is the ultimate custodian of all knowledge and wisdom. But, like our governments, God doesn't control us. Like any good government, He has given us the power of self-determination. He only advises that as we determine our destiny, He has placed before us life and death and has urged us to choose the path of life. That alone means we choose what to do and what not to do on earth. That makes us responsible for what happens on earth. When He advises us not to lean on our own understanding but to trust in Him, it means we can choose either to or not to rely on Him. Whatever we choose, we, not God, will have controlled what takes place here. As such, we can't place that responsibility on God or else we would be insinuating that God is manipulating us from behind the scenes, which is a dangerous assertion again. In that case, we can't say God controls us or what happens here. We control ourselves based on who we choose to listen to-God or satan. <u>Out of love and generosity, God has given us limited sovereignty over the earth.</u> We determine what goes on here. I say limited because He expects us to run this planet according to His counsel, not our own. We have limited sovereignty in the sense that ultimately, what happens on earth depends on us, not God, although He expects us to run the planet according to His dictates. If we choose to listen to Him and do His will, heaven shapes the earth. We also have freedom to choose against His will as we often do and in such cases, heaven loses and hell determines what passes here. So, our sovereignty doesn't mean independence. In fact, <u>God doesn't want our independence because we are not omniscient and self-sustaining like Him. He wants cooperation. He wants ruler-ship through fellowship with Him.</u> He wants us to reign on earth in an arrangement of moment to moment relationship with Him. He will not act on earth independent of us, and we can't act properly independent of Him. We need Him like the air we breathe, and He wants our submission to Him. For people who take sovereignty of God to mean that God controls and determines everything and everybody on earth, one of the texts they latch onto to develop that twisted doctrine is the book of Job. They assume satan still has access to the presence of God where they can have a conversation and God allows that wicked fellow to come and attack His children. He no longer has such chance in the post Jesus era. In Job's time, Satan could come before God because Adam gave up his place of authority on earth and of fellowship with God but that completely changed after the last Adam (Jesus) came. After Jesus ascended to heaven, He sprinkled His blood and cleansed the things of heaven-Hebrews 9:22–24. His blood even cleansed and redeemed the unclean place where Satan walked and stood before God. As a result, there remains no place in heaven for Satan. He cannot come before God anymore because Jesus who whipped him badly in hell is seated there and we are in Him. No one can now accuse us before God because it is that same God who even after knowing all our shortcomings, He still justifies us perfectly because we are in Christ.

Romans 8: 33 *Who shall lay anything to the charge of God's elect? It is God that justifieth. 34 Who is he that condemneth? It is Christ that died, yea rather, that is risen again, who is even at the right hand of God, who also maketh intercession for us.* (KJV)

Job is not a New Testament person and he certainly was not a new creation. He was ignorant of God, of satan and of the scriptures and of the ways of the kingdom of God. Remember Job lived before Moses and before any part of the Bible was written. In fact, Job was most probably the first book of the Bible to be written. That is why you see him blaming God for his calamities. The thing that I cannot understand is why New Testament people who should know far better still sing that stupid piece of "God gave and God has taken away." Can you imagine New Testament people who have the full revelation of the activities behind the scenes which caused Job his misfortunes teaming up with Job to blame God for supposedly taking away anything? How foolish and how sad? This tragic lie that is perpetrated in religious Christianity of attributing to God what is obviously the work of the devil is a trap that has destroyed the lives of countless people. The sleekest and most devastating scheme of the devil is to get religious people mistake his dastardly operations for God's. If he succeeds in doing that as he has in large part, then they will not resist his dirty works for fear that they are resisting the will of God because they think He is teaching them something or working out some good cause. The other scripture people use to justify putting up with all the garbage from the devil is Romans 8:28. *And we know that all things work together for good to them that love God, to them who are the called according to his purpose.* (KJV)

A lot of Christians mistake that verse to be saying that God causes all things (including the bad and the ugly) to happen and then works to cause good to come out of it. Nothing could be more erroneous. That scripture is simply saying that if it happens that you find yourself in the devil's trap either for fault of your own or because the enemy got you, God will take the situation and turn it around and bring something glorious come out of it. And God will not just take any situation and turn it around for good. The previous verse says the person should be praying in tongues and groaning in the spirit so that the Holy Ghost takes up the matter and helps the person pray. That is the meaning of the conjunction 'and' in the beginning of verse 28. It doesn't mean God is the author of that evil. Because most people are just religious and are not tuned to the Spirit, praying and groaning in Him, that is part of the reason why they suffer for long and never quite see their circumstances turning around and panning out. God is holy and righteous and has no evil to mete out on His children. This satanic doctrine of religion which attributes disease, death, destructive weather and other terrible things to God is responsible for turning away many people from God. Most logical people don't want anything to do with an unreliable God who can put disease, poverty or other types of sufferings in a person just to teach them some lesson.

(ii) MEN ALLOW BAD THINGS IN THE EARTH, NOT GOD

When a preacher says at a funeral, "we all loved this child, mother, father, sibling, grandmother, friend, or whoever else; but God loved them more." What such a person really means is that God caused or allowed the death through whatever means and for whatever reasons. The danger with that common lie from the pit of hell is that it leads a Christian to believe that one day, everything could be going well and all of a sudden God either causes or allows suffering for reasons above our comprehension. Consider this, if you had a relative who contracted a terminal illness and suffered for years before they took a final bow, thinking God was in control, you may hate God or at the very least, not be intimate with Him any longer. If God is controlling your life and your life is in a mess, then who's to blame? God does not control anybody's life. Each person controls their own life. That is why God has equipped us with everything we will ever need for life and godliness in order for us to shape our own lives. That is why He has given us His word, His Holy Spirit, His authority, the tongue and the earth to rule. God is sovereign but He does not rule in the earth. You just need to go to heaven where He reigns supreme and you will very quickly learn that there is no single trace of evil there. God gave this property to the sons of men-Psalm 115:16. Because men are not using their authority to resist the devil but instead are cooperating with him, the earth finds itself in such a mess. Only a deluded person would assert that God is in control on earth. It goes without saying God wants to control the earth but not directly. He wants to do it by possessing and influencing men through whom He can have His will done on earth as it is in heaven. God is spirit and He gave the earth to human beings with bodies to rule it. God in His spirit form is illegal to carry out anything on earth. That is why He had to have a body to operate here and Christ afforded Him that legal way. After Jesus came and took the authority from satan which he had craftily usurped from Adam, He handed it back to men, went back to heaven and the only body He has to operate on earth through is the body of Christ, the church. satan himself is also illegal on earth and he too wants to possess and influence men to have his will done on earth through them. <u>Both God and satan want their wills carried out on earth but for totally different ends.</u> Religious people don't understand this and the devil would be happy to keep it that way because he likes it when men wait for God to come and do what He equipped and instructed them to do. With diminished opposition like that, he can even reward himself with a long holiday and he will still come back to find them "waiting on God." <u>Satan doesn't get his permission to oppress men from God. He gets it from the men themselves who either fail to exercise their authority or those who allow him to operate in their lives.</u> Men are the rightful wielders of authority to run the earth. If anything bad happens in your life, it's because you allowed it by not using your God given authority. We have been instructed not to give any place to the devil. It is not for God to do that. It is upon us.

Ephesians 4:27 *and do not give the devil a foothold.* (KJV)

1 Peter 5: 8 *Be sober, be vigilant; because your adversary the devil, as a roaring lion, walketh about, seeking whom he may devour: 9 Whom resist steadfast in the faith, knowing that the same afflictions are accomplished in your brethren that are in the world.* (KJV)

You can see here that afflictions come from the devil and he is doing it all over the world, not just to us. If you don't resist the roaming enemy, he will be all too happy to devour you with sickness, poverty, depression, stress, defeat and a whole range of the weapons he will throw at you. Christians are giving a foothold to the devil and blaming God for it! This is crazy! Heaping the blame of our afflictions on God is not resisting the devil but cooperating with and embracing him. The Bible is very clear that afflictions and attacks don't come from God but from the enemy and they are designed to steal the word.

Mark 4:17 *And have no root in themselves, and so endure but for a time: afterward, when affliction or persecution ariseth for the word's sake, immediately they are offended.* (KJV)

Did you read that? A lot of Christians argue that afflictions and tribulations come to strengthen us or to build patience in us. That is wrong. Patience is a ready fruit or nature we are born again with, not a virtue developed in the school of hard knocks. In fact, what usually tends to happen is that instead of developing patience as religion advances, some afflictions and tribulations make some Christians depart from faith. Now, don't get me wrong, I understand that although we are born full of patience, we must make it work by subjecting it to life's situations and it is possible to grow strong by its usage and practice. Part of the problem in understanding patience, how it is developed and how it works is in misinterpretation of the virtue itself. Most people take patience to mean putting up with suffering silently. That is not it. We are not called to endure suffering, especially one that doesn't come from persecution. Patience is simply prolonged faith. It is making our faith last through difficulties to the point where we ultimately see the breakthrough. Patience is consistency or staying on course and strong in faith through it all. Patience is not how long you can wait through a tough time but how well you handle yourself by keeping your faith strong while waiting. Although every Christian has the faith of Jesus, a lot of people don't let their faith last through life's tests. They let it snap too quickly. They let their faith do only a short burst then fizzle out instead of having it last through the whole period until they come out strong and successful. Patience is letting your faith do a marathon, not a short sprint. When Peter walked on water, he let his faith do only a short sprint and then he began sinking. If only he had let it run a marathon, he would have walked all the way to where Jesus was without trouble. That is what most people do. When trouble comes up as it will certainly do, they begin by exercising their faith. At the starting, their faith is usually strong. As time goes by, they begin listening to the voice of the enemy who whispers to them all manner of things. He may tell them that God is not hearing their prayers. He may accuse and condemn them in their hearts. He may fill them with guilt and sin-consciousness. He may tell them they don't deserve what they are asking for. He may lie to them that the problem they have is a punishment from God and that it is His will. He may tell them that the problem is of their own making and hence God won't help. He may tell them that if God was interested in answering them, He would have done it long time ago and that their wait is futile. He may tell them that what they are trying to bring to pass only happens to other people but not to them. One of the commonest lies he spreads is to tell people they are not good enough to receive what they expect or to last through the period. In the face of this barrage of onslaughts, some people cave in and lose the good fight of faith. <u>They are full of patience in their new spirits but their soul refuses to make use of it.</u> But we have veteran faith fighters who never give in until they receive their breakthrough and pull through no matter what. They don't pay attention to the enemy. They are like an experienced tree-cutter who persistently works with his axe to bring down a massive tree. When you find the fellow starting, if you are ignorant, you will think he will never bring down that giant tree with his seemingly small blows. But the worker who has been doing it for a while is not perturbed. He continues to work on the massive stem for days on end. With every small blow, he weakens the tree further. Eventually, the mighty tree is brought down by the last blow. The fellow knows all too well it is not that last strike which fell the tree but the accumulation of all those blows for days. Jesus had a similar experience with a blind man one time.

Mark 8: 24 *And he looked up, and said, I see men as trees, walking. 25 After that he put his hands again upon his eyes, and made him look up: and he was restored, and saw every man clearly.* (KJV)

Such is our faith. When facing a situation, we need to keep at it with prayer, meditation on the word and fellowship with the Holy Spirit until we see our desires met. With the kind of enemy we have, the old adage proves true in our encounters with him; "persistence wears out resistance." Persistent speaking with new tongues is usually the only way to go about it because then, the spirit who knows everything is the one praying and he knows where the problem is. As such, he prays perfectly. But if you insist on praying with your limited known language, I guarantee you will pray wrong prayers of unbelief and ignorance because your mind is the one praying and it is severely limited in knowledge. For example, if your finances are out of whack, it could be due to a huge number of factors. If you find yourself unable to put a finger on what is ailing you, it is only the Holy Spirit (who is one spirit with your spirit) who will know exactly what is happening behind the scenes. As such, it is futile to pray with your understanding because it is already disadvantaged and unfruitful. Only the spirit knows what is happening and what needs to be prayed precisely. That is an unassailable formula for breakthrough. Never forget that <u>patience is refusing to succumb to the bullying of physical circumstances but staying strong in faith in trying times.</u>

Romans 4: 19 *And being not weak in faith, he considered not his own body now dead, when he was about an hundred years old, neither yet the deadness of Sarah's womb: 20 He staggered not at the promise of God through unbelief; but was strong in faith, giving glory to God;* (KJV)

Now turning again to Job, the man had no authority over the devil and he was also in the dark about the will of God. Not only so, he was fearful, he was not at rest in God and he was sin-conscious.

Job 1: 5 *And it was so, when the days of their feasting were gone about, that Job sent and sanctified them, and rose up early in the morning, and offered burnt offerings according to the number of them all: for Job said,* **It may be that my sons have sinned, and cursed God in their hearts. Thus did Job continually.** (KJV) Emphasis added.

Job 3: 25 *For the thing which I greatly feared is come upon me, and that which I was afraid of is come unto me. 26 I was not in safety, neither had I rest, neither was I quiet; yet trouble came.* (KJV)

You need to understand several things here. One, satan is not God's errand boy whom He employs to carry out dirty business. Satan is not like a dog in God's leash released to do God's bidding. God doesn't have a shortage of holy angels to send to minister to His children. Plus, the Holy Spirit is the only teacher Jesus promised, never satan. For God to send satan to carry out evil would mean He is responsible for that evil. There would be no difference between

Him allowing satan to do it or carrying it out Himself. Jesus revealed to us the heart of God. He said He came to give life abundant but the devil is out to steal, kill and destroy. There is nowhere in the Bible where Jesus took anything from anyone, except with the intention to multiply it and bless the owner. Jesus never put disease on anyone. If anything, He healed all who came to Him oppressed by the devil, not God. As John Alexander Dowie put it; "sickness is the foul offspring of its mother sin, and its father the devil." Jesus never killed anyone but only raised the dead. Even when He asked for water to drink from the Samaritan woman, He blessed her in turn with springs of living water. Jesus never issued any instruction to anyone for His sole benefit but only to bless those He addressed. He didn't come to be served but to serve men and even offer for them His very life. On the other hand, the devil has never given anything to anyone if not diseases, lies and death. He has no capacity to give anything but to take only. He only steals, kills, destroys and makes away with. <u>Religion is insinuating that God also steals, kills and destroys or allows the devil to do it.</u> If that was the case, what would be the point of alerting us to resist the devil and equipping us to do so? God is light and in Him is no darkness. The rampant and unfortunate belief that God allows satan to test our faith or teach us some lessons is one reason many believers in Christ have departed from the faith, resent God or have no faith in Him to protect them. Even where Job the Old Testament fellow is concerned, God did not allow satan into his poor life. Job let in satan by his own fears, restlessness and sin-consciousness. Satan didn't even need to ask for permission from God. He had the authority to operate on earth which he received from Adam. He was not coming to heaven to ask for permission but actually wanted God to be the one to afflict Job. Satan was actually tempting God to attack Job, just like he would tempt Jesus later. If it is true God was responsible for allowing satan to attack His children for whatever reason religion gives, then satan would not be doing evil and God would not judge him because he would have permission from God. Also, if satan took his permission from God to tempt, test and attack people, God would not judge all those who fall for the enemy's temptations, tests and other attacks because He would have carried them out, initiated them or allowed them. In that case, the devil would'nt be sinning by doing the dirty things he does but we know he is busy on earth carrying out his wicked will and opposing God and His people. God cannot give the devil permission and power to oppose Him and to attack, kill and destroy His children. In fact, even to entertain the thought of God permitting satan to do dirty things on His behalf is very wicked. Only an absolutely deluded person can entertain that. The crooked fellow is on his own mission. Ultimately, if you believe God has allowed the devil to carry out his dirty operations in your life, why would He again charge us to resist him and not give him a foothold? And why would you strive to get out of what the devil is doing because in overall, it would be God's will for you to go through it? People who subscribe to this twisted viewpoint occur to me as very dishonest and hypocritical. God does not control everything that happens on earth. People who advance that position defend their argument with scriptures like these ones:

Isaiah 45:7 *I form the light, and create darkness: I make peace, and create evil: I the LORD do all these things.* (KJV)

1 Samuel 19: 9 *And the evil spirit from the LORD was upon Saul, as he sat in his house with his javelin in his hand: and David played with his hand.* (KJV)

Psalm 78:49 *He cast upon them the fierceness of his anger, wrath, and indignation, and trouble, by sending evil angels among them.* (KJV)

When religious people read scriptures like those, without any further thought, they immediately rush to conclude that God is responsible for releasing or allowing wickedness into the universe. None of these verses means that God is responsible for bad things. By God saying He creates evil, He doesn't mean He is responsible for wickedness. When you read it in its context, God is simply saying that He is a God of justice and will avenge His people Israel and do them good even though they don't acknowledge Him. He says He will do those things to prove that only He is God and only He can do that. Because there were some people who had mistreated the Jews, by giving judging His people and doing them good, He would also deal with oppressors of His people. God is saying that He is the one who blesses His chosen people and also visits the terror of His judgment to those who don't do what is right. Evil in this verse means judgment for those who are against God. It doesn't mean wickedness. For those people receiving that judgment, it was of course not sweet but evil and painful. God is never wicked and He has no capacity to be so. But, He is a God of Justice and He must punish sin or else He will be unrighteous. Woe unto the people who say God originates or allows death, carnage, diseases and violent weather because they call evil good and good evil.

Isaiah 5:20 *Woe to those who call evil good, and good evil; Who substitute darkness for light and light for darkness; Who substitute bitter for sweet and sweet for bitter!* (KJV)

Isaiah 45:7 can carry other applications as well. First, the prophet is not saying anything we don't know already. Who doesn't know God created light and darkness in the beginning? Who doesn't know that after God created everything He declared it was all very good? What this verse is saying is that although God is the one who created everything that is, there was possibility for corruption and perversion. We can't blame God for such corruption and perversion any more than we can blame the internet creators for online pornography. God originally created all the pathogens which we seek to eliminate from the catalogue of human experience but they were all good and useful creatures. They just got corrupted.

For those who point to Saul and say God can send evil spirits, they are wrong. Again, evil here doesn't mean wicked. There is a big difference. It simply means he was a spirit of God who was sent to carry out judgment against Saul for his disobedience. To Saul, the spirit was evil because he caused pain but to God, he was holy and sent to administer His justice.

God doesn't have a reservoir of evil spirits who He can send to do things similar to those of the devil. There is a whole lot of difference between God and satan but when you hear religious people speak in funeral ceremonies or when they preach on their interpretation of the 'sovereignty of God,' you can't tell the difference. It is the same thing with Psalm 78:49. God is describing the terrible things He wrought in Egypt when He saved Israel. He narrates how He sent His angels to carry out destructive work in judgment against Egypt for oppressing and terrorizing His people. It doesn't mean they are wicked angels. It just means they were administering the justice of God. Their work was terrible and painful to the Egyptians but according to God who sent them, it was fit. The recipients deserved it. Make no mistake; seven of those 'evil angels' will be released again in the end times and cause such carnage on earth as has never been witnessed according to Revelation chapter 16. They will still be evil angels in the sense that they will carry out terrible acts of God's judgment but they will be holy angels, not wicked.

They are just like the police force or the army. No one can call them wicked because they are sent by the state to administer justice. There is another scripture the protagonists of the doctrine of the 'sovereignty of God' choose to conveniently forget or sweep under the carpet:

Jeremiah 24: 2 *One basket had very good figs, even like the figs that are first ripe: and the other basket had very naughty figs, which could not be eaten, they were so bad. 3 Then said the LORD unto me, What seest thou, Jeremiah? And I said, Figs; the good figs, very good; and the evil, very evil, that cannot be eaten, they are so evil.* (KJV)

Does it mean the figs Jeremiah saw were satanic or wicked? Of course no! They were just bad or rotten figs. We need to understand that the English language has evolved since the first English Bible translations were produced. Back then, the word evil didn't mean satanic as it has come to be almost universally applied. It simply meant having terrible effects.

We can argue from morning to evening when it comes to how God appears to be operating in the Old Testament but the ultimate nature of God is revealed by Jesus in the New Testament. Jesus is the brightness of God's glory and the express image of His person. Jesus was God in human flesh. To see Jesus is to see God personified. There is nowhere in the New Testament where we find Jesus doing anything wicked, participating in anything wicked or even suggesting any such thing. Wherever Jesus went He did good. He only gave life, prosperity, victory, liberty and health. Jesus was God in action. Someone may be asking; does that mean if we disobey God He can still send these evil angels to mete His justice against us? No. There is a vast difference between the old and New Testaments.

Jesus made all the difference. He became our sin so that we can be made the righteousness of God in Him. There is now no sin in our spirit (although there is sin in our flesh) because Jesus took it all away and we were born afresh in the spirit. We are forever redeemed from sin by the perfect work of Jesus who was judged for all the sins of all men of all time. Those who believe in Him receive the eternal forgiveness of sins and sin can never be imputed unto them again. They have passed from judgment and death to life. There is no more judgment for them and their sins and lawless deeds God remembers no more. They cannot be judged again for the same sins Jesus was judged for. Fire never burns where it has burnt completely before as there is nothing more to burn. When the Israelites departed from Egypt, even before they crossed the first barrier which was the Red Sea, they began murmuring, rebelling, complaining, were afraid and engaged in all manner of folly and sin. They had no faith in God at all and were behaving like pagans. The many wrong things they did were very disgusting to God and He did not like it at all. Nevertheless, He put up with them and blessed them amidst their murmurs, complaints, rebellion and unbelief. His wrath did flare up at times to consume His adversaries among them but it would be quickly quenched when Aaron atoned for their sins. When they got to the plains of Moab and camped there, Balak king of Moab was threatened by them and he summoned for Balaam to come over and curse the Israelites if peradventure that could make him defeat them. When Balaam uttered what he was instructed to say by God, it was mind blowing. With all their cursing, with all their rebellion against God's appointed authority, with all their complaints, murmurs, unbelief, thanklessness and foolishness; what God said about them was literally out of this world and it would be almost unimaginable and unacceptable to a contemporary religious man.

Numbers 23: 21 *He hath not beheld iniquity in Jacob, neither hath he seen perverseness in Israel: the LORD his God is with him, and the shout of a king is among them.* (KJV)

Notice God didn't say there is no perverseness and iniquity in Israel. There were those things in plenty and in fact, the Israelites deserved to be wiped out of the face of the earth for their very unbecoming conduct. But, as long as Aaron and his family continued to offer sacrifices for the Israelites, God would not see any of those because they were covered. The Lord is echoing the same thing to us today. There is no doubt that even for the best of us, we err every day but the Lord does not see iniquity and perverseness in us because we live in Zion where there is the blood of sprinkling of the messiah which speaks forgiveness, not vengeance, judgment and condemnation-Hebrews 12:24. The Lord is not dealing with us according to our sins but according to the riches of His mercy and grace. He can now afford to do that in this testament because Christ came and by one sacrifice at once paid the bitter penalty for all our sins for all time.

(iii) NEITHER GOD NOR SATAN IS TO BLAME FOR TROUBLES ON EARTH, MEN ARE

Back now to this destructive doctrine of sovereignty of God and I like how one brother put it when he commented on this fallacious mentality of religion called the sovereignty of God; where they define sovereignty as meaning that God controls everything and everybody everywhere. He said, "Why do you think God controls everything and everybody? He doesn't control you!" I like that. If God controlled everything, He would control you. If God controlled everything and everybody, He would control them to come to Him and believe in His son with the end result of receiving eternal life. In that case, nobody would go against the will of God or choose the path to hell and if any did, then God would be responsible for it because according to religious people, He would have controlled them to follow that course! You see, proponents of the God's sovereignty argument would reject this line of reasoning arguing that it is fallacious and yet that is exactly what they mean when they argue for God's sovereignty. They attribute everything that happens (no matter how weird and evil) to being the work and "sovereign will" of God. It is just absurd. We know God doesn't exercise such control. I mean you sin when you want; you do what you want, when you want, where you want, how you want, with whom you want and for as long as you want. You say what you want to, you can choose to obey or disobey God yet He doesn't force anyone to do His will, or else, everybody on earth would be doing God's will.

If that is so and it is, why would anybody think God is in control on earth? If God was in total control, He would start by controlling you. The Bible says that if you are willing and obedient, you shall eat the best of the land. There is a huge element of personal choice there. It means you choose and determine how your life turns out to be and that has nothing to do with God or satan. This is tough but I repeat again to remove all doubt that the way your life is, you have designed it so and it is not the product of God's sovereign work or satan's interference. The only part those two have played in shaping your life is the part you've invited and allowed them to. <u>Your life is a sum total of your choices up to this point. You can't blame God or satan if your life is in a mess but you can thank God if you involved Him and things are glorious.</u> Your decisions determine your circumstances. Please note that I am not saying that satan is not at work. He is. My argument is that he needs not succeed where you are concerned because you are the one with the authority on earth to put him where he belongs. He cannot force you to do anything. He can only trick and tempt you to allow him to carry out his dirty work or cooperate with him in any other way. If you think satan is actively ruining your life, he is not to blame because he is there by your invitation. When serious students are hard at work, you refuse to study hard in school and therefore flop your exams then you say, "God is in Control." You lose your Job or are demoted because of your ineffectiveness, stinking attitude, inability to improve and slothfulness and you say, "God is in Control." A friend or relative dies by sickness because you didn't heal them and you say "God is in control." Due to recklessness and avoidable human error, someone perishes in an accident and you say, "God is in control." Your health is failing because of irresponsibility and poor choices and you say, "God is in control." Things are falling apart all around you because you are too lazy and ignorant to put to work your God-given authority yet you say, "God is in Control." Here is the good news: God is not in control because He has given you the control. He has given you the authority; so stop putting the responsibility back on God. On top of authority, God has given us the Holy Ghost to teach and remind us all things; lead us into all the truth and help us make the right decisions. What more would

God have done after putting in our hands all things we would ever need for life and godliness? Life and death are not in God's hands but in your own tongue. In many instances, our problems are of our own making although at others, the devil does attack. Whichever the case, it is not God's part to put the devil to flight but ours. Resist the devil and he will flee from You-James 4:7.

God has equipped us with more than enough weapons to resist that unpleasant fellow and run him totally out of our lives. When we talk about resisting the devil, some people don't know what we mean. Some think it is saying; 'devil I resist you.' Others think it is praying hard, fasting, doing vigils, getting physical with him and many such religious exercises. That is not it. We resist the devil the way Jesus did during the famous temptations. Jesus didn't change His tone, stamp His feet on the ground, sweat, jump or perform some other weird calisthenics. He simply stood on the word. He met every temptation with the written word of God until the devil threw all the weapons in his wicked arsenal and had to flee. But before we resist with the word, we start with word-based thinking. As a man thinks, so will his life go. If your thinking is not word based but carnal, the devil will have a field day with you. For you, the battle will be lost between your ears. Let me give you a practical example: Let's assume you have a stronghold in your life in the form of a recurring negative habit like entertaining evil thoughts. You know very well what the Bible says we meditate on. We are to think on whatsoever things which are true, noble, right, pure, lovely, admirable, excellent or praiseworthy. When you catch yourself thinking on retrogressive things, you don't need to try to get them off your mind. The more you try to do that, the more you will find yourself thinking harder on them. The thing to do is to first affirm and believe that you have the mind of Christ and are the very righteousness of God in Christ, even in the midst of those dirty thoughts. That is important because it shields you from the guilt and condemnation generated by the devil. The next step after that is to shift your thoughts to the things of God. The more you meditate on the word, the more the dirty thoughts disappear. Not only so, as you continue to behold Jesus in the word, you are transformed into His image and His thoughts. The arena of what is called spiritual warfare is the mind and it is not fought physically but with the word.

2 Corinthians 10: 4 *(For the weapons of our warfare are not carnal, but mighty through God to the pulling down of strong holds;) 5 Casting down imaginations, and every high thing that exalteth itself against the knowledge of God, and bringing into captivity every thought to the obedience of Christ;* (KJV)

Notice here how the Bible is very clear that the struggle we have is in the mind and it involves wicked imaginations and suggestions originating from the devil! Remember also the word instructs us to guard our minds because out of the same flow the issues of life. The entry point for satan in your life is your mind and that is where the supreme guard of the word is supposed to be ever ready.

Colossians 3:16 *Let the word of Christ dwell in you richly in all wisdom; teaching and admonishing one another in psalms and hymns and spiritual songs, singing with grace in your hearts to the Lord.* (KJV)

Now, one thing God will not do is to resist the devil for you. You have to take the word and your faith to put that crook where he belongs. If God was in control on earth as religious people aver, His will would automatically be done throughout the earth. Yet, we know what we see all around us is not God's will but man's will guided by that deceiver called satan. God's will is very rarely done on earth. That is why the earth is a far cry from the perfect heaven where God is in total control and His will is done without question.

1 John 5:19 *We know that we are of God, and that the whole world lies in the power of the evil one.* (NASB)

Right here it says the devil is the one trying to sway the earth, not God. God's will is only done on earth when a Christian decides to put God's word to work. To say God is in control of the earth and everything that happens here is to say God allows all the wars, terrorism, genocides, rapes, stealing and other crimes and all the wickedness that is so pervasive in the world today. That would mean we cannot prosecute the perpetrators of these heinous and beastly acts because God is in control. If God is in control and His will must happen in everything as religious people say, then why do the many things we do to make the earth a better and safer place to live in? If God's will must still carry the day, then why pray? Why read the Bible? Why renew our minds? If God controls everything, why evangelize or try to change the world for the better? All these things and many more that we do would be unnecessary because they would all be trounced by God's strong control. In that case, God would override and prevent anything that's not according to His will. Yet, we don't see that happen because God ceded control of the earth to men. We decide what happens on earth. We decide whether there will be war or peace. We decide whether we will go by God's will or ours. Even when we decide against God's will, He doesn't rush to stop us. That is why He didn't rush to stop Adam and Eve from sinning and plunging humanity into millennia of chaos. One would ask, is God then evil, aloof, ignorant, disinterested or uncaring? He is none of the above and that is how and why most people do not understand God and His nature. He is a God of is His word. He is also a God of love and that is why He created men with ability or will to choose, not puppets to control and manipulate. If God had created us like robots or marionettes with no will, Adam would never have sinned and we would all be towing His line without question. You certainly do not want that. Do you like robots? What would you rather have, a robot or a pet? If we were created robots, how would we ever choose to love and how would we appreciate love? God is love, not a controller and love liberates as opposed to controlling. In marriages where there is prevalent control and monitoring, we know that there is no love. I certainly would detest my spouse trying to control, manipulate and monitor me. In fact, I wouldn't take that kindly. Likewise, God had no pleasure in creating toys that He could control. He wanted a family to relate with on the basis of love. Now where love is, there must also of necessity be choices otherwise love would no longer be love. That is why even today, He doesn't force us to love Him. He just let's His goodness lead us to repentance. God also gave the earth to man and He cannot take it back because that would constitute breach of His word; something He is incapable of doing. If you had any doubt that God has let men to exercise their freedom of choice to put their lives in the path of life, then check out these verses:

2 Peter 3:9*The Lord is not slack concerning his promise,*

as some men count slackness; but is longsuffering to us-ward, not willing that any should perish, but that all should come to repentance. (KJV)

Deuteronomy 30: 15 S*ee, I have set before thee this day life and good, and death and evil... 19 I call heaven and earth to record this day against you, that I have set before you life and death, blessing and cursing: therefore choose life, that both thou and thy seed may live:* (KJV)

God is not willing that any should perish yet people are perishing by droves. They are perishing not because God chooses it for them or He controls things that way, but because they choose it for themselves. As a matter of fact, everyone who finds themselves in hell will have to literally climb over Jesus to get in there. The other verse says that life is a choice and so is death, God therefore advises, choose life. <u>God does not make choices for men and then shoves them down their throats like a cruel tyrant. He lovingly points to them the path of life, empowers them to choose it and lets them exercise their liberty to do so.</u> People who subscribe to this faulty doctrine of sovereignty of God rarely evangelize to the lost because they tie it to another doctrine of their own making called predestination. They argue that whoever was decided for by God to be saved, will be saved and nothing can prevent him to be saved, just as nothing can be done to the person God never chose. You see how dangerous this doctrine is? These people think that God chose some people for salvation and didn't choose others. Is it not written that God shows no favoritism and that His will is for every single person to repent and turn away from destruction? Does it not explain that for this latter reason, God (who is not slow in executing His word) has not wrapped up time but is patient with His people if peradventure, all may come to the saving knowledge of Christ, not willing that any should perish?

1 Timothy 2: 4 *Who will have all men to be saved, and to come unto the knowledge of the truth.* (KJV)

You see, if you subscribe to these faulty doctrines of sovereignty of God and predestination, you will find it hard to evangelize because you will imagine that those who God chose to be saved, will be somehow saved and those He did not choose, will be damned even if they were preached to daily. That is not true. God does not even choose people per se. He does not really choose individuals directly. What happened is that God chose Christ before the foundation of the earth and whoever chooses Christ, is also automatically chosen by God.

Ephesians 1: 4 *According as he hath chosen us **in him** before the foundation of the world, that we should be holy and without blame before him in love…6 To the praise of the glory of his grace, wherein he hath made us **accepted in the beloved**.* (KJV) Emphasis added.

Although ultimately God initiated and completed the grand work of salvation through Christ, the initiative to respond positively to that grace begins with us and until we hear the gospel, heed to it and believe in it, by our own engineering, we will keep ourselves outside the kingdom of God and God is not to blame for our destruction. The Bible asks how they will call on whom they haven't believed, how they will believe on whom they haven't heard and how they will hear without a preacher. God is not the one who controls whether people come to Him or not. He has invited all to Him but they must exercise their privilege of choice to accept His invitation. <u>Predestination means by His omniscience, God foreknew all those who would believe in Christ and those are the people He called, justified and ultimately glorified</u>-Romans 8:29-30. Our work is very clear-cut in that we are to make Christ known. Whether those who hear us will ever accept Him or not is really not our business.

To say God controls everything is to mean that God is responsible for all the rot, all the darkness, and all the wickedness that earth swims in and it's an insult to God. If God is in control on earth, then He sure is doing a pathetic job because the world is in complete disarray and it is actually going to hell in a hand basket. The truth is, man chooses what happens on earth –good or bad. That is why we must choose to accept Christ. That is why we must choose to pray, read and meditate on the word. That is why we must choose to be filled with the Holy Spirit. Ultimately, that is why, we must choose to practice the word of God and be led of the Holy Ghost. There are fellows who have chosen not to do the above things and they are the ones troubling the earth. Those of us who have chosen to do them are the ones preserving the earth and shining the light that can still be witnessed in all the darkness around. The only trace of God in that equation is when the new creation chooses to depend on God and not lean on their understanding. It is when we submit to the Holy Spirit for wisdom, power and guidance that we carry out God's will on earth. It is when through the new birth, we receive the abundance of grace and the gift of righteousness to reign in this life. When we do that, then we can comfortably say that God is in control. Otherwise, the rest of the folks are carrying out Satan's will. God is not involved in what they are doing and He should be not dragged there. So, once we are walking in the Spirit and not in the flesh, Heaven has absolute sanction on the decisions we make on earth. That way, God has faith in us.

(iv) WHAT IS AUTHORITY?

Let us now define authority. It is the discretion, the mandate, the leeway to exercise power. In Matthew 28:18-19, Jesus said that we have the discretion to exercise all of God's power on earth. Yes, we have the unlimited power of God at our disposal to function on earth.

Ephesians 1:19...*and the unlimited greatness of his power for us who believe, according to the working of his mighty strength......*

We have access to as much power as we want to use. God is not the one who has placed the limit. We place it on ourselves by not renewing our minds and aligning our thinking with His word.

The New creation has access to limitless power. Jesus said the new creation should be busy doing not just the things Jesus did but greater things even. Jesus raised dead people, multiplied food supernaturally, walked on water, cast out demons and did so many other things that if they were to be put down in writing, there would be no enough space on earth to hold them. To begin with, every believer should already be doing all these things listed above that Jesus did. And we should not stop there. We should gear up to do greater things than the master. This is for every believer, not just for the apostles, pastors, prophets or other perceived "super saints."

The qualification Jesus put is to believe only.

John 14:12 *Verily, verily, I say unto you, He that believeth on me, the works that I do shall he do also; and greater works than these shall he do; because I go unto my Father.* (KJV)

You can repeat this ultra-powerful confession after me: "Dear loving Father, I thank you for your word which is true and constant in all circumstances. I am who you say I am, I can do what you say I can do and I have what you say I have. Period! You told me that if I believe in Jesus I will do the exceedingly mighty things that He did and even greater things. I believe every letter of that promise because you are not a man to lie. So, I will do the things Jesus did. I will raise the dead, heal the sick, cleanse the infected, feed multitudes miraculously, speak to creation and it heeds, prophesy and much more. I will not stop at that. I will do greater works. I may be able to travel at the speed of thought without using man-made contraptions. I may be able to speak to millions of people without requiring man-made gadgets like microphones. I may just show up like Peter and Paul and people receive healing without a single word from me. These and many more will I do. Thank you Jesus for your help as I walk that journey. Amen."

A lot of people have been trying to justify their mediocre performance in relation to John 14:12 by proposing all manner of ridiculous things. I have heard some say that their greater work is preaching on Television or radio because Jesus didn't use those mediums. I do not for one moment think that argument and others like it hold any water. I think that is trying to cope with failure. May be the greater works include some of the few listed above. You can add to that list and believe God for it. You see, you get what you believe for. A lot of Christians are not even doing the works Jesus did, not to talk of greater works.

Most Christians are praying in their homes or churches and sending God to go and do what He told them to do. They pray, "Father save, heal, deliver, help that person, do this, do that." As they pray, they are not willing to go out and preach the Gospel, work miracles, heal the sick, save the oppressed and do all the other things Jesus instructed us to do. That is called escapism. That is why I have a problem with the way what they call ministries of prayer warfare and intercession are mostly run. This poses several problems: first, if you only pray and never share Bible truths and revelation with people, those people will never get help. What helps people is a direct touch of ministry, not so much a remote prayer. You can pray for your roommate for life but if you don't share the gospel physically with him or her, they will never be saved, healed, delivered and matured in Christ. With that kind of approach, the church will only have bare minimum impact and society will continue on its rotten path. Imagine if the late nineteenth century missionaries had only been praying in Europe but never risked everything. Imagine if they didn't pour themselves out as drink offerings to spread the Gospel in distant lands. People in Asia, Africa and other unreached places would never have seen the light. There is a place for prayer, but after prayer, it is time to rise up and do something practical to actualize that prayer. We can pray for centuries about the lost but the Lord will never violate His word to come and preach to anyone or send an angel to do so. That's our job. That's why Paul the apostle said woe to him if he didn't preach the gospel because necessity was laid upon him to preach. The privilege of preaching the gospel to convert men, to heal them or minister to them in any way is not God's and it hasn't been given to angels or any other celestial beings. It is men's. Why do you think that angel of the Lord who appeared to Cornelius in a vision could only point him to Apostle Peter to have him come and preach and not preach to him directly?

Secondly, those prayer warriors tend to always imagine their work is to fight with devils. As a result, they end up spending very little time with God and most of their time involved with satan- real or perceived. In actual sense, they end up being more satan conscious than God conscious. Thirdly and very importantly, that practice of setting apart a few people called prayer warriors to be praying for the rest of the people heaps pressure on them and makes the rest of the people relax. Why pray when you have "warriors" who have your back? In the New Testament, we have only one very able and perfect intercessor and mediator called Jesus Christ. We can pray for other people, but we must always draw a line as to how far a man's prayer ministry for another man can go and where Jesus' starts. Those who imagine they are called to be prayer warriors, with whom are they warring, about what and for whom? If they wrestled with answering those questions, they would most likely find they have no answers and they would rise up to go and touch people's lives literally.

If anybody will be saved, healed, delivered or helped in any other way, God will have to use a human agent to touch and change the life of that person. God doesn't just come to earth to work independent of humans. If He did, then Jesus would not have sent us to do those same things. We would never have to do anything because God with His infinite ability would do everything. He would just come and independently, touch everybody at once and finish all our problems in one fell swoop. Yet He doesn't do that because He doesn't have the authority on earth to do that here. He has to employ a man. To defeat satan and save humanity, He had to send a man-Jesus. Jesus gave God authority to operate on earth and do what sons of Adam could not have done. How do you explain all the people who are suffering in hospitals yet God is everywhere including in those hospitals? Either God is unwilling to help them, or someone else is not at work in their post. The latter applies. You see, God excluded Himself from the equation of running the earth:

Genesis 1:26 *And God said, Let us make man in our image, after our likeness: and let them have dominion over the fish of the sea, and over the fowl of the air, and over the cattle, and over all the earth, and over every creeping thing that creepeth upon the earth... 28 And God blessed them, and God said unto them, Be fruitful, and multiply, and replenish the earth, and subdue it: and have dominion over the fish of the sea, and over the fowl of the air, and over every living thing that moveth upon the earth.* (KJV)

Psalms 115:16 *The heaven, even the heavens, are the LORD's: but the earth hath he given to the children of men.* (KJV)

(v) GOD HAS THE POWER, WE HAVE THE AUTHORITY.

In other words, God has the power on earth, but we have the authority. If we are mean in using our authority to exercise His power, nothing happens on earth. That is precisely the reason why you see things going wrong all around you and you wonder where God is. Frankly, this very thing unsettles and even destabilizes very many ignorant Christians. They wonder why God looks on as things deteriorate so badly yet He is omnipotent, omnipresent and omniscient. I will surprise you with the news that your feeling of frustration is shared by God. He is wondering why you are sitting on authority while things go stale. He is right there in that confusion and wickedness but He will do nothing on earth alone. He has to operate through a human with a body. That is the only entity with legal right to operate on earth. So, things are going wrong around you because you've not taken the initiative to engage the power of God through either prayer, declaration of the word or commanding things to line up with God's will. <u>Prayer is simply permitting God to bring to pass or to manifestation what He has already done concerning any situation that may be out of order.</u> Remember God does not react to circumstances like men who lack foreknowledge. He already anticipated everything that would ever happen and made adequate preparations to remedy it. That is why the lamb of God was slain from the foundation of the world. God has already seen and known what needed to be done about any problem and provided for it in Christ Jesus. Prayer doesn't move God in the sense that He rises up and begins to act. God is resting now with Christ at His right hand and we are seated in Christ. Although Jesus said His Father is always working, it is important to understand the nature of God's work. First, the work God is doing is not hard labor as man is accustomed to. After creation, God released His word to sustain creation and went to rest. His word is packed with the power and intelligence required to do all His work for Him. Also, God's work is what we are doing whereby He releases His power and we mix it with authority for results to be made manifest on earth. Two, Jesus may have meant that God was working until the time of His death and resurrection and finished everything when Jesus declared, "it is finished!" It is strange to think that God is working and Jesus is resting at His right hand. Prayer is simply a tool for receiving what God has by grace provided for. Prayer is also our avenue to thank God for doing everything for us and all we do is to receive. Grateful people are receivers as well. A prayer of faith is a positive response to what God has already done and it is only a means to access it. We have not because we ask not or should I add that we receive not? One would ask, how then should we pray correctly if God has finished all the work and given us all things? Well, prayer is not an occasion for asking things from God. What is it you are asking for if all things are yours and God has given you everything you will ever need for life and godliness and has also blessed you with all spiritual blessings in heavenly places in Christ Jesus? Well, if is healing you need, you can go about it this way: "Father, I thank you because you saw this attack on my health before the foundation of the world. It doesn't catch you by surprise and neither does it surprise me. Thank you because you've healed me already. You've provided for my healing in Christ. I need it now and I receive it with thanksgiving in the name of Jesus Christ. Amen." After that prayer, you then need to take your authority and order the disease to vacate your body in Jesus' name. Afterwards, you can also command your body to be restored to wholeness again and to gain strength after the disease is gone. If you do that in faith, there is no reason why any disease can stick in you no matter how terminal it is. The power of God does not differentiate between terminal and lesser diseases. All are cleared in the same way and it is easy although it is impossible with men. God is unaware that there is anything that goes by the name of terminal disease. Impossibilities only occur in the vocabulary of men. He has already anticipated everything He will ever need to do and He has done it in Christ. His part is finished. Our part is what remains and that part is called receiving through the prayer of faith. With prayer, we also take out any devil who may be obstructing or delaying our answers. Prayer is our participation in the program of God of carrying out His will on earth. Without our participation, God will do nothing on earth and without His power, we can do nothing. Prayer is one of the most important God-given tools there is of releasing our authority on earth. <u>God doesn't just come to work on earth without our cooperation. He must work with human agents. That is why He needed people like Moses, Joshua, Aaron, David, the prophets, the judges and ultimately Jesus!</u> God could not just intervene and redeem the Israelites from slavery or later save mankind. If God could function on earth by sidestepping man, He would have come way earlier than He did through Jesus, whipped satan and stripped him of the power he usurped from Adam, and restored it to man. Yet, He didn't do it without taking the form of a man. It was man who gave authority away because it was his to exercise, and it was man who had to take it back.

If God could work independent of man on earth, then why should we bother to pray and fast? Why bother to preach, rebuke the devil and study the word if God will still carry out His will on earth in spite of us? If God called the shots on earth sovereignly as religion preaches, we wouldn't need to do anything. We would only have to just sit passively and wait for what God has in store to come hurtling towards us and we would all get similar results because God would be the only factor. But, we know that Jesus said that men ought always to pray-Luke 18:1.

Ephesians 6:18 *And pray in the Spirit on all occasions with all kinds of prayers and requests. With this in mind, be alert and always keep on praying for all the Lord's people.* (KJV)

It is only when we pray that what God has prepared for His people is released. That is why we should pray for all men at all times. Not only should we pray, but we should pray with other tongues because only God knows who needs what.

Now, if God doesn't provide the power, our authority is in vain. But praise Him because by His love, He has provided that power unreservedly. It is men who are sleeping on the job. God has already provided salvation freely for everybody. But, someone has to preach to the lost. It is not the job of God or of angels to preach. He did His part already. We are the ones to spread the good news of what God in Christ did to save mankind from sin, sickness, lack, bondage and every other product of the fall.

Romans 10:14 *How then shall they call on him in whom they have not believed? and how shall they believe in him of whom they have not heard? and how shall they hear without a preacher?* (KJV)

Men are not saved through prayer, just as children don't come through prayer. A seed has to be planted for a baby to come. Similarly, the incorruptible, living and abiding seed of the word of God has to be planted in the heart of man for saving faith to be born.

Please don't get me wrong. There is a place for prayer in people getting saved but it is not the way people have made it to be. We cannot pray for God to save people as if He had refused to save them in the first place. He provided salvation for everybody but the evil one has blinded them so that they cannot see and respond positively to the glorious gospel of our Lord Jesus. They think they are independent or free thinkers but actually they are pitiful captives of the enemy. These need more than preaching to and that brings us to the first need for prayer in the process of getting someone born again. We need to get behind them and bind the devil who is blinding them and once their blindfolds fall off, then they will see clearly and surrender to Jesus so that He can free them. Secondly, if the individual has shut out some people from engaging him or her in regard to the gospel, prayer can help direct to their path an alternative laborer they can pay attention to. That much, prayer can do. Otherwise, the spiritual rebirth is just like the first and carnal birth. Both occur when a seed is planted. Only that one seed is physical and corruptible, the other spiritual and incorruptible. Prayer does not negate the need for a seed of the word to be planted, it merely aids it.

1 Peter 1:23 *Being born again, not of corruptible seed, but of incorruptible, by the word of God, which liveth and abideth forever.* (KJV)

John 1:12-13 *But as many as received him, to them gave he power to become the sons of God, even to them that believe on his name: 13 Which were born, not of blood, nor of the will of the flesh, nor of the will of man, but of God.* (KJV)

Those who say that God is sovereign and that sovereignty means He does on earth anything He wants with and for anybody at any time are actually ignorantly implying that God is partial. That is to say, God moves and does whatever He pleases, for who He pleases, however He pleases. If He wants to heal, He heals. If it pleases Him to save, then He saves. The problem with this faulty theology is that it means that God chooses to save, heal and bless some people and not others. That is far from the truth. God tells us that it is not His will that any one perishes but that all should come to the saving knowledge of and faith in His son. That should mean that anyone who goes to hell chooses it himself and the one who is saved chose the path of faith as well. Likewise, people choose to be healed or to stay sick. They also choose to collect their blessings from God or to let them stay. Someone may say, but I am sick and I have not chosen it! Well, you may not have overtly said, 'I want to remain sick' or lived in open rebellion against God. But, you just need to harbor this unbiblical line of thinking which says God will heal or bless you if He wills and if He doesn't, then, you will just stay with the sickness. That way you will surely die because you've chosen to believe a lie and to adopt faulty traditions of men which make the word of God of none effect. God has already provided salvation and all blessings for everybody by grace, but He doesn't force anyone to be saved or to collect their blessings. People have to hear the Gospel and choose to believe in order to appropriate what is theirs in Christ. If the custodians of Kingdom information sit on it and don't pass it around, then the people die in their sins. On the other hand, if the people get the good news but disregard it, they also die in their sins. God doesn't enforce His will on earth. If He did, then everybody would be born again and living triumphantly because His will is that none gets lost but all come to salvation according to 2 Peter 3:9 above. Although the love of God is currently available to everybody on planet earth, it is useless to the man who does not believe in Christ. In fact, that love is deadly to such a person because they will be held to account for what they did with the most precious gift in the whole universe. You can't have what you don't receive. God can't force His love on people or else that wouldn't be love. Love liberates instead of possessing. People have to make a conscious decision to accept the love of God in Christ.

God does not micromanage man to ensure that if he is not performing his duties, then He recalls His authority.

His gifts and callings are without recall-Romans 11:29. So, now that we are in charge on earth, God will not come and say. "You people have refused to expend the authority I gave you. I will overrule you and apply it instead myself." God is orderly. Plus, thanks to Jesus, God has already provided salvation and all manner of blessings for everyone everywhere for all time. God is not waiting, or wanting to bless you. He has already graciously blessed you with everything you would ever need and the greatest waste in life is to do nothing and let what Jesus toiled so hard for to remain unutilized.

Every move God ever wanted to do He has done already. Our part is to find out what He did and provided and put it to work. For example, the Holy Ghost is not just now being released. He has been around and in plenty for over 2000 years for anyone who cared to engage Him. Even during the dark ages, He was still here waiting to work with anyone who was willing. There is so much religious talk of, "a coming visitation or coming move of the Holy Ghost, or the newest move of God." God moved in Christ and in His signature modus operandi, completed all His work. After He poured down the Holy Spirit in the day of Pentecost, He has never taken Him back. It is men who blow hot and cold in terms of manifesting the presence of God. It is not God who hides and emerges based on His whims. That means everything you see happening in Christendom and you think is new, its potential has been there since Jesus resurrected and the Holy Spirit was poured upon men. God has not been asleep and is just waking up now to do what you think is new. It has been around for the whole time but men were in the dark about it. It is men who are just waking up now to what God did over two millennia ago. Furthermore, there's nothing new under the sun. A lot of what is happening in the body of Christ now was happening with the first century believers. God did not just pause it at some point for some reason just at the onset of the dark ages and He's just reopening the floodgates of grace. That would be like saying that the forces of electricity, telecommunication and other scientific and technological marvels were released in the nineteenth century. They were all here since the days of Adam. Cain and Abel could have been flying! It is men who are always playing catch-up with God. I can also not downplay the role of satan in blinding men to the glorious things God has in store for His children. For example, if you get born again today, it doesn't mean God had been waiting all along to release your salvation at a particular day. You could have been saved years or decades ago. However, you were either too busy for God, or you hardened your heart, or you were ignorant, or someone was sent to deliver to you the gospel but they refused, or, there was some other factor but not God. That is tough for the religious mind but it is the truth. Religion says when the day of your salvation, death or blessing comes, you can't resist it. There is no such a thing as a particular day of salvation, death or blessing. Every day is a day of salvation and blessing. Every day is also a day to say no to death because the devil wants to kill you at any opportunity. Tragically, a lot of Christians will not let the Word of God get in the way of their religion. The thing is, God made everything ready for everybody over 2000 years ago when Jesus said "it is finished." What happens is that when you realize you are lacking in anything, you just turn to your heavenly account and make a withdrawal of your divine gift. This fairly new revelation of grace was here since the days of Paul just immediately after Jesus left. The devil kept it concealed in piles of religious garbage until men began to critically examine the truth and the things we are discovering are mind-blowing. There was no better time to be a Christian than now. The devil will never rest again. We will keep him on his toes and fleeing until Jesus comes. We can't allow him to carry out his dirty operations again in our watch.

One of the other strongholds that makes religion such a boring, unattractive, ineffective and futuristic exercise is this whole talk and anticipation of revival. Revival is a very common word in the charismatic movement of Christianity. But, did you know most of the people talking about revival do not even know what it is?

There is a lot of activity and agitation towards preparing and planning for it and there are innumerable meetings organized to pray towards that end.

What these people ignorantly call revival is actually the mission Jesus Christ left us to do. Revival should be simply studying the scriptures to find out the truth and then spreading that truth to dispel darkness and set men free. Revival happens as we preach the gospel of grace so that people are set free from the dominion of darkness and translated to the kingdom of God's dear son. That includes disseminating the truth of the gospel, reconciling people with God, getting them Spirit filled, training them in the ways of righteousness, healing the sick, raising the dead and casting out demons. That is simply what revival is. The revival we need is for the church to deepen in personal relationship with God, to grow in the understanding, appreciation and interaction with His love. Revelation of His love is what causes us to be filled with all the fullness of God- Ephesians 3:19. *Trust me, you don't need the pie in the sky or carnal emotion that religion calls revival; all you need is revelation of God's grace.* Religion has been "banging the doors of heaven" asking for revival as if God is the one holding it back and waiting for us to do more, pray more, fast more, confess sins more and behave well so that He can release it. None of the things above that Jesus instructed us to do is dependent on God doing anything more than what He has done already. He has already saved us, healed us, provided for us, blessed us with everything we will ever need for life and godliness, filled us with the Holy Spirit and power, given us His word and sent us. In fact, I will venture to say here that <u>satan has used this pursuit and expectation of revival as a red-herring to keep many Christians busy doing nothing and expecting a pie that seems to be perpetually floating in the sky.</u> What more revival are these religious people waiting for? If you are in Christ, you are revived already. You just need to stop lazing around, shake yourself from your slumber, smell the coffee and start spreading the word of grace, making disciples, healing the sick, raising the dead and casting out demons. If you do that, you will see more revival than you can contain. I will soundly echo the words of brother Curry Blake who grew tired of all this religious talk about some coming move of God and said that <u>the only next move of God we will see will be the move of God's people or what I call Jesus-men.</u> God is not just about to move independent of the church. He only moves through the church. If the church goes to sleep like it had done for centuries, His power becomes potential energy only, waiting for when the church wakes up again. People are all over praying and organizing revival meetings yet they sit idly and never share the gospel, never try to heal the sick, rarely pray or study the word, never exorcise demons and have no idea they can raise the dead. Where are they expecting the revival to manifest? What do they understand by revival? Do they even understand what they are waiting or praying for? If revival showed up at their door steps, would they really recognize it? People who are ever holding meetings praying for revival and waiting for it are some of the most disillusioned and frustrated people on the earth because they never see what they are waiting for and that makes them very exasperated. What happens is that they continue to sink deeper into religious rituals and performance and become more tired and frustrated. Every year, they hold these meetings but the results are the same and they keep wondering where they go wrong. The reason is they are waiting for that which came over 2000 years ago and has never left. Ever since God poured out His Spirit on the church's birthday, He has never withdrawn Him again and He will never do because lo, He is with us up to the end of the age. Revival is simply making use of the Holy Spirit who abides in us continually to do work of God on earth and bring His will to bear in our circumstances. The Bible says that for those who believe in Christ, out of their bellies shall flow rivers of living water. Christ said that referring to the Holy Spirit. Those rivers are what constitute revival and they continue to flow from the bellies of those who step out in courage and faith to do the things which Christ did, and greater things. Revival is when the power in those rivers is harnessed and channeled to kingdom work. Revival is not some religious, ritualistic, nebulous or even magical concept that we keep chanting in expectation that God will hear and sent down His power. <u>Revival is not some futuristic and independent move of God but a present hour reality for those who take steps to send the gospel to the ends of the earth with accompanying signs and wonders.</u> It is happening every time to and for those who are in action for God. For those who sit and wait for God to visit them in their homes or in their religious worship places, it will remain to be a chimera throughout their lives.

    This religious pastime of organizing meetings to pray for revival is not only a waste of time but a futile exercise of chasing a mirage. In fact, I believe this craze and unending stampede around revival activities is from the devil. He is the one who specializes in keeping people busy chasing things that they either possess already, or do not exist. You see, if that dirty fellow can engage your time by getting you busy with things that are neither here nor there, he can keep you from doing the things that really matter or that add value to your destiny. You do not find the early church locking themselves up in churches and praying for an imaginary thing called revival. They dispersed and spread the word throughout the world and that is how they were able to turn upside down the known world then. <u>Praying for revival without a clear intention of springing on your feet to go and take the gospel to the ends of the earth with accompanying signs and wonders is rebellion.</u> Revival follows those who go to work in the field of God which is now overripe with ready fruit. Revival is actually just the act of going out by the power of God to bring in the harvest. <u>The new creation is not only revived, he is reborn.</u> He carries revival in his belly. All he needs to do is to renew his mind and make use of the Holy Spirit. That is what genuine revival is.

You see, after Jesus' complete work at the cross, God made available for us everything we require. He put it in Jesus, who lives in us by His Spirit and is now one with our born-again spirit. That is what we mean when we say God has blessed us with all spiritual blessings in heavenly places in Christ. So, all the while you've been praying and looking to God to bring help from above, you have everything for this life and divine life right inside your new spirit. You must understand that all things consist in Christ who lives in you and in whom you live. To have Christ is to have everything. That is why paul tells us all things are ours and that we are heirs of God-joint heirs with Christ. Why and how would you lack anything when you are heir of the one who owns all things? That is why God is not aware that you are lacking anything. As a gracious, foreknowing, wealthy, loving and generous Father, He has released everything for you already. No good thing has He withheld from you. If He gave Christ-Heaven's best-how will He not with Him give us all things? Withholding any other thing from you would mean that thing is more valuable than Christ! I hear people talking about a double portion anointing, double portion provision, double portion conference or any other double portion blessing. I say to myself, all those double portions are fallacies! This is not the Old Testament when people needed to receive a double portion of anything. God has given us everything. He has given us His Holy Spirit without measure. He has even given us His entire Kingdom.

John 1: 14 *And the Word was made flesh, and dwelt among us, (and we beheld his glory, the glory as of the only begotten of the Father,) full of grace and truth... 16 And of his fulness have all we received, and grace for grace.* (KJV)

Ephesians 3:19 *And to know the love of Christ, which passeth knowledge, that ye might be filled with all the fulness of God.* (KJV)

The Holy Spirit did not come into you in a limited measure. He is in you wholly. He is occupying your spirit with His full power and weight. You use as much of His power as you want to. He is not the limit, you are. We have received of the fullness of Jesus. We also receive all the fullness of God as we increase in the revelation and experience of the love of God. What more double portion can you receive? The question of double portion of whatever it is does not arise. In the Old Testament, Christ had not come and so they could not receive the fullness of the godhead bodily. For us, of His fullness have we all received, and grace for grace (grace heaped upon even more grace). The question is, how do you make a withdrawal from your heavenly account? The Bible is not silent about that either. We receive everything God has availed for us freely through faith. We must first acknowledge what God has granted us; and that is found in His word.

After we identify and acknowledge all that we have, we must believe we receive it, then it will manifest in the physical. It is that simple. <u>Faith is the divine force that makes things to jump from the pages of the Bible to manifest physically in our lives.</u>

12. THE NEW CREATION IS A CHAMPION FOR EVER

Satan's number one goal on the planet is to neutralize and overcome the church of Christ which is the salt and light of the world. If he can succeed to put out their light, then he can stamp out their influence here. Satan is not really so much after people who are not born again because they are already his. Those ones are easy to deal with. He has innumerable demons of busyness to keep such folks involved in endless activities including work, pleasure, entertainment, crime, addictions and even all the religions of the world other than true Christianity. The people satan is mostly out to steal from, kill and destroy are the new creation in Christ Jesus. Those are his most prized targets. Most of his plans, plots and schemes are targeted at the elect of Christ. You see, when you go hunting and shoot one game dead but another escapes wounded, you will obviously leave behind the dead game and pursue the wounded one in the hope of getting it. The dead one is in your hands already. Likewise, satan has hopes that he can still recapture those who are not in his grasp. He does that by trying to steal the word from them, clouding their understanding so that they do not comprehend the word, keeping them busy so that they do not have time for the word, attacking their health and families, contradicting the word, sowing seeds of doubt of the word and persecution. All these onslaughts are aimed at one thing: weakening the believer's resolve and faith to a point where it is easy to give up. All the activities of Satan: the persecutions, the contradictions against the word of grace and those who believe it, the accidents, the social unrest, the false religions, cults, violent weather, economic and political upheavals, LGBT promotions and general escalation of wickedness: They are all intended to swallow up and overwhelm the believer to a point where he will think his faith is needless.

Matthew 24:12 *And because iniquity shall abound, the love of many shall wax cold... 24 For there shall arise false Christs, and false prophets, and shall shew great signs and wonders; insomuch that, if it were possible, they shall deceive the very elect.* (KJV)

Mathew 13: 20 *But he that received the seed into stony places, the same is he that heareth the word, and anon with joy receiveth it; 21 Yet hath he not root in himself, but dureth for a while:* **for when tribulation or persecution ariseth because of the word,** *by and by he is offended.* (KJV) Emphasis added.

That is why when Jude wrote to Christendom, he urged us to defend fiercely our faith.

Jude 1:3 *Dear friends, although I was eager to write to you about the salvation we share, I found it necessary to write to you and urge you to continue your vigorous defense of the faith that was passed down to the saints once and for all.* (ISV)

Our faith and hope in Jesus is always under attack. The earth is a very hostile place for the new creation. Satan has unleashed every tool he can muster to defeat the cause of Christ. It started as soon as the church was born in the day of Pentecost. Probably only a day or two after the church was born, Peter and John were arrested and threatened by religious men. The onslaught continued unabated as Stephen was brutally killed shortly thereafter. Without doubt, one of the most enduring weapon of choice for satan against the kingdom of God has been persecution. Satan believes he can beat believers to submission. Nearly every generation of Christians has had to contend with it.

However, I believe the devil is an idiot. More often than not, this route is usually counterproductive. While it is true some people decide to stay away from Christianity because of persecution, a yet vast majority become emboldened by it. Don't take my word for it:

Matthew 11: 12 *And from the days of John the Baptist until now the kingdom of heaven suffereth violence, and the violent take it by force.* (KJV)

Matthew 13: 33 *Another parable spake he unto them; The kingdom of heaven is like unto leaven, which a woman took, and hid in three measures of meal, till the whole was leavened.* (KJV)

<u>The new creation is an unstoppable juggernaut. Contrary winds don't dampen our spirit. Far from it, they drive our roots deeper.</u> In fact, they serve to facilitate our promotion. Persecution causes the Gospel to spread faster than its absence. Persecution also strengthens the resolve of the new creation.

Acts 20: 22 *"And now, compelled by the Spirit, I am going to Jerusalem, not knowing what will happen to me there. 23 I only know that in every city the Holy Spirit warns me that prison and hardships are facing me. 24 However, I consider my life worth nothing to me; my only aim is to finish the race and complete the task the Lord Jesus has given me—the task of testifying to the good news of God's grace.* (NIV)

The new creation is not afraid of Satan and his activities. He advances forcefully in spite of the enemy. In fact, the new creation does not recognize the presence of enemies. He prospers in spite of them and even feasts in their presence. The new creation has the attitude of Joshua, Moses' successor. Hardships and obstacles are the new creation's bread for food.

Psalm 23: 4 *Yea, though I walk through the valley of the shadow of death, I will fear no evil: for thou art with me; thy rod and thy staff they comfort me. 5Thou preparest a table before me in the presence of mine enemies: thou anointest my head with oil; my cup runneth over.* (KJV)

Numbers 14:9 *Only rebel not ye against the LORD, neither fear ye the people of the land; for they are bread for us: their defence is departed from them, and the LORD is with us: fear them not.* (KJV)

The new creation is not bothered about some wicked principalities operating "above his area." <u>The new creation is the chief principality in his area.</u> He is the one who calls the shots. What he forbids heaven forbids as well and no one can overrule it. To the New creation, the devil is not even a factor. We do not let that fallen spirit and his sympathizers occupy our time so that we try to fight him, defeat him, exorcise him or even preach about him. We don't let him dampen our spirit for a moment.

We thrive hand over fist in spite of his empty rants. Empty tins make a lot of noise and satan is the ultimate empty tin. To use the words of our Lord Jesus, Satan has nothing in us-John 14:30.

In other words, we are not bothered about Satan. He has no claim on us because we have been taken by our suitor, Jesus. He is of no effect to us and neither do we have any business dealing with him. The worst that Satan can do is to harm our bodies but he can never come anywhere near our new spirits. Our bodies are only houses where in we dwell. If someone damaged your house but could never harm you in person, that could sure cause some level of discomfort but it would not be a very big deal. With your health intact, you can always put up an even bigger and better house. Likewise for us, to die is gain and to live is Christ. No Christian should be so attached to this life on earth that they are afraid of death. If you are so concerned about preserving this temporary life, Jesus said it is the surest way to lose it-Matthew 16:24-27. Your life is worth nothing if it is not used to serve God's eternal purposes. Sow your life as a seed into the kingdom and you will not have enough room to store the harvest when eventually you face God. Whatever you invest into His kingdom here, you will find it multiplied infinitely in His hand in heaven. This life is not all there is for the new creation. It is only a gateway to a higher dimension of eternal life. For those outside Christ, they have cause to be afraid, very afraid.

With that background, you now understand why Paul could be so bold.

Romans 8: 35*Who shall separate us from the love of Christ? shall tribulation, or distress, or persecution, or famine, or nakedness, or peril, or sword? 36As it is written, For thy sake we are killed all the day long; we are accounted as sheep for the slaughter. 37Nay, in all these things we are more than conquerors through him that loved us. 38For I am persuaded, that neither death, nor life, nor angels, nor principalities, nor powers, nor things present, nor things to come, 39Nor height, nor depth, nor any other creature, shall be able to separate us from the love of God, which is in Christ Jesus our Lord.* (KJV)

In everything we have victory already! We are not trying to be victorious. We are not trying to wage a battle whose outcome may swing either way. We start from a position of victory and all we do is stand our ground and guard our faith against corruption and theft.

Hebrews 10:39 B*ut we are not of them who draw back unto perdition; but of them that believe to the saving of the soul.* (KJV)

Furthermore, we do not exist in our own. Our lives are hidden with Christ in God. Out of God's hand, no one can snatch us.

Jude 1:1 *Jude, the servant of Jesus Christ, and brother of James, to them that are sanctified by God the Father,* **and preserved in Jesus Christ,** *and called:* (KJV) Emphasis added.

John 10: 28-29 *And I give unto them eternal life; and they shall never perish, neither shall any man pluck them out of my hand. My Father, which gave them me, is greater than all; and no man is able to pluck them out of my Father's hand.* (KJV)

Colossians 3:3 *For ye are dead, and your life is hid with Christ in God.* (KJV)

It doesn't matter even if satan stirs up trouble and violence. We are more than ready for it. In fact, as satan keeps increasing the intensity of violence across the world, Christianity grows by leaps and bounds as it spreads like wildfire. Right now, his most usefultool is a religion called radical Islam.

These fundamentalists are so violent, so cruel, so mean and so wicked that I think sometimes satan takes notes from them. In the midst of all the violence, economic upheavals, diseases and madness raging on, the Christian is safe in the secret place of the Most High. No evil can come near us. There is no trap that our Father has not made adequate provisions to protect us from. Whether it is an earthquake, a stray bullet, a sniper shot, a drunk driver, a grisly accident, a plane crash, an unknown virus lurking in the shadows, an undetected disease or a terrorist attack; the Lord has our back. He never sleeps or slumbers watching over us. His angels are under instruction to not let any danger befall us. No evil can befall us and no plague can come near our dwelling because we have made the Lord our refuge; the most High our habitation. The angels have been assigned responsibility to keep us in all our ways, that is, in every step we take. Other people can expect danger but you are different. You are in this world but not of this world. We live in this world but according to the provisions of our Heavenly country. We are under God's protection because we are His and in Him. There is absolutely nothing to fear in this world. The Lord is our strong tower. The righteous live in Him and are safe from any evil and danger, known and unknown. We do not even fear death because even death has been defeated by Jesus and He made it our property-1 Corinthians 3:22. *The fear of danger, of the future and of death will rob you of the joy of living.*

We must always bear in mind that we are in the earth but not of the earth. We have been send here as ambassadors from heaven. That means we have diplomatic immunity from any harm with the exception of persecution and even that one we only go through it because we allow for it. It is not that heaven can't protect us. We welcome it and highly anticipate it. It multiplies our reward and helps us conform to Christ at the point of His cross. Now, just because we have diplomatic immunity doesn't mean we won't have some hardcore criminals (read demons and the human agents they use) who attempt to make attacks against us while we are on duty in our country of posting. They will try. That is why they we must never let our guard down while we are in this hostile territory. We must keep speaking God's word and declaring upon our lives by faith what He has said about us because when we do that, angels are activated to go to work for us. Remember the Bible says in Psalm 103:20 that angels do God's commandments, hearkening unto the voice of His word. That means we have to give God's word voice by speaking forth scriptures in faith. That is exactly what we do when we declare upon ourselves scriptures like Psalm 91 which is about divine protection. If it was all up to God to protect us without any single role on our part to play, we would all get uniform protection yet we know it comes to each Christian differently.

Perhaps you are asking what sets the new creation apart from the ordinary people of the world. Well, there is one quality in the new creation person which sets him above other men and renders him not susceptible to the common troubles that afflict those who are not in Christ. That attribute is righteousness.

Isaiah 54: 14 *In righteousness shalt thou be established: thou shalt be far from oppression; for thou shalt not fear: and from terror; for it shall not come near thee. 15 Behold, they shall surely gather together, but not by me: whosoever shall gather together against thee shall fall for thy sake. 17 No weapon that is formed against thee shall prosper; and every tongue that shall rise against thee in judgment thou shalt condemn. This is the heritage of the servants of the LORD, and their righteousness is of me, saith the LORD.* (KJV)

Proverbs 12: 28 *In the way of righteousness is life: and in the pathway thereof there is no death.* (KJV)

There is no known way of defeating a word-speaking, tongue-talking new creation person. That is a source of no mean frustration to the enemy.

John 16: 33 *I have told you these things, so that in Me you may have [perfect] peace. In the world you have tribulation and distress and suffering, but be courageous [be confident, be undaunted, be filled with joy]; I have overcome the world." [My conquest is accomplished, My victory abiding.]* (AMP)

13. THE NEW CREATION CAN DEFY AGING.

One of the most dreaded things in this Life is aging. As

soon as humans hit 40 years of age and signs of aging become evident, they start to panic. That is for a good reason. Aging comes with its own share of complications. The human body system begins to get sluggish, organs start to malfunction, the immune system begins to give way, and general appearance appears set on course to disintegrate. That is a frightening specter and it can drive one to depression. The Good news is, it doesn't have to be like that. There is a better way for the new creation. The Bible advises that we constantly refer from our source- Abraham and Sarah. We are the seed of Abraham and what was true of this mighty couple is true of us as well because we are blessed with faithful Abraham. <u>The promises made to Abraham are our present-day reality by faith.</u>

In his journey to Egypt recounted in Genesis 12, Abraham was seventy five years of age and Sarah was sixty five. When they got to Egypt, Pharaoh did not hesitate to take her as part of his harem. We do not have to guess why even the princes of Pharaoh commended her before him. Abraham tells us she was a fair woman to look at. At sixty five in the deserts of middle East? Wow! That speaks volumes. Pharaoh had an entire population of youthful, beautiful women to choose from yet among all those, he was helplessly smitten by a sixty five year old? That attests to the stunning beauty and youth that was Sarah even at advanced years. She must have looked considerably very young and fresh for her age. That is not all. Decades later, they journeyed again to Abimelech's territory at Gerar. Abimelech was attracted to Sarah who was now 90 years old. It seems as if very little had changed in twenty five years as far as Sarah's appearance was concerned. As if that is not enough, at 90, Sarah bore her Son Isaac. That is astounding. At more than double the age when biologists ascribe menopause to women, Sarah was just in time for her big break. That is just like our God. His ways are far from men's. To think that these are our patriarchs in the faith is highly encouraging. At past a century, Abraham was still very strong, vibrant and biologically viable. He remarried after Sarah's death and had six more sons. That is the man with whom we are blessed. He was strong, age-defying and productive to the end. That is not the only biblical promise we have. In a number of other places in the holy book, we have promises to the same effect. These promises are only for those who belong to the Lord, under whose refuge they abide and those who believe in literal youth renewal.

Isaiah 40: 29*He giveth power to the faint; and to them that have no might he increaseth strength. 30Even the youths shall faint and be weary, and the young men shall utterly fall: 31But they that wait upon the Lord shall renew their strength; they shall mount up with wings as eagles; they shall run, and not be weary; and they shall walk, and not faint.* (KJV)

Romans 8:11 *But if the Spirit of him that raised up Jesus from the dead dwell in you, he that raised up Christ from the dead shall also quicken your mortal bodies by his Spirit that dwelleth in you.* (KJV)

Some people tell us that this verse refers to when we will receive new bodies at the coming of Christ. This verse does not say the Spirit of the Lord quickens our immortal bodies which are what we will receive then. It is referring to our current mortal bodies. The Lord is promising to keep strengthening, refreshing and invigorating your mortal body even with advancement in age by His Spirit. Don't push it to the future like a religious person. Take it now and run with it.

Psalms 103:5 *Who satisfieth thy mouth with good things; so that thy youth is renewed like the eagle's.* (KJV)

Those who are in Christ and delight themselves in the Lord need not fear aging. They have clauses in the constitution of Heaven- God's own letter of Love to His children- they can stand on and defy aging.

But, you must have faith. It only works for those who dare to believe it and expect it. You see, <u>you don't automatically get what is promised in the Bible. You get only what you believe for from God's word.</u> If you believe for and expect nothing, verily verily I say unto you, you get nothing. You will still age and die disgracefully like a mortal man. You will have brought it to yourself. If you are the kind that joins natural men to talk how you are preparing to age and have all the complications that come with it; if you think in your mind, "surely all of us must grow old and decrepit because it is only natural;" if you begin preparing unconsciously for a tough future without teeth, sickly and full of problems; if you believe and say those terrible things of yourself and agree with others of similar conviction; you will only get natural results. The Bible will not work for you. Conversely, if you believe that as your years increase, so will your strength, then your life will be as glorious as Caleb's.

Joshua 14:11 *As yet I am as strong this day as I was in the day that Moses sent me: as my strength was then, even so is my strength now, for war, both to go out, and to come in.* (KJV)

Deuteronomy 33:25 *Thy shoes shall be iron and brass; and as thy days, so shall thy strength be.* (KJV)

Isaiah 40:31 *But they that wait upon the LORD shall renew their strength; they shall mount up with wings as eagles; they shall run, and not be weary; and they shall walk, and not faint.* (KJV)

Don't allow yourself to age like a natural man. You don't have to deteriorate, become sickly, lose memory, develop joint problems, become slow and grumpy, lose vision, lose strength, develop degenerative diseases and look forward to death. Caleb showed us we can maintain our strength even with increase in years, instead of diminishing and vanishing ingloriously like a dying ember. We belong to the same God and He has no favouritism. We can be as strong in old age as Caleb and with as powerful sight as Moses at 120 years old. Speak life to your mortal body. Speak to it restoration, youth renewal and strength. Learn to speak to your body and tell it what to do. Speak life and not death to it.

Again, don't swallow Satan's lies. When he says, 'this is what happens normally or naturally as you age: diseases attack you, your strength diminishes and your eyesight takes a beating.' Tell that defeated old foe that you are not ordinary, normal or natural. You are a new creation, a child of God. All things of diseases are passed away and all things are become new. All things are of God. So, all things are of health, strength, renewal of youth, peace and prosperity. Say to yourself that the same Spirit who raised Jesus from the dead indwells you and God through Him makes alive your mortal body. Be a talking Christian! Silent Christians suffer much in life and grow old like ordinary people. Don't feed on lies whether they be perpetrated by satan himself or by the so-called experts. Feed only on the word of God. Even in old age, the new creation still bears fruit. His entire life is of unceasing fruitfulness.

Psalm 92: 12 The righteous shall flourish like the palm tree: he shall grow like a cedar in Lebanon. 13 Those that be planted in the house of the LORD shall flourish in the courts of our God. 14 They shall still bring forth fruit in old age; they shall be fat and flourishing; (KJV)

What a scripture! Everybody must repeat this Psalm daily and put faith in it as if their life depends on it because, it really does. Ultimately, when it is time to check out of earth, whether the new creation will go by a chariot of fire or through sleep if the Lord tarries; the Lord is pleased with the departure from earth of a believer. It is not death. It is transition to full and complete glory. That is the kind of mindset early Christians had when they defied governments and religious authorities openly only to be thrown alive (but singing) to ravenous beasts and fierce fires. They literally availed themselves readily to be murdered so cruelly because they had set their sights on something infinitely more glorious than anything this sorely sorry earth can offer. They did not value their lives but actually started the Christian journey by offering themselves as sacrifices, choosing notto live for themselves but for the one who died for them.

Acts 20: 24 But none of these things move me, neither count I my life dear unto myself, so that I might finish my course with joy, and the ministry, which I have received of the Lord Jesus, to testify the gospel of the grace of God. (KJV) Emphasis added.

Romans 8: 36 As it is written, For thy sake we are killed all the day long; we are accounted as sheep for the slaughter. (KJV)

14. THE NEW CREATION IS IN ETERNITY ALREADY

You need to know that the new creation is not a slave of time. I say the new creation does not wait to be told what time it is. Instead, he tells time what time it is. We are in Christ and Christ is not in time. He is in the 'eternal now.' Eternal now has no beginning and no end, it just is. 'Now' is eternal and is spiritual. NOW is distinct from "past" and "future." When Moses enquired of God about whom he should say sent him to deliver the Israelites, God had a strange answer. *"And God said unto Moses, I AM THAT I*

AM: and he said, Thus shalt thou say unto the children of Israel, I AM hath sent me unto you." -Ex 3:14. When Jesus disputed with the bothersome religious leaders called the scribes and Pharisees, He said, "Verily, verily, I say unto you, Before Abraham was, I AM." -John 8:58. Jesus just told them He was the very great I AM who sent Moses. Now we are in Him. When you are in the speed-monster we call supersonic fighter jet, you don't travel at the speed of mere mortals. You defy all established limits and travel at supersonic speeds in that fearsome instrument. The distance that takes men hours to cover you do in common seconds. We are in the one who is infinitely swifter than any supersonic jet that will ever be designed. He travels and operates at the speed of thought. We operate at His speed, the speed of the Holy Ghost! Please arm yourself with this mentality and your life will never be ordinary again.

1 Kings 18: 45 *And it came to pass in the meanwhile, that the heaven was black with clouds and wind, and there was a great rain. And Ahab rode, and went to Jezreel. 46 And the hand of the LORD was on Elijah; and he girded up his loins, and ran before Ahab to the entrance of Jezreel.* (KJV)

From this account, Elijah outran the royal horses of King Ahab and reached Jezreel ahead of the king who had departed much earlier. If that happened with people who were not in Christ, what speed can we move with in this testament?

<u>The new creation was never intended to be a slave of time because he lives by faith. Faith cancels the restrictions of time because it is a higher law than time.</u> Time is a terrible task master that we must overcome by faith in order to enjoy our God-given inheritance even while we are in this side of eternity. Those without faith are forced to wait on time. When they need a family home, they have to acquire it over twenty five years servicing a punitive mortgage. When they are sick, they have to queue to see a human doctor whose knowledge is severely limited and they have to wait for their healing for some time, if ever it will come. But, for the new creation who is loaded with faith, all he needs to do is take that which lies in the future and bring it to now. When Jesus went to raise Lazarus from the dead, Martha tried to tell Jesus that she knew her brother would rise again in resurrection on the last day. Jesus immediately corrected her that

the resurrection and life Himself was standing there talking to her. They didn't need to wait for some future resurrection day. Likewise, you don't need to wait for your healing or financial breakthrough for years and decades. Jesus, who is everything you need has made His abode inside you and you can benefit from Him right now! It all depends on you, not Him. <u>If you are sick, you determine when you receive your healing. You can decide to receive it now or ten years from now.</u> You can even elect to forgo it altogether. One of the reasons why religious Christianity is so off-putting and many people are resisting it and giving it a wide berth is because it oscillates between being very futuristic and very historical. It doesn't seem to have any tangible application and relevance for the now. Religion is still stuck in presenting a historical Jesus who is still a baby held by "Mary," or, one who is still hanging on a tree or even one who is dead in a grave. Another section of religion presents a Jesus who used to heal back then but who cannot really help now because He is gone and healing or miracles seem to have left with Him. Then, a yet third wing of religion presents a futuristic Jesus who is irrelevant now but is only waiting in heaven to receive us, wipe our tears and relieve us from the crushing weights and burdens of this dark and groaning world. I present to you that we believe in a very current, relevant, updated and real Jesus. I present to you a resurrected Jesus who is almighty. He is seated by God's right hand and we are seated in Him. He is our source and we draw from Him whatever we need. We do not deal with some distant Jesus who is detached from what we are going through but one who is in it with us. He is our High priest who has been through everything we experience and who is able to help and save us to the uttermost. Everything you need has been prepared and made ready for you right now. All you need to do is reach inwardly into your spirit where everything is and withdraw your breakthrough. You don't need to wait for anything because Jesus is here now. He is with you, in you and one with you. You are not waiting for Him to show up. He is waiting for you to let Him loose on your situation through faith in His word, faith confessions and professions, faith declarations of the word, authoritative decrees, prayer and speaking in tongues. There is no need to wait on time for one more day. Right away, engage Christ and take what you need from Him now! The Bible says we must seize or apprehend (as if by force) our inheritance in Christ. The element of force comes in because there is an enemy on the loose who works hard to obstruct our blessings from manifesting and whom we must rebuke in the name of Jesus and speaking in tongues to put him to flight. All said, <u>faith bypasses time and takes what could have been achieved a hundred years in the future and delivers it to you now and here.</u> We need to recalibrate our thinking to be in tandem with this new reality of who we are in Christ. When we do that, we will even begin seeing literal physical translations to where sometimes we are not encumbered by all these limitations and travel restrictions of men to where we can transact kingdom business at the speed of the Holy Spirit.

15. THE NEW CREATION IS UNLIMITED: KNOWS NO IMPOSSIBILITIES

Ordinary human beings dwell in the realm of impossibilities. In fact, their lives are defined and governed by their limitations or what they can't do. They know all too well the myriad of things they can't do and they are very hopeless because they also know there's nothing they can do about it. They know of all the terminal diseases they can't cure or be cured from. They know of all the financial, social, educational and legal constraints and barriers they can't remove or negotiate safely to get to their destiny. That is the most terrible position to find oneself in. The new creation man is the original superman. He sees the invisible and does the impossible. He does not recognise such impediments. *While ordinary men who walk by senses operate by money, education, class or other carnal means; the new creation operates by a mountain-moving and forcefully-advancing juggernaut called faith.* Faith knows no impossibilities. Faith never takes no for an answer. Faith never gives up. It is never intimidated and neither is it ever negative. Faith can never be overcome. It doesn't cry or give excuses but only gets the job done. Faith is the force of the new creation kingdom man who no longer fears the devil by rolling over and playing dead like an opossum. This new man advances by the fire and force of the Holy

Ghost.

Matthew 11:12 *From the time of John the Baptizer until now, the kingdom of heaven has been forcefully advancing, and forceful people have been seizing it.* (GOD'S WORD® Translation)

Consider Paul whom some men were dissuading from going to Jerusalem to preach the gospel. He became furious and stopped them from stepping in his way of accomplishing his God-given mission.

Acts 21: 12 *When we heard this, we and the people there pleaded with Paul not to go up to Jerusalem. 13 Then Paul answered, "Why are you weeping and breaking my heart? I am ready not only to be bound, but also to die in Jerusalem for the name of the Lord Jesus." 14 When he would not be dissuaded, we gave up and said, "The Lord's will be done."* (NIV)

Even when the earthly forces are elevating the pressure too much and they think they are winning, we defy even death itself and simply stand up and continue walking, working and advancing forcefully.

Acts 14:19-20 *"A group of Jews from Antioch and Iconium came to Lystra and won over the crowds. Then they stoned Paul, and dragged him out of the city, supposing he was dead. But as the disciples stood around him, he rose up, and entered into the city. On the next day he left with Barnabas for Derbe"*

This is the very thing that explains why Christianity always seems to thrive even more where there is pressure of persecution. You see, the gospel of the good news of Jesus' grace is like fire shut up in the bones of the new creation. We can't sustain the pressure of that fire and that is why we have to let off that steam by releasing it to those who still sit in spiritual darkness. If you are a Christian and you are just glad and comfortable "going to heaven" alone and never share the gospel with those in need of it around you, something is definitely wrong somewhere. Necessity is laid upon you to share the good news of Jesus' resurrection and the subsequent glory that is afforded to all who believe in Him. The kingdom of God encapsulated in the new creation is like yeast which although it may appear tiny judged by the size of the dough, it spreads and takes over the whole thing.

Luke 13:20-21 *It is like the yeast a woman used in making bread. Even though she put only a little yeast in three measures of flour, it permeated every part of the dough."* (NLT)

Kingdom people have a radically different worldview from normal men. These two groups of people look at things very differently. While ordinary men view things from ground up, supermen view things from God's point in Heaven where they are seated in Christ. When ordinary men say there is a casting down, we boldly assert against all odds that there is a lifting up. We have a bird's eye view. So, even the things that appear like imposing heaps of problems still look like tiny anthills. Supermen look at challenges with the eyes of faith, not the physical ones.

Matthew 19:26 *But Jesus beheld them, and said unto them, with men this is impossible; but with God all things are possible.* (KJV)

This verse is very important because it tells us why there is no impossibility for the new creation: it is because the superman is not alone but with God. This verse does not just mean that God can do everything as most people take it to mean. More specifically, it means that for the man who is with God, there is no known impossibility. Dare to believe that. God operates in this man; He walks in Him and dwells in Him- 2 Corinthians 6:16.

Our Father is the God of all possibilities. What He can do through the new creation, natural men can only behold in bewilderment. Also, very significantly, the word says, all things are possible to him that believes- Mark 9:23. The life of a Christian is one of limitless possibilities and endless victories.

2 Corinthians 2:14 *Now thanks be unto God, which always causeth us to triumph in Christ, and maketh manifest the savour of his knowledge by us in every place.* (KJV)

When Jesus made the statement to the effect that all things are possible to the one that believes, He didn't even try to qualify it. He didn't say all things are possible only if the situation is not so severe or if you have a lot of power, or, if you have been living very holy and have tithed, prayed a lot, fasted and done other religious works. It was that clear and straight forward. He just said if you believe, all things will be possible with you. If only you believe you are in Christ and He is carrying out His work in you to the extent you allow Him, it is impossible to see any impossibility. It is possible for you to see every disease healed (including the most terminal one). It is possible to cast out any demon. It is possible to raise a dead person back to life. It is possible to do greater works than Jesus did. It is possible to handle any emergency, anywhere and at any time. All these things are possible because the greater one lives in the new creation. They happen not by might or human power but by the Spirit who indwells us and who does them all through us. If you can believe that, then you can expunge the word impossible from your daily vocabulary. Now, believing isn't expecting it to happen in some future date as many people take it to mean. That is hope. And this is the difference between faith and hope. Hope is spiritual reality that will be manifested at a future date. Faith is the power or force that transports hope from the spiritual realm to physical reality. Believing is acting on your faith. Faith is what gets you immediately what you believe for, although it may manifest progressively. <u>Faith either supersedes or even where necessary cancels the law of time which governs the natural universe. It does so by crossing over from the natural to the supernatural realm to deliver reality that would either have naturally been impossible to attain or would have taken long.</u>

When the world says "this or that is impossible," or that a particular ailment is incurable, they are just defining the ceiling of their acutely limited and natural understanding. Your life should not be dependent on the limitations of the carnal men's thinking. <u>There's no ailment that is incurable and there is no problem that is insurmountable.</u> There's nothing that is impossible to God and the believer. If you are tempted to think your condition is beyond fixing, don't become despondent. Christ in you is the hope of glory, deliverance, healing, health, preservation and prosperity. Even now, proclaim that every fibre of your being is subject to the impact and influence of the life of Christ in you! Christ is your life and your righteousness and has ushered you into a realm of unlimited possibilities, victories and dominion! I can do all things through Him who is my strength, salvation and wisdom, glory to His name for ever. Amen

The Marvel Of The New Creation Superman

CHAPTER FOUR
AN EARNEST INVITATION TO JOIN THE GOD CLASS

God so loved the world that He sent Jesus His son to come and take away the sin of men so that they can have His acceptance and receive His goodwill, peace and fellowship. Profound love comes with profound responsibility on the part of the receiver of that love. However, God did not burden us with any grievous responsibility other than that we believe in His son only and receive the abundance of His love and eternal life. There will be no excuse for anyone who refuses or fails to acknowledge Jesus Christ as the only saviour and way to the Father. Do not listen to the voice of religious, legalistic people who tell you that salvation is by trying to keep every law and please God. God was already more than pleased by Christ for your sake. All you need to do is just get into Christ by believing in Him. He is like the Noah's ark. For many days, people of Noah's time had been warned of the impending judgment of God but they despised the warning. Everyone that was found outside the ark faced a very cruel death from the devastating deluge that enveloped the entire earth. Likewise, everyone who will not be found in Christ in these end times will be damned eternally when the wrath of God is visited upon all unbelievers. The time to accept Christ is now while you can still make a decision. Anytime from now can be too late. Don't play Russian roulette with your life. <u>The greatest gift from God is His son to those who believe in Him. However, the greatest unquantifiable tragedy and loss is to not believe in that gift.</u> It amounts to a rude rejection of such a precious offer of love. God can never take that kindly. If God is not asking even for a dime to save anyone, what excuse will you have for being found outside Christ when He returns?

Hebrews 10: 28 *He that despised Moses' law died without mercy under two or three witnesses: 29 Of how much sorer punishment, suppose ye, shall he be thought worthy, who hath trodden underfoot the Son of God, and hath counted the blood of the covenant, wherewith he was sanctified, an unholy thing, and hath done despite unto the Spirit of grace? 30 For we know him that hath said, Vengeance belongeth unto me, I will recompense, saith the Lord. And again, The Lord shall judge his people. 31 It is a fearful thing to fall into the hands of the living God.* (KJV)

Salvation is for everybody. As long as one is breathing, they are prime candidates for salvation. It is for all; from the least to the greatest; from the lowliest slave to the noblest elite; from the utterly illiterate to the most learned; from the poorest to the wealthiest; from the most powerless to the most powerful and, from the most clueless to the most informed. Salvation is so simple nobody will have any excuse if found outside Christ.

Let me at this point specifically address the lowliest group of people who are derogatorily referred to as 'nobodies.' If you number yourself among that group, then God is aggressively looking for you to transform you from whatever you think your state is now to His own beloved glorious child and a brand He will be proud of. As many as receive Jesus, He gives them power to become sons of God. God is not interested in one's beauty, intellect, education, wealth, success, physical strength or any other physical attribute as a condition for salvation. He says you come as you are. Can you imagine God Almighty, the creator of the universe, He who is all powerful, knows all things and is everywhere at once; is pleading with every human being everywhere and of every generation to receive His forgiveness of sins and be reconciled to Him? -2 Corinthians 5:20.

That is a staggering reality! However, we stand informed that He will not beseech us forever. That window of grace and benevolence will at some point be shut and it will be too late to seek this reconciliation to God that is so abundantly and freely available now. Make plenty of hay while the sun still shines.

According to God, it is easier for the powerless, the poor, the not so educated, the weak, the sick, the meek and lowly, the not so attractive and the not so successful to become sons of God.

1 Corinthians 1: 26 *For ye see your calling, brethren, how that not many wise men after the flesh, not many mighty, not many noble, are called: 27 But God hath chosen the foolish things of the world to confound the wise; and God hath chosen the weak things of the world to confound the things which are mighty; 28 And base things of the world, and things which are despised, hath God chosen, yea, and things which are not, to bring to nought things that are:* (KJV)

James 2: 5 *Hearken, my beloved brethren, Hath not God chosen the poor of this world rich in faith, and heirs of the kingdom which he hath promised to them that love him?* (KJV)

If you belong to the categories listed here above, the greatest favour you can do yourself is to get baptized into Jesus by believing in Him. Then, you will you have gained eternal life. The greatest unquantifiable tragedy and loss of all time is to suffer and be a nobody in this world, and again suffer damnation in eternity. Because life on earth is full of suffering and misery even for the affluent, at least, purpose to live large in eternity. What is the point of suffering in this life and suffering immeasurably in the hereafter? That is why God is looking for every single person to be reconciled to Him- 2 Peter 3:9.

He alone knows how perilous eternity will be in hell. No wonder, He is beseeching us to take full advantage of His extravagant grace. God is looking for the poor, the slow, the fearful, the unsuccessful, the foolish, the uneducated, the inconsequential in the natural, those who don't amount to anything, the sick, the lazy, the despised of the society, the disabled, the defeated, those beat by life, the homeless, the mentally unstable, the tired, the heavy laden, the hungry, those not considered attractive, those struggling with all manner of sins and addictions, those written off by society, the lowest of the low, the drunkards and drug abusers. God has His eyes on those who have reached the end of their lives; the hopeless, those who wish for death, those contemplating suicide and those who muse over why they were even born. He wants them to first let His son Jesus into their hearts, before carrying out their wish, then we will see whether they will really proceed with their plans.

The Lord is inviting all to eternal life. This broad invitation is extended to fornicators, adulterers, atheists, agnostics, pagans, homosexuals, thugs, terrorists, and people of the earth's pagan religions whose saviour is not Jesus. The Lord seeks to win to Himself the corrupt, the perverts, the murderers, the liars, pathological gossipers, the guilt-ridden, the condemned and the jail birds. The Lord is calling to Himself through Christ people of all races, creed, color, religion, profession, background and history. Do you feel so condemned and so guilt-ridden that you don't believe the Lord will have anything to do with you? The Lord is looking for especially you. He says where sin increases, grace super abounds to save and to clean to the uttermost. Do you feel like a total failure and a reject in life who cannot get anything right? Do you feel like someone who cannot amount to anything, who provide for his own family? The Lord is saying you don't need to do many things right, but there is one thing you can do perfectly right- believe in Jesus Christ for the forgiveness of your sins and attainment of eternal life. If you come to Him, He guarantees He will by no means cast you away- John 6:37. As long as you are still breathing, the Lord is saying there is more hope for you than in a dead king. Don't squander this opportunity of eternity. If you are reading this material and are yet to be born again, the Lord is knocking at the entrance of your heart. When you open for Him by saying yes to Jesus, He will open for you a new page in life so panoramic and so breath taking it will blow you away. If you harden your heart and remain indifferent, He will be exactly indifferent to you in the Day of Judgment: nothing in all existence is more sad and chilling. There is only one chief aim of life- to know God, and to know and believe in Christ whom He sent. Every other thing men are chasing is vanity.

If you are reading this and you do not want your lot to be everlasting reproach and eternal suffering, then pray this prayer: "Father in Heaven, I confess the Lordship of Jesus Christ over my life. I believe He is your son and I accept Him as my saviour and Lord. I believe He came in the likeness of sinful flesh, died for my sins, and you raised Him from the dead for my justification. I am now your righteousness in Christ Jesus. I am no longer an ordinary man but an original superman in Christ. Amen" Scripture references of that all-important prayer are as follows: 1 John 4:15; John 1:12; 1John 5: 11-13; and, Acts 10:43 just but to list a few.

If you have prayed that prayer and meant it from the bottom of your heart, you just instantly was translated from the dominion of darkness into the kingdom of God's dear son as a bona fide citizen. You immediately became an eternal son of God. You are a junior brother of Jesus. Nothing shall ever change that position. Nothing shall separate you from Him henceforth - not men, not spirits, not sin, not failure, not addiction, not wealth, not poverty, not hunger, not life, not death, not even angels can adversely affect your sure salvation in Jesus Christ. Nothing past, nothing now, nothing in future can nullify your divine son-ship. You are now helplessly saved and not even you can reverse it.

Jeremiah 32: 40 *And I will make an everlasting covenant with them, that I will not turn away from them, to do them good; but I will put my fear in their hearts, that they shall not depart from me.* (KJV)

You have just undergone what we call the second birth or spiritual re-birth. Your sin nature just disappeared and in its place came a brand new spirit which is incorruptible by sin, and is as holy and as righteous as Jesus is Himself. You can't see that spirit man with your eyes but He is right in there. In fact, He is more real than your physical being. You now have to walk by faith not by sight. <u>In your former life in darkness, seeing with your physical eyes occasioned believing. From now on, seeing it in the Bible leads to believing and when you believe it, then you see it with your physical eyes.</u> That is a critical difference! The way Jesus benefits you is by believing that he is in you and one with you, not by trying to feel him with your senses- 1 Corinthians 2:14. That spirit man who is the new you is full of spiritual food called grace. He will feed your soul as you continue to understand and grow in the grace of our Lord Jesus. The only food your soul can flourish on is the word of grace, not law. Don't entangle yourself with the bondage of the law. That way, you will have done yourself a favour. The law kills, but the spirit of God, through your new spirit gives life. The new you is a righteous and holy spirit called the new creation. He can do everything Jesus can do; he has the mind of Christ and knows all things. He will renew your soul as you meditate on the word of God. The law stunts the growth of the believer, but grace hastens it. All what remains for you to do is to be transformed in your soul by the renewing of your mind. That is done through reading the good news of the grace of Jesus Christ. Most of it is packed in the Pauline letters to the various churches of his day. If you grow in grace by growing in the knowledge and appreciation of God's great goodness and mercy, sin shall not have dominion over you. Sin has only dominion over those who elect to put themselves under the Old Testament commandments. As from me an apostle of His grace, grace to you and peace from God our Father, and from the Lord Jesus Christ. Grow from grace to grace, and from glory to glory until the glorious appearing of our Lord Jesus Christ with whom we will reign in the universe for eternity. Amen.

Watch out for other revolutionary works from this author.

www.ingramcontent.com/pod-product-compliance
Lightning Source LLC
Chambersburg PA
CBHW021140080526
44588CB00008B/149